WRITING IN GOLD

The gospels were "writing in words",
but icons are "writing in gold".

St Theodore, Abbot of the monastery of Studios in
Constantinople in the late eighth and early ninth centuries.

WRITING IN GOLD

BYZANTINE SOCIETY AND ITS ICONS

ROBIN CORMACK

OXFORD UNIVERSITY PRESS
NEW YORK 1985

Published in Great Britain by George Philip,
12–14 Long Acre, London WC2E 9LP

Published in the United States by Oxford University
Press, Inc., 200 Madison Avenue, New York, New York 10016

ISBN 0-19-520486-7

Library of Congress Catalog Card Number 85-42886

British Library Cataloguing in Publication Data

Cormack, Robin
    Writing in Gold: Byzantine society and its icons
    1. Art, Byzantine
    I. Title
709'.02   N6250

Printing (last digit) 9   8   7   6   5   4   3   2   1

Printed in Great Britain

CONTENTS

PREFACE

BYZANTIUM is not a lost world. Considerable evidence of its vast empire remains—documents and works of literature written in medieval Greek are still available in substantial numbers and its material remains, dating over a period of many centuries, are to be found over a great area. Yet all sorts of difficulties confront any attempt such as this one to write for non-specialist readers. How does one select from this vast range of material when not even professional Byzantinists are agreed on what is important or even typical? How does one avoid simply skating over the enormous surface, or on the other hand entering into narrow and hopelessly specialized arguments? I have taken an admittedly cavalier approach and I have chosen a series of texts and images which seemed to me to offer a pattern through which it is possible to make sense of the history of Byzantine art and culture. I have tried to ensure that most of the chosen texts are available in modern editions, and so can be consulted by those who can read modern Greek; but I have not of course assumed any knowledge of Greek on the part of the reader, and, where details of the text are important, I have included extended English versions of their content.

The evidence of the Byzantine world and the problems this raises are of outstanding interest. Its art, for example, cannot easily be studied along the traditional lines of the history of western European art; and cannot be seen in terms of a continual attempt to recreate the natural world in the artificial media of art. Byzantine art needs to be interpreted, not just to be perceived. Its literature, too, cannot be read in a straightforward way. In this book I have tried to point to one way of entering this complex society.

Note on Dates

The Byzantine year ran from September to August of the modern year. In the text Byzantine years have been translated into modern years where this has been possible, but in those cases where the month of the Byzantine year is not known the date is shown as, for example, 681/2, indicating that the event took place some time between September 681 and August 682.

ACKNOWLEDGEMENTS

To write acknowledgements is to face the moment of truth at the end of a book; the assistance that has been given and its necessity becomes all too clear.

The time to write was granted to me through the British Academy Readership scheme, which has allowed me to leave most of my teaching duties at the Courtauld Institute of Art for an extended period. I am a grateful beneficiary of the scheme and thank Professor P. Lasko, the Director of the Courtauld, for his agreement to my leave.

During the writing of the book, I was fortunate to have an office in the Warburg Institute, the best library in London for the Byzantine art historian, and I thank the Director, Professor J. Trapp, for this arrangement. The book was completed in Cambridge, while I was a Bye Fellow at Robinson College.

In obtaining photographs, I relied on the help of several individuals. At the Courtauld Institute of Art, particular assistance came from Constance Hill, the Conway Librarian, Geoffrey Fisher (Conway Library) and Jane Cunningham (Photographic Survey); this included access to the riches of the R.G. Searight Collection (London), some of which I am glad to be able to reproduce. At the Center for Byzantine Studies, Dumbarton Oaks, Washington DC, I owe thanks to Charlotte Kroll Burk for sending me photographs for use here; without these photographs it would have been impossible to illustrate successfully the wall-paintings of the *Enkleistra* of S.Neophytos. In the British Museum, I was helped by David Buckton with photographs of the S.Demetrios reliquary and by John Kent with photographs of coins. The staff of the British School at Athens and The Royal Institute of British Architects also gave assistance in providing access to some of the valuable material in their collections. Other photographs are due to the enterprises of Ernest Hawkins (St Sophia), Judith Herrin (Thessaloniki), Timothy Potts (Albania), Beat Brenk (Mar Saba), and Laskarina Bouras. The photographs taken by me owe much to the help of travelling companions, particularly Ernest Hawkins and Ann Epstein.

To Michael Crawford I owe thanks for setting out a conceptual framework within which I was able to formulate a book; and later for his historical observations. At George Philip and Son Ltd, I was fortunate to have in Lydia Greeves a publisher who not only showed proverbial patience but who was ready to devote her attention to every aspect of the book and to every detail to which I should have devoted more attention myself. This book is dedicated to Mary Beard. This is not the first book to contain an acknowledgement of her constructive cricitism of a text, but in this case her help included the demonstration that many of the questions that a historian of ancient history might ask can inform the Byzantinist too.

For Mary Beard

I

THE VISIBLE SAINT: ST THEODORE OF SYKEON

'This worthless history contains nothing but declamations and miracles. It is a disgrace to the human mind.'

So Voltaire described the history of Byzantium, and his sentiments have been repeated, echoed or regretted by later historians. The historical facts which this writer denounced in support of his attempts to reform the established church in France in the eighteenth century are the same ones which are confronted in this book; but the aim here is to interpret and to understand, not to pass judgement on a civilization. The society which is observed in the following pages is Byzantine. The word Byzantine today immediately conjures up an image of remoteness, obscurity, and labyrinthine complexity. It is often handled as a useful term of abuse—anybody frustrated by the machinery of an organization is likely to criticize it as a Byzantine bureaucracy, and a London University professor who recently wanted to quote some subject which everyone would instantly recognize as quite useless hit upon Byzantine botany. As a subject of possible study, Byzantium therefore may inspire reactions of fascination or repellence. Why find out about this society? What is still interesting about an empire which dominated the Eastern Mediterranean from 330 to 1453? What *was* Byzantium?

This book attempts something more than the correction of conventional images of Byzantine society. The evidence on which it will rely is not principally documentary evidence of economic or political activity, but to a large extent the works of art produced by Byzantine artists. None of this material, neither the writings nor the objects of art, survives from any part of the period in its entirety. For example, thousands of official documents which once existed in church and state archives (as can be demonstrated from the lead seals, once attached to them, which have survived) have been lost through the vicissitudes of history: after 1453 most regions of the former Byzantine empire were

9

for centuries occupied by a new empire with different religious and political beliefs; under this Islamic Ottoman empire conditions were not conducive to the survival of medieval Christian material, and this is one reason why only a fraction of it remains. The survivals of art are also patchy, though a significant amount is still to be seen; this is scattered geographically in monuments around the Mediterranean or in museums and libraries all over the world. The most serious shortage of material is of that from the capital of the empire itself. From what is available a selection of material has been made which allows an argument to be constructed not only through the works of art themselves but also through contemporary written texts.

The aim of this argument is to offer new insights into the way that the visual arts functioned in this society, and so, by analogy, in many other societies. Byzantium is not the only society to have been in daily contact with its art; nor is it the only society in which visual experience was an integral part of its members' consciousness of the world. The book provides, in one sense, a case study for the use of art as fundamental to the understanding of any society. It explores the operation of visual images within society, approaching art not just as another source of information somehow on a parallel with literature, but as a means of opening up levels of understanding inaccessible from the study of written texts. Of course the writings of Byzantines take a prominent part in this book, but it is the conjunction of art and literature that offers the most possibilities for a new analysis.

The visual material has been chosen from the domain of religious art, not just because this is the area where most has survived, but because of the active role of Christianity in Byzantium. The period of the Byzantine empire can be seen as quite as significant for the development of modern Europe as the period of classical antiquity. It was here that the idea of a Christian state was first worked out; one particular version of that idea was successfully developed and formed the basis of what is now called Orthodox Christianity. The church was the dominating intellectual and moral institution, which controlled (or attempted to control) the patronage of art, and ensured that its range of subject-matter was limited to Christian themes. Art was one medium through which it could promote and control allowable emotions and values. Art was a part of the system through which the church carried out its role in disciplining and regulating society. The visual environment of Byzantium was as a result a carefully constructed one and a study of it offers a way of decoding values and attitudes, and the ways they were promoted and maintained.

So far the visual production of Byzantium has been mentioned in general terms, but the one particular type of artistic production commonly supposed to be characteristic of the society is the 'icon'. To some extent this supposition is justified: icons, in the sense of panel paintings on a wooden support, were in use in most periods of Byzantine history and large numbers of these panels have (exceptionally) survived in the remote monastery of St Catherine on Mt Sinai, in Egypt. Yet there is a problem of terms. The widespread modern definition of 'icon', which includes only such panel paintings, will be impossible to maintain throughout this book. The Greek word *eikon* (of which the modern spelling 'icon' is only a variant) is used in Byzantine writings to refer to any image whatsoever, from portable icons in the modern sense to monumental mosaics set on to walls or vaults. When the word 'icon' is met in these pages, it will have been used in the Byzantine sense and will refer to any product of the visual arts, often, but not always, a panel painting. This is not in fact so broad a usage of the word as it may at first sight appear. In comparison with the modern world, the visual production of Byzantium was distinctly limited in its types of media: there was much painting and mosaic, but a very limited production of large-scale sculpture. We are dealing with a society which had less variety of expression than the modern world, but in which, conversely, each visual production had greater potential influence over those in its presence.

Art was essential to the functioning of Byzantium—it would have been a different culture without icons. Moreover as Byzantine society changed over the centuries, so also did the visual culture of Byzantium. This study will be concerned with both changes and continuities in the role of visual images. Underlying its argument is a series of questions through which (it is hoped) the innovations and the traditions may be more precisely defined. What was the part played by icons in Christian worship and prayer? How do icons express beliefs and reflect devotional practices? How was art used by the church to confirm doctrines and codes of behaviour? What can be said of the mental habits of the users and spectators of religious art? These questions are formulated in terms of the Byzantine material, but the reader will see that they are fundamental for the study of any society.

★   ★   ★   ★

The heart of the Byzantine empire lay in the coastal regions and countries of the eastern Mediterranean, in Asia Minor, Cyprus and Greece (see map, p. 12). In time it extended from the fourth to the fifteenth century, although the people and their surroundings to be studied in detail here belong only to the central period between the sixth and the twelfth centuries. The capital city of the Byzantine empire was Constantinople (*Constantinopolis*), often called simply the *polis*, the city, or even the Queen of Cities. This city is now Istanbul, the largest conurbation in modern Turkey, sprawling from the Sea of Marmara to the Black Sea.

The site of Constantinople had a long history before the Middle Ages. A city first appears in the historical record with the name Byzantion, founded as a colony of the Greek city of Megara, in the seventh century BC. Its site was a strategic one on the Bosporus, and it was soon able to derive wealth from levying tolls on passing ships and from fishing. Later, under its Latin name of Byzantium, it increased in importance and status as part of the Roman empire; and it benefited still further when as an outcome of the administrative division of the Roman empire

OVERLEAF *The Byzantine empire showing its extent (a) at the death of Justinian I in 565; (b) in the reign of Leo III (717–741); (c) at the death of Basil II (1025); and (d) at the death of Manuel I Comnenos (1180).*

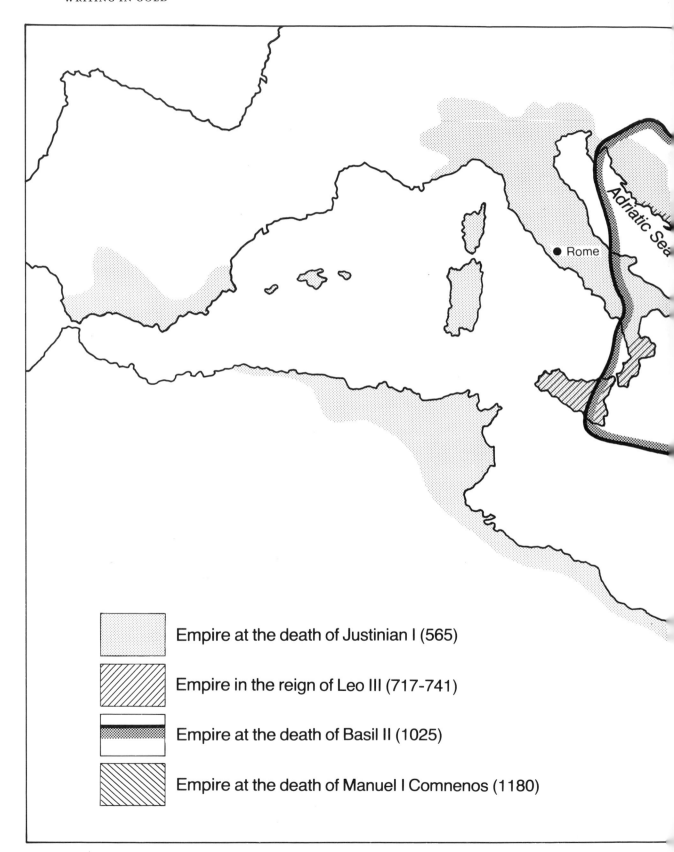

Empire at the death of Justinian I (565)

Empire in the reign of Leo III (717-741)

Empire at the death of Basil II (1025)

Empire at the death of Manuel I Comnenos (1180)

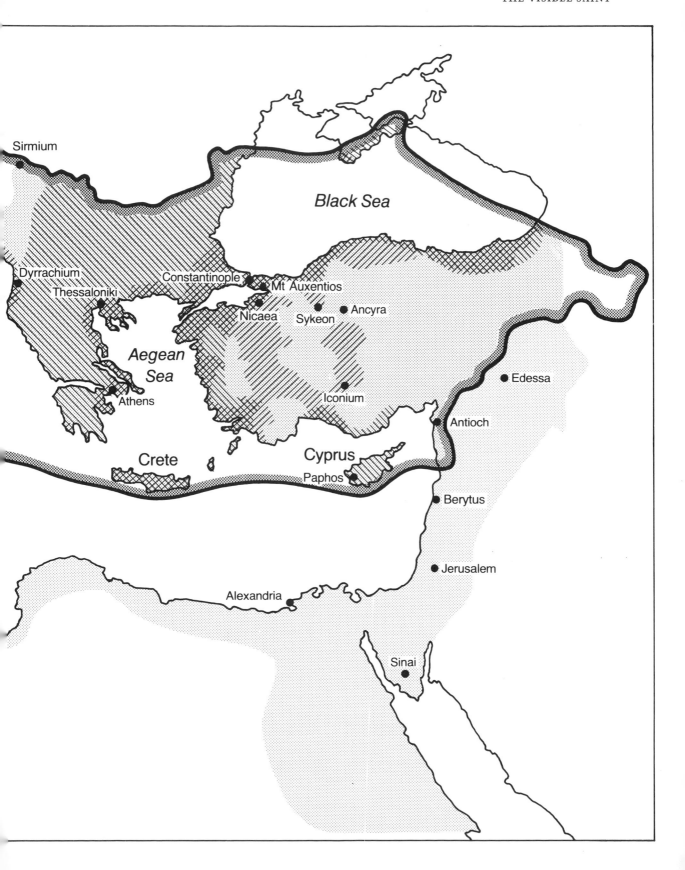

Sirmium

Black Sea

Dyrrachium

Constantinople

Mt Auxentios

Thessaloniki

Nicaea

Sykeon

Ancyra

*Aegean
Sea*

Edessa

Athens

Iconium

Antioch

Crete

Cyprus

Paphos

Berytus

Jerusalem

Alexandria

Sinai

into two sectors, one western and one eastern, Byzantium was 'refounded' as the capital city of the eastern half of the Roman empire by the emperor Constantine the Great (285–337). It was then (in 330) that it gained its official title of Constantinople or, alternatively, New Rome.

The independent empire which developed around this capital was in some senses the direct continuation of the Roman empire in the Greek-speaking provinces of the eastern Mediterranean. Not only were various of the political institutions of Byzantium modelled, at least formally, on Roman predecessors, but also the Byzantines viewed their own history as essentially Roman. Indeed they normally referred to themselves as *Romaioi* (Romans). Yet from the beginning the society of Constantinople—in a city redeveloped by Constantine, the first Roman emperor who became a Christian—was one with a predominant commitment to Christianity and its institutions.

Partly as a consequence of this official ideology, theologians and mystics gained a prominent role in Byzantine society and influenced behaviour and beliefs in this eastern half of the Roman empire; and the position of the emperor was understood and justified by a Christian interpretation of the order of the universe. The acceptance of such views owed much to the initial formulations of a bishop who was a prominent supporter of Constantine, Eusebius (260–340), and to the popularity of his *Ecclesiastical History*; his account of the history of the world ended with the triumph of Constantine as the ideal Christian emperor. By the sixth century the emperor was perceived to have a special and symbolic relationship with God. This perception can be found expressed in the court propaganda of the sixth century, as, for example, in the Latin verses of the epic poet Corippus *In praise of Justin II* (emperor from 565 to 578):

> *terrarum dominis Christus dedit omnia posse.*
> *ille est omnipotens, hic omnipotentis imago.*
> (Bk III, 427–8)
>
> *(Christ gave earthly rulers power over all.*
> *He is omnipotent, and the earthly lord is the image of the omnipotent)*

The power structure of the Byzantine state remained, at least formally, similar throughout the centuries of its existence, although many details of organization changed both as the extent of its territory contracted or altered and as the administration was adjusted to new circumstances. The key to everything was the emperor, justly titled the sole ruler and monarch—*Autocrator* and *Basileus*—from the seventh century onwards. The emperor made the laws and all decisions, including declarations of war. He was not elected but chosen by God. In effect this meant most commonly that he was designated by his predecessor (probably his father) and endorsed by the army and senate, following the procedures of accession under the Roman empire. But it was in theory possible for anyone to be chosen for the position, and there were cases of unexpected elevations—perhaps the most notorious example of opportunism was the ninth-century emperor Basil I who, as we shall find in Chapter 4, was an illiterate peasant who rose to found a major dynasty.

The emperor was beyond human criticism; everyone had to obey him and pray for him. A good emperor was acknowledged as a just judge of his subjects. He lived in the vast complex of buildings known as the Sacred Palace (or the Great Palace) which spread over an enormous area of the centre of the city of Constantinople. This lay to the south of the church of St Sophia, the destination of many imperial processions and the location of the most solemn religious ritual in which he participated in public view; and to the east of the Hippodrome, the largest arena in the city, which attracted large crowds for entertainment at the regular chariot racing. At an audience with the emperor, visitors were bound to silence and had to prostrate themselves on the ground in front of him (the act of *proskynesis*). Those allowed to enter into the palace—the military and civil elites and foreign ambassadors—saw icons of the emperor among all the splendour, surrounded by candles and incense, a parallel to the images of saints in Byzantine churches. The palace was the home of the emperor and his family, and the centre of the administration of the empire; it was the model from which the Russian Kremlin was later to be derived.

Such a state can fairly be described as an absolute monarchy, but there were nevertheless restrictions on the emperor's freedom of action. He was expected to agree to the laws enacted by his predecessors, and was required to make a profession of Christian faith. There were also other ways in which his accession, behaviour or policies could be influenced by groups of his subjects. The Senate, the traditional aristocratic council of Rome itself, continued in existence throughout the period and retained the role of approving the succession of a new emperor. The people as a body came regularly to the Hippodrome, and could make their approval or disapproval of the emperor and his policies known through vocal demonstration or even rioting. Their outbursts were not to be dismissed as mere high spirits at the races—an emperor could ignore the violent demonstrations of thousands of his subjects only at his peril.

All senior officials were appointed by the emperor—there were no elections. The civil administration was concentrated in the court at Constantinople where all the officials were considered servants of the emperor and bound to him by an oath of loyalty. It is this organization which has given rise to the characterization of a Byzantine civil service in terms of a centralized bureaucracy. In theory access to high office was open to all, but in practice the powerful landowning families were most likely to be chosen—and from the twelfth century onwards kinship with the imperial family provided the easiest access to the top posts. In some respects in the administration there was a further continuity with the traditions of Rome. Some of the positions at court, for instance, retained the names of the magistracies of the Roman empire—*praitor* is just one example; and among the attainments expected of a senior official (just as had been the case in the Roman empire) was a working knowledge of traditional rhetoric, itself learned through a formal classical education. Yet much more about the system was characteristically 'Byzantine' and quite different from its predecessor. Not only did a range of quite different magistracies develop, some limited to eunuchs, but also a series of graded honorific court titles emerged, in return for a regulated system of fees to be paid to the emperor.

The church may be considered, in some senses, to be a branch of the services of the Byzantine state, and it is hard to draw the boundary between 'church' and 'state'. For example, even the choice of the Patriarch of Constantinople, one of the five major bishops and in effect the head of the Byzantine church, was not under the internal control of the ecclesiastical organization. His election, although nominally in the hands of the principal bishops, was in practice under imperial control. The electors met and submitted a list of three names to the emperor for his final approval; but he was allowed to substitute a fourth nomination and entirely to sidestep the expressed wishes of the bishops. He took this prerogative on more than one occasion.

In the course of time the organization of the main branches of the Byzantine state (finance, justice, diplomacy, and the military) underwent a number of changes, particularly felt in the administration of its provinces. If there was a general trend over the period studied here, it was from a system of control by the military towards the greater delegation of responsibilities to a combination of military and civil authorities. Up to the seventh century there was a relatively small number of great ministers of state and commanders-in-chief of the army; they were personally responsible to the emperor but had a staff subordinate to them. For example, the two areas of the Balkans and Greece on the one hand and Asia Minor and the eastern provinces on the other were controlled by just two main military posts—the *Praefectus Praetorio Illyrici* and the *Praefectus Praetorio Orientis*, the Praetorian Prefect of Illyricum and the Praetorian Prefect of the East, titles derived from the offices of the Roman empire.

This organization was changing at the time of the events of our first two chapters; the regions were broken down into smaller units of organization, which were called 'themes'. These districts were under the control of a military governor, the *strategos* or general, who also ran the civil jurisdiction. One result of this reorganization was an increase in the number of officials, all of whom were now individually directly responsible to the emperor. A similar pattern of change between the sixth and the eighth centuries occurred within the palace hierarchy in the capital: a small number of central administrative offices concerned with the administration of Constantinople was then broken up into a large number of departments each with a limited competence. Further changes took place in the late tenth century, a time of the renewed expansion of the empire after centuries of contraction and defensive warfare. The military commander of the theme was from this time called a duke or a *katepan* (the latter title usually being employed in a frontier region); his staff included several generals (*strategoi*). The civil administration was now separately managed by a *praitor* or *krites* (judge), who was now the civil governor. This was the organization current in the closing chapters of this book, though adjustments had to be made in the governance of Asia Minor as it fell into Turkish hands in the course of the twelfth century.

The Byzantines saw their society in two divisions: the emperor and the ruling class on one side, the ruled on the other. They saw the Christian heaven in the same way: God and his chosen saints above the faithful. If Byzantine society was bureaucratic, so was that of God.

★ ★ ★ ★

When Theodore, the subject of this chapter, was born in the middle of the sixth century, the empire centred on Constantinople had already been established for two centuries. The emperor at the time, Justinian I (527–565), came to be regarded by Byzantines as of equal importance in their history as Constantine the Great, with whom he is coupled in a prominent mosaic in the church of St Sophia (Figures 54–56). His reign, however, must be regarded as an ambivalent moment in Byzantine history, a time of attempted consolidation combined with ominous collapse. Justinian has been characterized as the emperor who tried to unite the whole of Europe as a Christian empire, to standardize Christian belief, to redefine the legal code (published as the *Digesta*, a full compilation of existing Roman law) and to construct a new physical environment for his Christian subjects through his massive programme of building and church decoration. The paradox is that this renovated empire fell apart in the last years of the Justinianic Age when it was confronted with the foreign invasions, plagues and other disasters which can be seen to mark the transition from Antiquity to Medieval Europe. The life of Theodore was therefore spent in what seemed to contemporaries a time of collapse after years of security and which is still called the 'Dark Ages' of Byzantium—his birth was in the lifetime of Justinian and his death in the year 613. He therefore lived through various foreign threats against his region and the appearance of the Persian armies, and also through the most severe epidemics of bubonic plague to occur in Europe before the Black Death of the fourteenth century. Crisis in various forms was the continual experience of the society of this period.

Theodore was born in the country village of Sykeon in Asia Minor and spent the bulk of his life in this region. In the course of his life he was accepted by his contemporaries as a saint, and their verdict was confirmed by later generations who concurred in the belief that he was one of the major saints of the Byzantine church. To become a Byzantine saint in this period did not require canonization by a council decree (the bureaucratic organization of canonization developed first in the Western church, from the eleventh century, and only from the thirteenth century influenced the attitudes of the Orthodox church); but it did require the performance of miracles in public, and so such miracles must feature prominently in the life of any person who was successfully to gain public assent to his sanctity.

Theodore can only be observed through the written *Life*. It follows that our knowledge of the man and his society has already been processed through the selective writing of his biographer. One has to remember the inherent difficulties of using such a medieval document. There is the question of the quality of the biography, and how close the biographer was to his subject and how well-informed. There is the question of whether the text which we now have is what it purports to be. And there is the question at rather a different level of whether biography can ever be accurate. The text cannot be used until answers are given to each of these questions.

A full title of the biography is given in one of the several medieval manuscripts with a version of the text. This title is (in a manuscript now in Venice, Marciana Library, gr. 359): *Life of our father Saint Theodore Abbot (Archimandrite) of Sykeon: written by his disciple Georgios, priest and abbot of the same monastery*. These terms offer a certain amount of information in themselves, if for the moment it is assumed that these represent the original title. The biography must be posthumous because Theodore is specifically called a saint. The term archimandrite is a special term of honour confined to monks, and indicates that Theodore was the abbot of an important community. The name of the biographer is Georgios, and he was an educated monk, as he could write this text, which is one which shows a good grasp of language and Christian literature. He was himself now the head of the community, and he was an ordained priest—unless a monk had been ordained he could not celebrate the eucharist (or the liturgy as the mass is more commonly described in Byzantine writings), but could only participate as a helper or an observer. Ordination also meant that the priest was subject to the control of the church in a more obvious way than the ordinary monk who could live independently of strict authority and without responsibilities to a community.

What more can be discovered about the biographer Georgios? He gives snippets of information about himself (found in the *Life* in chapters 22, 75, 126, 165B and 170), though several of his remarks are no more than the standard clichés of Christian authors of the time—protesting his own unworthiness and making other such expected disclaimers which cannot be taken at face value. This information needs to be briefly collected together, as his character must be part of our assessment of the evidence about Theodore of Sykeon. The baptismal name of the author was Eleusios; his parents (from a local village) attributed his birth to the personal agency of the saint, for the pregnancy occurred after several years of childlessness and after a blessing from him. In thanks they sent their son to the monastery to be brought up and educated there—he was in the monastery during the last twelve years of the saint's life (601–613), and the saint gave him the new name of Georgios.

Georgios began to write the biography of the saint at some time during these years—Theodore once came across him at work on the text—when he had reached the age of seventeen (he was probably born in the decade of the 590s). He obviously did not complete the work until after the death of the saint. He understands that his reader will ask about the documentation of the *Life*, and makes a statement on the subject. He claims that his information for the last years of the saint's life derived from his own observation; and that he learned the events of childhood and middle age from eye-witness accounts, both from those who saw the miracles and from those who were healed by Theodore; and also from his contemporaries and schoolfellows. Furthermore one of the major sources of information was the saint himself: apparently he was happy to narrate the events of his own life for the edification of his monastic community—showing a lack of selfconsciousness which recurs in other holy men, most noticeably in the case of St Neophytos of Cyprus, the holy man with whose life this book will close.

From the information disclosed about himself by the author Eleusios/ Georgios, it can be said that he was born in the region of Sykeon and received his education in a rural monastery; he never went on to 'further education'. The result of the type of education he received can be observed in his literary style which is direct and full of Biblical allusions—it lacks artificial references to the language or contents of the classics of pagan Antiquity. The structure of the *Life* is of course influenced by earlier models of biography.

The second question is how close the modern printed text of the *Life* is to what Georgios actually wrote. It might for example actually represent a later, possibly much altered and embroidered, version composed by some anonymous author without historical contact with his subject. This problem must always arise in a period before the invention of printing when any scribe could copy out an earlier text and make any additions or subtractions as he wished. There is also endless scope for errors or inventions when books are transmitted under these conditions. This is a particularly obvious problem in this case, for there are no manuscripts which survive from the time of the attributed authorship; worse still, the texts which we do have (coming from seven manuscripts) differ in length (and purpose) from each other. This leads to such questions as whether the surviving 'short' *Life* is the original biography and whether the 'long' *Life* (preserved in manuscripts of the tenth and eleventh centuries: the text which is followed in this chapter) is a later, doctored version.

The main reason for accepting that the modern printed text of the 'long' *Life* is substantially the work of Georgios (even if he revised the work at various points in the course of his own life) is the detail of the historical information which it contains about the period, particularly of the early seventh century. This detail, which makes the text a valuable source for the modern historian of the time, could hardly have entered the text except through the hand of a man who lived through the events narrated. The style and language of the writing also fit the conclusion that we have a good source of information.

The *Life of St Theodore of Sykeon* is therefore treated from now on as a text which existed in the seventh century in a form very similar to that in which we can now read it. But this assumption does not relieve us of consideration of the third and final question raised before. In what sense does a biography give an 'accurate' picture of its subject? Once the problem is stated, it is obvious that this text, although written under excellent conditions for the observation of the saint and the reporting of his miracles and other actions, cannot be supposed to be a literally true and accurate account of what happened—what writing of any period could be? The special hazards of this text can be easily recognized. The rhetoric of a saintly biography must involve the exaggeration of human perfection. It must manipulate the readers' emotions and beliefs to encourage admiration, praise and even imitation. It will inevitably distort, omit and invent 'facts' in order to prove the sanctity of the subject. All the possible devices were well developed by the seventh century when authors could build on numerous models, including the New Testament. It must therefore not be forgotten that Georgios completed his text with the hindsight of someone who saw the sainthood of his hero as an established fact, which needed to be recorded in order to inspire the next generation (and others) living through a time of greater social crisis than Theodore (and of course foretold by him!).

The text of the *Life* is long and the consideration of its contents here is obviously selective; the focus will be on the ways in which it can give answers to an enquiry about the role of the visual in its period. Although dozens of miracles are recorded, many concerned with the cure of illnesses, only limited reference will be made to them. The structure of the text must be unravelled, and this can be done by setting out its contents in sketch form. The figures in brackets give the numbers of the chapters in the printed edition of Festugière (see Bibliography). The biography scans across the main regions of the eastern provinces of the Byzantine empire in the second half of the sixth century and the early years of the seventh century as Theodore travels in many parts of rural Asia Minor (modern Turkey) and makes a number of visits to both Constantinople and Jerusalem. All levels of society are involved in the events, from emperors to village idiots. As a narrative it records the remarkable powers that in the perceptions of this period could be attributed to a man from a poor and deprived background.

Theodore was born during the reign of the emperor Justinian (527–565), and he lived through six reigns, those of Justin II (565–578), Tiberios (578–582), Maurice (582–602), Phocas (602–610) and finally Heraclios (610–641). He was born in Sykeon, not a village whose precise location many inhabitants of the Byzantine world were likely to have known at the time; it was somewhere on the main road between Constantinople and Ancyra (modern Ankara), and nearer to the latter. It is exactly located by the biographer: twelve miles from Anastasioupolis, a city which was the capital city of the province which the Romans had called Galatia; the citizens of some part of Galatia had been addressed by St Paul in his Epistle to the Galatians (Figures 1 and 2 show the landscape of Asia Minor through the eyes of nineteenth-century watercolourists).

Theodore was the son of a prostitute, Mary, who operated together with her mother and sister at an inn at Sykeon. The inn had the practical advantage for their trade of acting as a stopping-place on the trunk road between the capital of the empire, Constantinople, and the eastern

1 Konya—the Byzantine city
of Iconium—lay on one side of
the main road through
southern Anatolia. Its setting is
typical of the landscape of the
high plateau of Anatolia in
which Theodore of Sykeon
often journeyed.

OVERLEAF 2 Although the
Islamic mosques and minarets
which arose all over Turkey
after the fall of Constantinople
in 1453 and the end of the
Byzantine empire changed the
face of the landscape, much has
remained from the Middle
Ages—walls, houses and
churches. Watercolour sketches
by travellers of the nineteenth
century instantly convey this
mixture of civilizations in
Asia Minor through which
elements of Byzantium can still
be glimpsed.

provinces. According to his mother, Theodore's father was an overnight
visitor at the inn who was on a journey from Constantinople as a mess-
enger in the imperial service of Justinian. The story she told was that
in the night she spent with this man she had a dream in which a star
descended from Heaven into her womb; and this was, according to
the biographer, duly interpreted for her both by a local holy man and
by the bishop of Anastasioupolis to mean that the baby was favoured
with heavenly virtues. The parallel with Jesus would certainly have been
lost on no Byzantine.

The child was (pointedly) baptized with the name of Theodore (gift
of God). When Theodore reached the age of six, his mother Mary made
plans to take him and her savings to Constantinople; but after a dream
in which St George appeared, she abandoned the idea. When he was
eight, there was sufficient money for her to pay for him to go to a
teacher to learn to read. Mary was still living at the inn, but she had
given up her erstwhile trade and the inn itself had changed its character;
it had become a noted gastronomic centre frequented by the influential
patrons who travelled along the road. Theodore came under the influence of the chef (Stephen), who, despite his profession, was a man deeply
committed to fasting and asceticism. Admiration for the chef led
Theodore to decide to spend his free time out of school in church and

to undergo fasts. He studied scriptures in the church of St George rather than go home for lunch.

At the age of twelve Theodore came near to death with an attack of bubonic plague (the plague was one of the major horrors of the second half of the sixth century). He was carried to a church of St John the Baptist near the village and laid down inside it at the entrance to the sanctuary. There he recovered. He attributed his cure to the agency of an icon [chap. 8 of the *Life*]: drops of dew fell on to him from an icon of Christ which happened to be above him. (Figure 3 is one of the few icons of Christ which have been attributed to a date during the lifetime of Theodore.)

After his recovery he took to going at dawn to the church of St George; and he started the practice of shutting himself up in the period between Epiphany (6 January) and Palm Sunday. As he grew more and more committed to a life of deprivation (and as a mark of his commitment he gave his mother his gold belt, necklace and bracelet), he was determined to learn all the Psalms off by heart (one of the necessary attainments of a monk). This enterprise did not go smoothly; he found them difficult to learn, and he got stuck at the seventeenth psalm (not surprisingly as this happens to be one of the longest in the psalter). He made no progress at all until he prayed for a better memory in a church of St Christopher near the village. He addressed his request to an icon of Christ [chap. 13]—and found his request granted.

By the age of fourteen he was determined to live as a monk, and he left home to reside in the church of St George. He dug himself a cave below the sanctuary to act as his living place for the weeks between Epiphany and Palm Sunday. The asceticism of his way of life was commended by the bishop of nearby Anastasioupolis. It was at this time that he performed the first of his many renowned healing miracles. A man brought to him his son, ailing (it was believed) under the possession of demons. Theodore effected a cure by expelling the demons after a fashion which was to become a formula used on later occasions in the *Life*. He took oil from a lamp in the church and anointed the head of the boy in the sign of a cross.

The next major event in Theodore's life was his disappearance for two years. He had hidden himself in a cave on the mountain, revealing his whereabouts only to a pious deacon who kept the secret and brought him food. In the end it was the deacon who revealed his place of concealment. Theodore was carried out in a poor condition, covered in disgusting sores, to the church of St George, and was visited there by bishop Theodosios who decided to ordain him as a Reader, the first step towards holy orders. On the next day the bishop promoted him to subdeacon and then ordained him priest, explaining that this gave Theodore licence to celebrate the liturgy in his church; the ordination also anticipated his eventual formal acceptance as a monk. The ordination was quite contrary to the normal practice as laid down by the church: the rules for the minimum ages of ordination were 20 for a subdeacon, 25 for a deacon, 30 for a priest, and 40 for a bishop. Indeed the biographer inserts a defence by the bishop against criticisms of his action in making

3 This painting of Christ (probably produced in Constantinople in the sixth or seventh century, but touched up by a later Byzantine painter) is an icon of great quality contemporary with Theodore of Sykeon. Christ holds the Book of Gospels, with his right hand extended in greeting or blessing towards the viewer. He is depicted long-haired and bearded, like a monk.

Theodore a priest at the uncanonical age of eighteen, although it is in fact not difficult to find parallels in other *Lives* of saints for premature ordination of this kind.

The ordination of Theodore ends the first section of the narrative. This ecclesiastical event is seen as a turning point by the biographer and it is marked by him with the insertion of the chapter [22] in which he discusses himself and his method of research.

The chronological biography of the saint continues with his first taking up residence beside the church of St George, but soon deciding his strategy for officially entering the monastic state. The method which appealed to him was this. He left Sykeon and went off to the Holy Land, where he systematically visited the holy sites connected with the life of Christ, and called on monasteries and hermits' cells in and around Jerusalem and Bethlehem. (Figure 4 shows the major pilgrimage site, the Tomb of the Holy Sepulchre, as it was in 1901; Figure 5 shows the type of souvenir that could be acquired there at the time of Theodore's visit and Figure 6 shows a nineteenth-century view of the

BELOW LEFT 4 *The goal of Christian pilgrims to the Holy Land has always been the Holy Sepulchre, the supposed tomb of Christ on the hill of Golgotha and the place where the relics of the Holy Cross were found. The church on the site in Jerusalem is today thoroughly restored and renovated, and the structure around the supposed tomb in the rock was rebuilt in the nineteenth century. Theodore of Sykeon and Neophytos of Paphos visited the Holy Sepulchre, and the emperor Constantine IX Monomachos arranged for the rebuilding of the Rotunda around the tomb in the eleventh century.*

RIGHT 5 *The ampullae which were acquired by pilgrims to Jerusalem in the time of Theodore of Sykeon contained oil from the lamps which hung in the holy places because it was believed that proximity to sanctity conferred special powers on the contents of the flasks. They were decorated with scenes connected with Christ and the pilgrimage sites. In this example, two scenes are shown: Christ crucified between the two thieves (Christ is shown bearded in a medallion, similar in form to the representation on the later coins of Justinian II) and Christ's appearance to the Virgin Mary and Mary Magdalene when they visited his tomb.*

OVERLEAF 6 *The fortified monastery of Mount Sinai— on the site of the Burning Bush and below the mountain where Moses received the Law—was constructed with the help of a donation from the emperor Justinian I in the middle of the sixth century. The complex has much of its original architecture intact and the church still contains much of the medieval decoration; its community of Greek monks now has the use of the largest and most important collection of Byzantine icons.*

fortified monastery on Sinai as built for this remote community in the middle of the sixth century.) He interviewed the most extreme ascetics about their mode of life. Finally, at the monastery of the Virgin at Choziba near Jericho, he persuaded the archimandrite to dress him in the 'angelic' habit of a monk and happily travelled back to his home at the church of St George at Sykeon.

Armed with all the inside information about the ascetic practices of Palestinian monks which he had picked up on his travels, Theodore now planned his own individual challenge of endurance, though first he took the wise precaution of hiring himself a servant and accepting another monk as a disciple. He spent one winter from Christmas to Palm Sunday standing inside a wooden cage in the church of St John the Baptist; and parts of the next three or more years in an iron cage suspended in the open air on the mountain, wearing heavy iron fetters, cross, shirt and belt. One of the unpleasant physical consequences mentioned in the text is the fact that his feet froze to the floor of the cage in times of severe frost. When he lifted them up, the skin on his soles was left behind on the iron strips (at least until his servant took to throwing warm water on to his feet to thaw off the ice).

With these prominent feats of endurance and numerous attendant miracles, Theodore increased his reputation as a holy man; he was believed to have the gift of second sight in giving advice and to have supernatural abilities to cure illnesses. Yet for the second time in his life he fell seriously ill and came near to death. He recovered, but the account of his restoration to health once again brings in a reference to an icon. It is clear that beside his sick-bed there was an icon of the famous medical saints Cosmas and Damian. These saints were known in Greek as the *Anargyroi* ('taking no payment') because, even though doctors, they took no fees [chap. 39]. He imagined that he saw the saints looking exactly as they did in the icon; they felt his pulse and asked the angels of death to wait while they went off to Heaven where they petitioned the 'King' and managed to obtain an extension of life for Theodore.

The monastic community at Sykeon continued to grow and this meant that Theodore had to organize building operations in order to house the community as well as visiting pilgrims and patients waiting for a cure. The community was further brought into the control of the organized church when one of the monks was sent to the bishop of Anastasioupolis to be ordained priest and abbot of the monastery, so relieving Theodore of these duties. The monk chosen, Philoumenos, was the first monk to have been accepted as a disciple by Theodore, and he was abbot until the reign of Phocas when he was succeeded by John (who in turn, presumably, was succeeded by the biographer Georgios). The main achievement of Philoumenos was to write out most of the liturgical books used in the monastery, and it was he who taught reading and writing to the other monks, including the author of the *Life*.

The material expansion of the community at this time is very marked and is signified by the fact that Theodore could afford the cost and com-

7 *This paten, made of silver and gilded, is decorated with representations of Christ giving first bread and then wine to the Twelve Apostles. He is shown standing behind an altar and below a ciborion. This decoration was considered appropriate for the shallow dish on which the bread was offered at the liturgy and on which the consecrated host was placed after the division of the bread. Most patens had matching chalices.*

plications of becoming a consumer of the art of Constantinople. He decided to replace the altar vessels used for the eucharist in the monastery because these were made out of marble, a cheap material in Asia Minor. He dispatched an archdeacon to the capital to purchase new silver vessels, a chalice for the communion wine and a paten for the bread (Figures 7 and 8 illustrate two silver patens from the period of Theodore). On its arrival at the monastery Theodore inspected the new silverware but declared that the metal had been recycled. Despite the archdeacon's protestation that the quality of the metal was guaranteed by the five hallmarks stamped on it (like those in Figure 9 on the paten in the Istanbul Archaeological Museum), Theodore proved to the satisfaction

of the community that there was something definitely wrong with the manufacture when both objects turned black upon first being used in the liturgy. The archdeacon was sent back again to the shop in Constantinople, and found out from the records that Theodore had been right in claiming that the silver had been melted down from a previous use. Indeed it was admitted that the silver had come from the chamber-pot of a prostitute. A replacement set was taken back to the monastery [chap. 42].

As the community grew and its organization was delegated to the abbot, Theodore was free to travel widely, not only in Galatia and other provinces of Asia Minor, but also to Jerusalem (where he further proved his powers when people and church believed he caused the rainfall which ended a drought). Conversely his fame ensured that while he was in residence at Sykeon people travelled to visit him. One visitor was the future emperor Maurice, who called on him while making his

8 *This paten, also silver gilt, was, like the previous example, made in the lifetime of Theodore of Sykeon. The composition of the decoration—Christ giving Communion to the Twelve Apostles—is also the same, but in detail there are differences of emphasis and treatment.*

9 This photograph of the reverse side of the paten of Figure 8 shows the five silver-stamps of the reign of Justin II (565–578), which authenticated its silver content. This object is one of several which illustrate the five stamps used by the silversmiths of Constantinople that were mentioned in the text of the Life of Theodore of Sykeon.

way back from the east after a successful military campaign on behalf of the reigning emperor Tiberios. Theodore foretold his rise to the imperial throne. It was this prophecy which (according to the *Life*), led to the enhancement of his status through his court contacts in Constantinople and the imperial administration. On the accession of Maurice, Theodore was in a position to send letters to an emperor; the material result was an annual subsidy of corn as well as another chalice and paten. Additional building operations followed to enlarge the church in the monastery.

With the death of the bishop of Anastasioupolis Theodore's ecclesiastical status was changed; he accepted the position of bishop and moved to the city, but soon complained that he spent more time in the administration of the bishopric than in proper monastic life. So, in a bid to resolve the problem, he went off for the third time in his life to Jerusalem and made his way to the monastery of Mar Saba in

33

the hills above the Dead Sea with the intention of retiring there (Figure 10 shows the present appearance of this sixth-century monastery). After some months there, which included the period from Christmas to Palm Sunday which he spent sitting down in one of the cells as an act of endurance, Theodore was ultimately persuaded to return to his see. Once reinstalled there, he continued his cycle of miraculous healings of extreme illnesses and afflictions; the text also shows how the duties of a bishop, with the round of services, processions, and administrative work, enhanced the public status of the saint.

After eleven years as bishop of Anastasioupolis, Theodore announced his intention of resigning and went to Ancyra to ask the metropolitan bishop of the region to agree to his permanent return to the monastery at Sykeon. The decision could not be made at this level, so they agreed that both should write to the patriarch of Constantinople for a ruling. Theodore, to the annoyance of his bishop, also wrote to the emperor Maurice with the same request and this was a successful manoeuvre for the emperor instructed the patriarch on the matter. Theodore was not only allowed to resign his position but was given an honorary bishop's cope (the *omophorion*) so that he would retain the status even in his monastery, though he was advised not to return there until the rumpus over his resignation had died down.

As a result of his contacts in Constantinople, Theodore now received letters from the emperor, patriarch and other influential citizens summoning him there in order to give them blessings. This was his first visit to the capital city and it was a short one (Figure 11 is a view of the Byzantine city, but as it was in the nineteenth century under Ottoman redevelopment). A notable series of healings was achieved in Constantinople according to the *Life*, and these occurred at all levels of society; he was even supposed to have healed one of the emperor's sons of an incurable disease. At the same time Theodore was granted various special privileges for his monastery, of which probably the most advantageous was that the abbot should always be appointed directly by the patriarch of Constantinople, independent of interference from any bishop.

On his return to Sykeon, Theodore was instrumental in the further embellishment of his monastery. Not only did he obtain relics of St George from the city of Germia, but after his healing of a cleric and his wife from Heliopolis (presumably Baalbek), they commissioned a painting, apparently of Theodore, in the oratory of one of the churches in the monastery where he used to sleep [chap. 103].

A third illness of Theodore is mentioned and this time it was a chronic affliction, probably hay-fever in the summer months. As in the other cases of illness, the narration centres around an icon [chap. 108]. The difference is that the outcome of the event is not, apparently, that the disease was healed, but that the icon itself was miraculously affected by his presence. To do something about his affliction, Theodore made the journey to the city of Sozopolis in Pisidia in western Asia Minor. There a famous icon from which exuded a sweet-smelling oil was kept in the church of the Virgin. When he prayed in front of the icon in

the church, the oil gathered into a bubble and poured down on to his eyes (this icon has not survived, but Figure 12 shows an icon of the Virgin painted in the sixth century, now in the collection on Sinai).

During the reign of the emperor Phocas, Theodore went to Constantinople for the second time. The reason for this visit appears to have been the death of the abbot Philoumenos and the need to follow the special protocol for the appointment of John as his successor, which now of course required the decision of the patriarch. The status of a holy man gave Theodore direct access to the emperor, whom in this

12 This small icon, an example of those produced during the lifetime of Theodore of Sykeon, depicts the Virgin and Child enthroned, with two angels in attendance. On each side is a saint holding a cross: probably St Theodore the General to the left, and St George or St Demetrios to the right.

case he had not met before. But the incentive for the emperor to see him was the hope that the holy man would cure the pain in his hands and feet. This cure was duly obtained, but Theodore also censured the emperor for the murders which had occurred in his reign.

While Theodore was in Constantinople, the monks of the monastery in which he was staying commissioned a painter to produce a portrait of him secretly [chap. 139]. This was done by the painter observing Theodore surreptitiously through a small opening in the wall of his room and this allowed him to produce what was required of him—a good likeness. After the painting was completed, the monks made the painter take it to the saint so that he might bless it. The saint made a joke to the effect that the painter was a thief and his presence seemed to suggest he was intending to steal something. Theodore blessed the painting, but with his remark he had betrayed a belief that an icon which copied a person could somehow take away something of the original and have a reality of its own in his image.

Theodore returned to his monastery at Sykeon to which he had by this time managed to attract more than fifty monks. The text shows no signs of running out of miraculous healings to record—or of the occasions when Theodore advised those who came to him that it was enough to have treatment or go to a doctor. He had reached the age—or status—where he was prepared to rebuke anybody if he disapproved of their way of life, even imperial officials if they came to him. After the death of Phocas he received letters of invitation to Constantinople from the new emperor Heraklios and from the patriarch Sergios. He found it prudent to go to the capital for the third time. On this occasion he resided in the patriarchal palace, next to the cathedral church of St Sophia; the public swarmed into the north gallery of the church to see him. Theodore was received in the palace and agreed to give his blessing to the heir to the throne, who had been carefully named Constantine.

The final chapters of the biography describe at some length Theodore's last illness, from which he made a temporary recovery. This time icons take no part in the narrative and the saint is offered no remission from death. Instead there are several accounts of his last dreams, including his visions of Heaven. Heraclios visited him while on the road past the monastery on his way to the Persian wars and received a blessing. Theodore foretold his own imminent death, but prophesied, correctly, a reign of thirty years for the emperor.

News of Theodore's death on 22 April 613 reached Constantinople very rapidly and the patriarch Sergios not only celebrated a special service in St Sophia but decreed an annual commemoration. This can be taken as equivalent to official canonization.

The 170 chapters of the *Life* of Theodore offer a vast amount of material for historical analysis. For the Byzantines themselves, they supplied a racy narrative as much as Christian edification. In the course of his life, Theodore is said to have achieved a remarkable number of miracles. It is the description of these which forms much of the narrative, though in the summary above no attempt has been made to list them.

The language of the *Life* is so often reminiscent of the New Testament that it can be difficult to decide whether an atmosphere of sanctity or a historical event is being conveyed. But however striking the miracles may seem, it is no part of the approach in this book to be concerned with questions about their authenticity.

Instead of asking about the truth of the miracles in the *Life*, an alternative approach is to consider how the biographer is depicting Theodore. Under his chronological scheme is concealed a structured pattern of development. This is revealed in three strands of description; the ways in which Theodore is portrayed as abnormal, the stages of his progression through a life of perceived holiness, and the sources of his power.

Theodore of Sykeon was not a 'normal' member of society. He was illegitimate, and gew up in a one-parent family with a mother who during his childhood developed from being a prostitute to being a relatively well-off member of the village community. The child slept with his mother and other women of the inn where they worked; possibly communal sleeping arrangements were normal. Theodore is distinguished from the other children of the community by his greater intelligence and speed of learning (though his biographer is quick to mention his popularity in order to forestall the reader's reaction that he might have been disliked). But Theodore does not follow a pattern of life which would lead to smooth integration into the community. His individuality and separateness are strikingly established by his adoption of an ascetic way of life—actually under the overt influence of the male member of his extended family in the inn. The chef Stephen not only is responsible for the prosperity of the inn and for the fact that the women were able to give up prostitution, but becomes the model for the young Theodore's attitudes to life.

Theodore's asceticism progressed through a series of rapid steps: first fasting, then solitary prayer, then confinement to a cave in a church, then two years hidden in a cave on the mountain from which he emerged as unattractive a figure as Job and like John the Baptist, the model for all monks. It was these feats of asceticism which earned him the grant of official status in the church through ordination as a priest, prematurely and without any official training. This recognition of his way of life by the local bishop became no more than a stage in his career which confirmed his decision to become a monk and helped him gain permission to wear the monastic habit from a monastery of Palestine, the region where the largest number of organized monasteries were located at this period. The source of the legitimation of Theodore's status came notably from the Holy Land, and this was confirmed by the further legitimacy given to his special position by the biographer's use of biblical language and parallels.

In the course of his life Theodore passed through a series of stages of recognition: he was accepted as a holy man of a special kind by the village of Sykeon, by the people of the nearest city, by the community of the monastery of Choziba, by the archbishop of Ancyra, and by successive emperors and patriarchs of Constantinople as well as a considerable number of people in the regions of Asia Minor. Yet his position as a holy man always meant he was regarded as abnormal in society; he was recognized by all levels of society but still lived outside the normal conventions of behaviour. Society worked better because of his existence, but he had no 'place' in it, although his gradual recognition gave him the basis of power. He is recognized as having within him special gifts which were supposed to have been given to him at conception, and which can be developed because of the manner of his life and his choice of environment. His pattern of life, because it is socially acceptable, enlarges his power. What began as personal moral and medical power becomes social power in certain spheres—ecclesiastical, monastic, and political.

Theodore, however, never exploits all his potential social powers to the full, but by his way of life diffuses them. He never, for example, acted as a parish priest but was given the rank in order that he might celebrate regular eucharist as a solitary; and when he was a bishop he was reluctant to give priority to the administrative or didactic duties of the office. As a didactic theologian he was unsystematic and he took a practical but unsophisticated approach. There is the example of the curious (though not unparalleled) piece of theology which Theodore expounded in Constantinople [chap. 137] when he condemned the habit, especially of the rich, of going to the baths after participating in the eucharist; the narrative introduces a certain element of irony in the reaction of the clergy of St Sophia who asked him whether his condemnation is based on scripture or personal revelation. This kind of homely theology was no doubt fairly typical of this kind of holy man, and in the case of Neophytos in the twelfth century (see Chapter 6), it was accompanied by a belief that the holy spirit spoke personally through the saint. In political life, Theodore could bestow moral authority on an emperor, but he had no practical advice to give and was in no position to make any kind of practical political decisions. His strongest practical position of power was in the monastery at Sykeon, and here one finds that he was capable of delegating so that others had the responsibilities of administration, of training the monks and of acting as priests at the liturgy.

The power given to him through the public acceptance of his healing powers, both for physical and psychological conditions, is the most subtle. He does not in fact replace secular doctors, but he does have an identifiable place in the 'hierarchy of resort' as the last possible help. Beyond him is only God, and he has a special relationship with God; he is an effective channel to God to which ordinary people can be given access. The holy man therefore is seen to make a decision whether he can treat patients or whether they should be referred to a lower level of treatment. He is prepared to refer such patients to particular specialist doctors and the advice he gave them was very precise and with all appearance of considerable experience. For example, people might ask whether he recommended bathing in the hot springs at Dablioi or taking the waters at Apsoda [chap. 146]. He might advise against both, and instead recommend purging drinks from one doctor or another whose names he would supply; alternatively he might recommend one or other of the springs, or even another spa.

A corollary of Theodore's publicly accepted position and social power was the acquisition of funds and material possessions, largely in return for his saintly services. The sources of all the funds which came into the monastery are not specified in the text. These must have been partly used by Theodore for his own purposes, such as his travel—just as he was helped by the monks of St Autonomos near Nicomedia who met Theodore with horses and equipment, a clear indication of the wealth of that community—but the obvious expenditure in the monastery was on the construction of the signs and symbols of the presence of a holy man. The nature of these and how their use punctuated the life of Theodore constitutes the most complex part of the way that the holy man was depicted in the biography; the role of the visual was essential in the establishment of his power in society.

As one looks through the text of the life of Theodore, it becomes clear that although he grew up and moved among a rural community—with occasional visits to the great cities of his time like Ancyra, Jerusalem and Constantinople—and although he was committed to continual acts of asceticism and deprived himself of luxuries, yet in the monastery and other ecclesiastical settings he was in the presence of the productions of artists. This art has more than one role in the life of the saint. One part which it plays is quite literal—it supplied a type of environment; but there are other, less obvious roles where art takes on a more complex significance. The most obvious literal function of art is in the decoration of the monastery: it is an unquestioned assumption in the text that this was not a place of bare walls or whitewashed settings but that art should be present.

A description of Theodore's clothing and personal decoration provides the first focus on the visual in the *Life*. The first mention of what we would call 'art', though no doubt the term 'minor art' might seem more applicable, comes when at the age of about six Theodore is to be sent to Constantinople by his mother to make his fortune. His outfit for the journey is described: he has a gold belt and rich clothing [chap. 5]. His mother wanted him to appear of high social status, and it was by the prominent display of these possessions that she thought this could be signified. The use of gold on the belt is specially noted, as a feature which showed both the material position of the wearer and how wealth could be tastefully used. The idea of conspicuous display of material possessions on the body and in particular of a preference for gold as the agent for this is of course not limited to this period and society. It is indeed still a prominent feature of the modern Turkish villages of Asia Minor, where street vendors display trays of gold ornaments and where these are commonly worn in public. Only a few chapters later [12] an action of the young Theodore further illustrates the point: when his mother tries to persuade him to leave the church of St George in which he had begun to spend most of his time and come down to their home to receive guests, he not only refuses to leave but makes a gesture to demonstrate his distaste for the material world by removing some of what he is wearing, namely a gold belt, necklace and bracelet. He was a boy aged between twelve and fourteen when his mother considered it appropriate to dress him in this way; her decision demonstrates again how important such signs of status were felt to be in this society. Much later in the *Life* the importance of denoting status by clothing is prominently reiterated when Theodore is allowed to resign as bishop but at the same time to retain his status by being given the right to wear the episcopal garment, the *omophorion*. He therefore had the choice of wearing as occasion fitted either the plain 'angelic' garment of the monk or the conspicuous garments of a bishop.

Icons first appear in the text early on in the narrative. The importance of the references to these icons is that they show how easily the biographer accepts the existence of such 'decoration' in a church, and, one can presume, indicate how Theodore from his childhood would have learned to accept these as the normal furnishings of a church; something he never questioned, even if in his way of life he rejected all luxuries. Two small churches of Sykeon where Theodore went in his boyhood contained an icon as part of their furnishings [chaps. 8, 13], and there is no suggestion in the text that this is anything unusual, or that they need special description for the reader. In both cases, the subject of the icon was a portrait of Christ (several such icons have survived from this period). The icons in Sykeon were most probably paintings on panels, and it is likely that they were placed in or beside the sanctuary rather than on a high screen between the sanctuary and the nave of the church. Although such an 'iconostasis' is a familiar feature of any Orthodox church today, where it results in the rites being carried out secretly behind a screen of icons, for most of the period covered in this book the arrangements were more open, and the sanctuary was divided from the nave of the church only by a barrier known as the *templon*. This was generally made of marble or wooden beams, and had the function of separating the congregation from the sanctuary, rather than of blocking their view of the altar. The idea of an opaque screen between nave and sanctuary seems to have developed only in the monasteries of the twelfth century, and this screen was made by fixing icons or curtains to the *templon*; the full icon screen of the iconostasis dates from the fourteenth century.

In the course of the biography of Theodore there are a number of other references to the existence of icons in churches and monasteries: a portrait icon of Cosmas and Damian above his bed when he was ill [39], a picture of the saint himself which was specially commissioned for the side-chapel of the church of St Michael where he slept [103], the miraculous icon in the church of the Virgin at Sozopolis, presumably an icon which portrayed the Virgin [108], and the portrait icon of Theodore specially made from life in Constantinople [139]. In addition to these references to paintings, other manufactured objects which were part of the furnishings of Christian buildings are mentioned. Theodore's monastery, for example, owns a set of marble liturgical vessels, to which he adds a more expensive pair of silver pieces, a chalice and paten, made in Constantinople [42]; later another chalice and paten is sent to the monastery from the emperor Maurice in Constantinople [54]. One church visited by Theodore has an ambo and chancel barrier, and one must assume that these sculptured fittings were part of all large churches in the period. The purpose of an ambo was to provide an elevated platform above the congregation from which to give the readings in the liturgy and for other ceremonial occasions; originally it was not intended as a place from which sermons might be given—these were spoken from the seating in the apse of the church—but in the course of time the ambo took on the function of a pulpit, and the seats in the apse, originally easily visible over the low chancel barrier of the early churches, became obscured firstly in part by the *templon* and then completely by the iconostasis. Other normal accessories of any church were lamps [112], candles [121, 157], censers [157], and processional crosses [127–8]. Works of art were of course not limited to the experience of those in church, but the only work of art outside the setting of a church to be specifically described is an antique marble sarcophagus. The lid of this object was used in a village as a trough and the base was left in its position on the outskirts [118]; antique plaques are also mentioned in the text [114, 115] since dangerous pagan spirits were supposed to emerge from them and Theodore was involved in their exorcism.

One notable production was a gold cross made for Theodore by one of his grateful and most powerful devotees, Domnitziolos, who was the nephew of Phocas and commander of the army in the Persian war. After he received the saint's blessing, he donated so much money to the monastery that it could afford to re-roof the church of St George with lead tiles and to acquire various sacred vessels [120]. In order to receive the gold cross promised by Domnitziolos, Theodore sent a deacon from the monastery off to Constantinople [128]. This man was required to wait while the jeweller made up the cross from the gold given to him by the donor. The method of production meant that the patriarch of Constantinople could also donate several major relics to be inserted in the boss at the centre of the cross—these included a piece of the True Cross, a piece of the rock of Golgotha, a piece of the tomb of Christ and a fringe from the garment of the Virgin Mary. The gold cross was intended for processional use and for adoration (*proskynesis*).

All these works of art are evidence of the fact that an embellished environment was felt to be necessary. It is also clear that the purposes of art were neither exclusively functional nor exclusively ornamental; attention was given to the materials and aesthetic appearance of liturgical vessels. Art was an essential adjunct to the ascetic life of the monk. At the same time it added to the power of the saint; he was given art as an acceptable token of thanks for his guidance and miraculous help, and in turn this art declared his powers both through the materials used and through its symbolism.

The influence of the visual is far more pervasive in the life of Theodore and his society than a simple increase in the beauty of the environment. Art moulded popular perceptions and the appearance and character of the holy—the 'unknowable' and 'unseeable'. When at the age of twelve Theodore had a vision in which he saw Christ and was encouraged by him to live the ascetic life, his perception of Christ was certainly fashioned by portrayals in art. In the same way icons were the source of his perceptions of the Virgin Mary, who appears in a vision [chap. 10] unnamed, but described unambiguously as a woman dressed in purple at the side of Christ. Art is in the same way likely to be the source of the way in which St George is seen in a dream [167] as mounted on a horse, a common rendering in the icons of this period (as for example in one of the icons in the collection of Sinai shown in Figure 13).

13 This folding three-part triptych (of which the central image has been lost) is a more complicated type of icon than that shown in Figure 12, but examples of this kind were probably produced in the time of Theodore of Sykeon. On the left wing is a representation of St Theodore the General and on the right St George. This particular triptych dates stylistically from a century or more after the time of Theodore of Sykeon, but its linear manner and the routine quality of the painting is probably similar to many of the icons painted locally for the churches of Asia Minor but now lost, among which the portrait of St George was a popular subject.

A number of turning-points in the narrative are highlighted by the introduction of icons. In part the references to art in these cases are a device for giving emphasis to key events in the personal life of the saint. The role of the visual in these examples is a complicated one, and they need to be considered in some detail in order to see how we may argue that power is sited in images.

It is through the agency of an icon that Theodore recovers from bubonic plague [8], and this is the first crisis in his life which is marked by a visual confrontation. The icon is a portrait of Christ, and so his recovery and future life are also to be attributed to the agency of God as icon; he owes his life to the concern of a supernatural being in the form of an image. The method of his cure is physical: he comes into contact with drops of dew which fall from the icon on to his body, and these are understood by his biographer to be signs of heavenly grace towards Theodore. The visualization is, then, to be construed as a symbol of the special concern of God for a particular individual; Theodore learns through it that a special place in society on earth is designated for him. Again it is an icon of Christ which gives him a further sign of his acceptability for a monastic life [13]. This is the implication of the way he learned the Psalms, something he had to accomplish if he was to be able to take part in the monastic office which is constructed around the psalter. Theodore is said to have gone into the church of St Christopher and to have prayed by 'throwing himself on his face' and asking God to make him good at learning the Psalms. But it is only when he gets up off the ground and prays directly to the icon of Christ that he receives the answer to the request, marked by a sweetness more pleasant than honey pouring into his mouth. It was through the sweet taste in his mouth that he realized that he had received an answer to his prayer and was able to learn the rest of the Psalms in a few days. In this account there are two stages of prayer, but the effective moment is when Theodore makes his request in front of an icon; the sense of taste is introduced into the account in addition to that of sight in order to confirm the answer to his prayer.

Again an icon takes a prominent part in Theodore's cure during his second dangerous illness [39], from which he was expected to die. He has above his bed a portrait icon of Cosmas and Damian. The story suggests that the two figures come out of the icon to act as doctors to Theodore and to go off to Heaven to gain on his behalf an extension of his life on earth. Theodore, then, makes his contact with the 'other world' through the activity of the inhabitants of an icon. In this particular narrative there is a sense of passing, like Alice, into a looking-glass world. Icons are perceived as the means through which direct contact is to be made with the supernatural world. In this kind of mediation Theodore would seem to be a privileged individual. The normal human being afflicted with illness would go to a doctor or would turn in desperation to the holy man, who might in the course of his treatment use oil from lamps which hung in church in front of relics or icons. The implication of the *Life* is that the effective treatment of illness through the agency of icons is limited to those of the holy man alone. This contrasts with the final days and death of Theodore when no icons are used at all; this exonerates them from any possibility of failure. Another case of the power of icons is that of the icon at Sozopolis [108] where the status of the holy man is proved by the quantity of perfumed oil which exudes from the panel, but there is no statement to the effect that his chronic eye affliction was permanently cured. This is a miraculous icon which represents the Virgin, but which appears to act in its own right. The powers apparently vested in this image may parallel Theodore's belief, as stated to the artist who painted his portrait icon in Constantinople, that the icon would take away some part of himself; the implication is that the icon might function independently of Theodore.

This examination of the functions of icons in the depiction of the life of Theodore has shown their part in the saint's sources of power. Icons were not only signs of the status and power of the holy man; they took on a special role in the mediation of prayers between the holy man and God and they are effectively agents in all the major crises of health in his life. In other Byzantine texts of the period, there is evidence that the conception of icons as 'supernatural' sources of power was accepted elsewhere, and that access to miraculous assistance from icons was often widely assumed, and was not limited to specially sanctified individuals. This was probably the case with such an icon as the Virgin of Sozopolis, and it is to some extent an exaggeration of the *Life* to focus on the power of this image towards Theodore. What was the purpose of the commission of the icon of the holy man himself by the community where he stayed in Constantinople except for future use in mediation with the 'other world'?

Some extreme cases of belief in the power of icons are known from other texts apparently from the seventh century. There is the case of a woman obtaining water from a dry well by lowering an image of a holy man into it; and of another who was cured by drinking a potion in which was mixed a painting of Cosmas and Damian which had been scraped off the wall. Such stories can often be seen to make the assumption that in some way the icon carries in it the presence of the holy figures portrayed on it. But such stories take us beyond the world of Theodore of Sykeon, which is, as conveyed to us, much more carefully ordered.

The stated aim of the *Life* [chap. 22] is to demonstrate the special powers of Theodore as an encouragement to the young to copy his virtuous life. To achieve his aim, the biographer offers a book full of miracles and of ascetic achievements. Through the resulting text the impression emerges of a well-ordered society with a number of set patterns of behaviour and communication.

Byzantine society at this time is one which has at its head a king on earth, who, as in the case of Phocas, can act with evil. This is set against the other society which has at its head the heavenly king, who is open to hearing appeals from his subjects and can change fate but who cannot act with evil. For the inhabitant of rural Asia Minor decisions are taken by the powerful elsewhere—in the earthly or heavenly capital. Even the established church has its head in Constantinople and it is here that major decisions must be taken. The theological status of the minor principle about baths after the eucharist made by Theodore presented some difficulty to the clergy of the capital, who could not decide whether it rested on the authority of scripture or on that of the saint himself. The workings of authority in this kind of community are given concrete illustrations in the *Life*, and one gains an insight into the social mobility of one individual. Once Theodore had gained a particular status in his own region, which was backed by conspicuous ecclesiastical rank, he was courted by the aristocracy and by the ruling classes, since he could add to their own social image—as well as allowing them to participate in his special powers when needed. He does himself show some practical political knowledge and is ready to comment on the government of the state.

Some of the buildings and works of art from the time of this society still survive. The church of St Sophia in Constantinople, the scene of some of the events of the narrative, can still be visited. Icons and liturgical vessels from precisely this time can be seen in several museums, and the modern visitor to the monastery of St Catherine on Mount Sinai can see a sixth-century monastic church still in use, and can look at icons contemporary with the events which took place in the narrative of this text. Little is said in the *Life* about who painted and who commissioned icons. There are icons in the local churches of Sykeon during the childhood of Theodore, but nothing is said about the artists who produced the icons or the donors who organized their manufacture. Although they were in public places, they could certainly be addressed in private by the individual at prayer.

The art which entered the monastery of Theodore, and which was therefore directly in contact with the holy man himself, was sponsored in the main by a small rich elite and was the work of the artists of Constantinople. The nature of the art which has so far been discussed was therefore substantially controlled in its type and method of production by a limited section of society which could impose its ideas on the public. Another effect of the patronage of this particular social group was that, perhaps imperceptibly, the wealth of the aristocracy can be observed to be passing into the domain of the monastery, a process which gained momentum in the later periods to be considered. A possible objection to the conclusions reached so far is that they are limited in their historical application because they devolve around a rural society in a predominantly urban empire. One answer to such criticism is to break down these opposed categories and to argue that the rigid distinction of town and country cannot be made in Byzantine society. But a more pragmatic way forward is to look at the evidence from a provincial city and to see how society works in this environment. The next chapter will therefore broaden the interpretation by turning to the evidence from a major city in the western part of the Byzantine empire.

By looking in this chapter at the conjunction of written text and works of art, the conclusion has been reached that the functions of the visual arts at this time can only be understood by considering their role on a number of levels. The surviving works of art do give direct evidence of the environment of Byzantine society in the period and all the images played an enormously active role in the perceptions of the population. In the sixth and seventh centuries, the range of possible stimulants to thinking was so much more limited than today when newspapers, printed books, radio, television, films etc are taken for granted and classified as the 'media'. In the time of Theodore the range and quantity of manuscript books was very limited, and the influence of church sermons or public orations, when these occurred, was likely to be enormous. The impact of works of art must also have been correspondingly greater than today, especially in the sphere of the holy. They were an essential part of life. In any church the atmosphere of reverence must have been perceived as heightened by the presence of manufactured objects such as liturgical vessels; these were even more effective when made from rarer materials and of better workmanship. Through his acquisition of works of art, Theodore contributed to such a conception of the proper appearance of a church.

But the works of art available to Theodore and to his society did not have a single function; their role changed according to the spiritual status of the viewer. For the holy man the icon could be treated as the most effective channel for prayers to the 'other world'. For society in general the icon was at this period one of the possible sources of help in moments of hope, trouble or illness. People hoped that a disease would be healed by going to see doctors, relics of the saints, icons, or a holy man himself, if there was one of proven abilities available. It seems likely that the result of this situation was an increasing dependence on icons for such purposes as time went on, but the kind of evidence available is not conclusive. The logic is that gradually icons could be trusted as more and more reliable sources of help if they were seen to produce repeated results. Unlike doctors and holy men they did not die, and unlike relics they were easily accessible and could be openly manufactured. Furthermore their remarkable effectiveness in helping Theodore cannot have escaped the notice of those with a knowledge of the *Life*.

2
THE SAINT IMAGINED: ST DEMETRIOS OF THESSALONIKI

THE *Life of Theodore of Sykeon* allowed the construction of a picture of the nature of life and the character of beliefs in a rural society in Byzantine Asia Minor. It was begun before the death of the saint in 613, and the bulk of the text was probably completed soon after that. It sees the historical events of the second half of the sixth century and the early seventh century through the eyes of a monk looking back over a time of apparently increasing crisis and leading up to a war in which the Persian armies were advancing closer and closer to Constantinople. The *Life* is a moralizing book, an invitation to follow a way of life which will lead to greater favour from God and conform to the ideal morality recommended by Christian ideology. Its recommendation is politically passive and it does not consider active responses to the crisis. It does not recommend, for example, joining the army, but rather an ascetic way of life—a less active solution, if hardly a soft option! The text also provides evidence for the production and veneration of icons, for belief in the power of icons to work miracles and for the part those icons played in helping men and women to structure and order the experiences of their lives.

One of the limitations for us of the *Life* of Theodore of Sykeon is that the icons mentioned in the text no longer exist; we can only visualize the art of Theodore's society through other works of a similar kind which have by chance survived. Elsewhere, however, we can find a situation where both a text and some of the related images and environment have survived and can be juxtaposed. This text is the *Miracles of St Demetrios* of Thessaloniki and through the evidence of this work we can look again at a society of the second half of the sixth century and beginning of the seventh. The text and the historical events recorded in it are precisely contemporary with the *Life of Theodore*; but they take us to another part of the Byzantine Empire, to the city of Thessaloniki (see map, p. 12). This city is in what is now the northern part of Greece, but had at that time become a place on the frontier between the empire and its invaders, the demarcation line between Christians and pagans. With hindsight we know that the city did not fall to the invaders, but was one of the few cities in the Balkans to survive over a century of sieges and attacks and of isolation from the rest of the empire. At the time we are interested in the outlook for the city must have seemed dire. The Byzantine army was based in Thessaloniki, and every citizen was involved in the war. There is no mention of the influence of a holy man like Theodore of Sykeon during this period of crisis, but a supernatural defender of a different kind did appear: St Demetrios. This saint was martyred in the early fourth century; but it is the stage which his cult had reached around the year 600, and the miracles connected with him at that time, which will form the focus of this chapter.

Initially the evidence that will be presented from Thessaloniki seems much more direct than that from Sykeon. The existing city and its medieval monuments act as a bridge between the present day and the detailed narrative of the texts; and the survival of one of the buildings, the church of St Demetrios, in which some of the actions and miracles took place, means that the surroundings of these can be visited (although the structure of the church has been substantially restored in recent years). Likewise the streets of the city can be followed and some of its walls still stand to mark the extent of the medieval area. Mosaics still exist which were set up in the church of St Demetrios around the time of the events described in the text of the *Miracles*. Yet the evidence of this visual material is less direct and easy to handle than it may at first appear. Ways of perception and responses to images have changed so much since the seventh century that it is inappropriate to rely on a modern intuitive approach to what remains. For the moment, though, one work of art will help to introduce the subject of this chapter. From this work we shall gain a first impression of how the citizens of Thessaloniki in the early seventh century perceived St Demetrios.

The church of St Demetrios in Thessaloniki, the major church in the centre of the city (and the location of many of the events to be described) contains a large mosaic icon. This is set on to the north face of the pier to the right of the sanctuary (Figure 14). The panel, it can be deduced, was set up soon after the year 620 and it is both a thank-offering to a saint on behalf of the city, and a commemoration of donations given to the church which led to its restoration. The panel is positioned some way above eye-level and the three figures it contains are symmetrically arranged, giving an impression of formality and order. Each figure is distinguished by his dress—a mark of his status and rank in society; but each one nevertheless is from the highest levels of society. Each is also distinguished physically from the others, most obviously by the presence or absence of a beard, or by the size of the beard.

The beardless and therefore presumably young figure at the centre is dressed in garments with a richly embroidered surface pattern, and with a panel inset over the waist. This garment is to be read as the dress of someone belonging to an aristocratic family—probably one whose members belonged to the 'senate', the direct continuation of the

14 This large mosaic is now the most prominent of those to survive inside the church of St Demetrios at Thessaloniki. It is accompanied by a text recording the restoration of the church and the salvation of the city by the saint. St Demetrios (centre) puts his arms around the bishop and the eparch: a sign of his supernatural favour towards the two men who rebuilt and redecorated his church, and towards their city.

major Roman council of state, but an institution of little power in the Byzantine period. This central figure is marked with a round halo which designates him as a saint. His age and rank fit those of the legendary descriptions of the patron saint of the church, St Demetrios, and this identification is confirmed by an inscription at the base of the panel, which will be given below. The saint has his arms around each of his companions, as if they were together at the same time. The man on the saint's right (our left) is in the place of greater honour according to biblical and Byzantine convention. He is wearing the *omophorion* of a bishop and has a full untrimmed beard. He carries the further mark of his office, the holy book of scripture which it is his duty to expound to the faithful. The facial type shown in this image is found in several other representations of bishops and monks at this period and was probably so strong a convention of the time that the lost icons of St Theodore (the *Life* reveals that a number were made in his lifetime) may well have resembled it. The third figure, with a fashioned beard, seems identifiable from his garments as the governor of the city; or, as he is called in the text to be studied, the 'eparch' (the prefect of the region), who was technically military commander with the additional responsibility of civil administration. This office was an adaptation of the earlier system of the military organization of the Balkans under the Praetorian Prefecture of Illyricum. This eparch holds as tokens of his office a sceptre and a purse.

These three mosaic figures stare outwards, in such a way that the observer can make contact with their eyes and the figures themselves seem less remote. Although St Demetrios has his arms around his two companions, and hence shows his benevolence towards them and through them to the city, yet to our eyes the message is conveyed with the utmost formality. Behind the three figures runs a wall with some kind of material laid along it; this might equally be interpreted as portraying the city walls, an interior setting, or even the square haloes sometimes used as a convention in the art of this period for the indication of a living personage. The text inscribed below demonstrates that it commemorates a particular historical event:

You see the donors of the glorious house on either side of the martyr Demetrios, who turned aside the barbarous wave of barbarian fleets and was the city's salvation.

From this icon and its inscription we may understand that the saint is being credited with some miraculous rescue of the city from attack by sea by an enemy fleet. The spiritual and temporal leaders of the city have made a donation to the church of St Demetrios to record their belief in the supernatural protection of the saint. The picture is part of that donation and has a double function: it exists both to record the event and as an icon to which future prayers can be directed and through which worshippers may hope for a miraculous answer from Heaven. By recording a miracle, the icon itself takes on the potentiality of a miracle-making image. The full implications of this icon and its range of evocations can only be appreciated by a deeper look at the times and circumstances of its production.

The *Miracles of St Demetrios* is the key text through which to enter into the society of Thessaloniki in the late sixth and early seventh centuries. It reveals the local popularity of St Demetrios in various ways. Not only would any visitor to early medieval Thessaloniki normally go straight away on his arrival to pray in the church of St Demetrios, but also the name Demetrios was the commonest choice for boys born in the city—as is demonstrated by the ridicule poured on an African bishop who went round Thessaloniki thinking he could easily find the house of a young man whom he knew simply as Demetrios. Yet the reasons for the popularity of St Demetrios are difficult to explain. There is even a problem in accounting for his appearance at all, since the evidence about the saint and the beginning of his cult is so limited. In fact the visual evidence here happens to be earlier than the written sources: the church and its decoration are themselves the best proof of the important role of the saint in the city from the fifth century onwards.

The story of the life and martyrdom of Demetrios is known to us from texts written down in the ninth century or later, and in the period with which we are concerned in this chapter it is impossible to be sure how far these stories had already been developed. Certain features of his cult do seem to belong to a period later than the seventh century; for example, the ability of the saint (or rather of his specially trained clergy) to produce in his church a flow of perfumed oil (the same 'myrrh' which the icon of the church of the Virgin at Sozopolis produced for Theodore of Sykeon) was only discovered at a later period. Likewise, the conception of Demetrios as a military general does not seem to be known in our period. The icons to be considered here help to reconstruct the form in which he was visualized up to the seventh century, although they do not allow us to arrive at a strict chronology of the various stages in the construction of the saint's supposed persona. Their principal value is in illustrating his powers.

The question 'who was Demetrios?' rapidly becomes a question of where and how his personality was invented. The first clear landmark in the cult is the foundation of the large church of St Demetrios in Thessaloniki, probably to be dated to the middle of the fifth century although this date rests only on the indications of architectural and sculptural style. In type the church is a large wooden-roofed basilica; it has a transept at the east end (below which lay a crypt) and galleries above the aisles. It could therefore house a considerable congregation at services and provide a major focus for pilgrimage. The considerable size of this church shows that by the date of its construction the cult was already an important one in the city (Figure 15 shows the church in its modern state; Figure 16 as it was after the fire of 1917 and before its reconstruction).

The appearance and development of the cult of St Demetrios can be related to the fortunes of Thessaloniki. The middle of the fifth century, when the church was built, was a time of material prosperity in

RIGHT *16 This photograph shows the condition of the church of St Demetrios after the fire of 1917. Thessaloniki was within the Turkish empire from the fifteenth century until 1912, and the minaret seen here dates from the conversion of the church into a mosque in 1492 (it was taken down during the restoration). All the mosaics were concealed during the Ottoman period; some were rediscovered in 1907 during works in the mosque, and the others after 1917.*

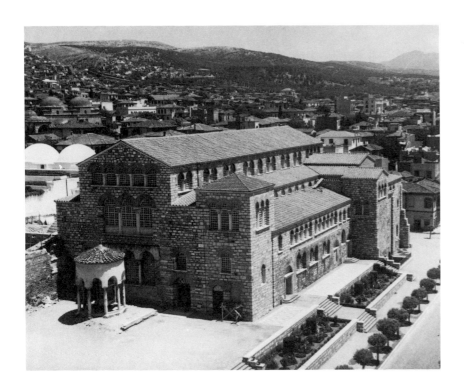

15 The church of St Demetrios in Thessaloniki has been substantially rebuilt since the devastating fire which destroyed much of the city in 1917. In this view from the southwest, several entrance doors can be seen on the west front and south side; the church was designed from the beginning to be used by a large congregation and to accommodate crowds of visitors. Its site was in the central part of the medieval city, around which the walls ran from the sea (to the right) up to the acropolis (to the left).

the chequered history of the region. A glance at the map (p. 12) might suggest that Thessaloniki ought to be one of the great capital cities of the Continent, situated as it is on the north side of the Aegean Sea, with a natural harbour and easy access by land into the interior of Europe. Since Constantine the Great is said to have considered Thessaloniki as a candidate for his new capital before finally deciding on Constantinople, he must have seen the possibilities and he went to the extent of developing the harbour. Yet the city remained relatively unimportant. Its potential for expansion always depended on a combined political control of the sea and the hinterland and this was seldom the situation in our period. As a result Thessaloniki was just one among several urban centres in Late Antiquity; its importance increased later as other cities succumbed to foreign conquest or declined for other reasons.

Thessaloniki was laid out as a city by Cassander, one of the rulers of the Macedonian empire in Greece after the death of Alexander the Great; under him (between 316 and 297 BC) it was given its first walls (Figure 17) and its grid system of streets. This city of the Hellenistic period was redeveloped by the eastern Roman emperor Galerius around AD 300. He built a hippodrome and an adjacent vast palace, triumphal arch and even a mausoleum (a vast rotunda to which his body was never taken for burial after his death in the Danube region in 311). The presence of Galerius in the city for these years was marked visually by his vast buildings of red brick and spiritually by his severe persecutions of Christians between 303 and 311. To this time and these buildings belongs the supposed martyrdom of Demetrios.

This environment of Hellenistic and Roman buildings marked the city until the changes of the middle of the fifth century. The political reason for the new development of Thessaloniki was its change in status. The city became the provincial capital of the whole region and the seat of the Prefect of Illyricum. The prefect and his army were evacuated from their previous base at Sirmium on the Danube in 441/2. The walls of the new command post were rapidly strengthened between 442/3 and 447, and it seems that it was at this time that the hippodrome was largely demolished—possibly to terminate the associations with Christian martyrdom, or, less symbolically, as a source of materials for strengthening the walls. The extent of the new administrative and Christian buildings made the city the main Byzantine centre in the Balkans. Several vast new churches were constructed with luxurious ornamentation made of marble brought from the Proconnesian quarries on the islands in the Sea of Marmara. One of these was the great basilica dedicated to St Demetrios.

During the first two centuries of the use of this church, the population of the city passed through one crisis after another, and it is against this background that the texts and icons must be set. There were various natural disasters, including severe earthquakes, and in the second half of the sixth century the city must also have lost a great proportion of its population through deaths from the plague; a recent estimate suggests that almost a third of the population of the cities of the Byzantine

PREVIOUS PAGE *17 Thessaloniki had protective walls throughout its history from Hellenistic times (this section is on the Acropolis). Their fabric belongs to several periods and they were kept in repair during the Byzantine period, but much of what can be seen today probably belongs to the massive building campaign of the middle of the fifth century.*

empire perished during this epidemic. Another problem was in Thessaloniki's constitutional status; the emperor Justinian, born in the Balkan hinterland, believed that under his military policy the region could once again be made entirely secure. He tried to move the military command and the ecclesiastical control of the region to a new city, which he built very close to his birthplace, and called Justiniana Prima (probably to be identified as the short-lived settlement excavated at Caričin Grad in Yugoslavia). The idea was not fully carried through, but Thessaloniki no doubt found imperial funds diverted to the new city, even though the eparch and the bishop stayed put. But the worst problems began when the city fell under constant attack from Slav and Avar-Slav tribes after the first assaults in 584 and 586—all these nomadic tribes had moved into the Balkans from Central Asia, the Avars, who were probably Mongolian, arriving first in the 550s. For over a century the citizens lived under continual siege conditions. It was during this period of crisis that the cult of Demetrios expanded apparently to dominate the minds of the people of Thessaloniki.

The story of the life of St Demetrios, as opposed to his posthumous miracles, is known, as we have seen, from accounts compiled in the ninth century and later. According to the shortest version of the various *Passions*, the emperor Galerius during his early fourth-century persecutions of the Christians imprisoned Demetrios in the Baths of Thessaloniki. In the course of public games at the Stadium, Galerius became so angry when his favourite gladiator Lyaios was killed in a duel with Nestor (described as a young disciple of Demetrios) that he retaliated by executing Demetrios, whom he ordered to be stabbed with lances. After his death miracles were attributed to the posthumous agency of Demetrios, and he gained the status of a saint. For this reason, it is said, an eparch of Illyricum called Leontios built in his honour a church which seems identifiable with the present church.

Other details, or variations, concerning the career of the saint are provided by later texts. Demetrios is described as a high-ranking officer in the army and a member of a senatorial family. Lyaios the gladiator is said to be a Vandal who began his career at Sirmium before moving to Thessaloniki. While Demetrios was imprisoned in the Baths, a scorpion attacked him, but he killed it by making the sign of the cross. An angel then descended from Heaven and placed a crown on his head. Nestor visited him in prison, and asked Demetrios to pray for him. After the duel, Galerius beheaded the successful Nestor, but learned that his victory was due to the prayers of Demetrios and so had him stabbed to death as well. The prefect Leontios is said to have built churches in honour of Demetrios not only at Thessaloniki but also at Sirmium. These longer literary versions were not necessarily inventions of the later Middle Ages, for the icons in the church of St Demetrios reflect some of their contents and consistently show him wearing the garments of senatorial rank; one panel in the north aisle may show his martyrdom.

The modern historian can build up a dossier of what was believed about Demetrios but there is no final test of the accuracy of any details of the life of Demetrios as there are no other records of his existence or of that of the other protagonists. There is indeed much ground for scepticism about the account and much temptation to reconcile the versions which have been transmitted in order to produce a straightforward 'rational' account of the material. One suggestion which has been pursued is that the cult of Demetrios was something limited to Sirmium until the middle of the fifth century, when it was translated and adapted to Thessaloniki by a prefect Leontios when the army was transferred there and the population of Sirmium was evacuated in 441/2. What is odd in this interpretation is that such a large church should be confidently built at Thessaloniki for an (as yet) unestablished cult. There is also a difficulty in documenting the existence of this Leontios; and his name might even be an invention in the Byzantine period, possibly suggested by the name Leo found in the seventh-century mosaics (Figures 28, 30). Other sources give the name of the prefect who transferred the army here as Apraeemius. We cannot in the circumstances be certain how and where the cult of Demetrios began.

The 'facts' of the legend, or even the historical existence of Demetrios, make no difference to the structure of social beliefs in Thessaloniki in the sixth and seventh century. The part that the cult played materially and physically in the lives of the citizens of Thessaloniki is documented in two different sets of literary texts: the first known as the *Miracles of St Demetrios* and the second as *Sermons of Praise*. These *Sermons* were the records of addresses regularly delivered in the church on 26 October to celebrate the supposed day of Demetrios' martyrdom, which had been declared a festival day of the church year. But this chapter is concerned only with the *Miracles*, the better source of narrative and information. The *Miracles of St Demetrios* consisted of a collection of stories about the saint (often derived from the sermons) which extend to a number of books. Only the sections compiled in the seventh century will be studied here: these are *Book 1* and *Book 2*. *Book 1* was assembled at about the same date as the pier mosaic of Demetrios and the donors was set up in the church (Figure 14); *Book 2* belongs later in the seventh century, but it describes, among other events, the sea battle to which the text below this mosaic refers. These texts give the empirical information on which the rest of this chapter depends; the account of the contents of the books must of necessity be fairly lengthy, but it is still highly selective for the purposes of the argument.

Book 1 according to a number of the manuscripts was put together by John, an archbishop of Thessaloniki known from various sources and the author of a number of other theological writings. The internal references in the *Miracles* can be combined with the other information about John to show that the compilation was made in the first years of the reign of Heraclios (610–641). He was a contemporary of Theodore of Sykeon and of his biographer Georgios. The information about the author of *Book 2* is much less clearly established from the clues in the text. He was apparently a citizen of Thessaloniki, presumably a churchman, and probably compiled his work at the end of the seventh century; some of his account probably derives from writings of John. John too had put together *Book 1* with the help of earlier writings, in particular sermons by Eusebios, his predecessor as archbishop. While the texts of the *Miracles* as we have them cannot simply be assumed to represent their exact original versions, the accuracy and quantity of historical detail confirm, as in the *Life of Theodore of Sykeon*, that they are substantially seventh-century texts.

The arrangement of both books of the *Miracles* is the same: a series of chapters ending with a standard public prayer. The chapters were therefore probably written with their delivery as sermons in mind; this would suggest they were a cycle of sermons to be delivered in the church of St Demetrios itself, with the audience surrounded by its rich visual ornament.

The purpose of *Book 1* of the *Miracles* was, according to John's prologue, to glorify God and St Demetrios, and to encourage the citizens of Thessaloniki to believe that they had available to them a saint who (though long dead) was always spiritually present as the guardian of their city. The proof of their special position could be shown through the miracles worked by St Demetrios. Since there are in all too many to describe, John admits he has made a selection, and has arranged his choice in order of types, starting for example with miraculous healings of the body. One criterion for his selection, he says, is to concentrate on those miracles of recent times, despite the availability of many earlier ones. This policy allows him to rely on the evidence of people who were present or involved, or on his own information. His conventions of reporting, like those of the biographer of Theodore of Sykeon, depend on the accepted credibility of oral witnesses. In both cases one feels in the presence of small communities where no private events can be concealed from public knowledge. John's text has fifteen sermons about miracles.

The prologue of *Book 2* has not survived in a complete form, but one part refers to archbishop John's writings and specifically offers this second book as a supplementary selection of miracles. They come from the last years of the life of John and from later on in the seventh century. The aim is to offer even more evidence to future generations for their continued trust in the abilities of Demetrios to protect the city. The second book is divided into six long chapters.

A summary of the two books is given here as this will be helpful later on in a comparison with the surviving icons, and also in order to present as clearly as possible the evidence of the role of the visual in the perception of the saint and the lives of the citizens of Thessaloniki. The way *Book 1* was composed, with miracles grouped according to their types, makes it difficult to relate the text directly to the material in the church. In this summary the contents of *Book 1* have therefore been rearranged to set the miracles in chronological order, so that they can be linked more easily with the historical evidence of the period and the surviving material. The dating of some events is very difficult and the solutions given here cannot all be taken as certain. The purpose of this account is to give some impression of this sort of text and of the kinds of miracles felt to be worth recording by the seventh-century writers. Most, but not all, the miracles will be mentioned. The focus for later comment will be on the place of the visual in the depiction of St Demetrios and his powers.

The earliest story chronologically is the miraculous healing of Marianos [Book 1: chap. 1]. For this story the writer, archbishop John, could not quote an eye-witness as his source, and instead justified its inclusion on the grounds of the notoriety of the miracle throughout the region of Thessaloniki and even in Constantinople. However he did support its truth by another kind of witness: any doubter of his account of the miracle may go to the church of St Demetrios and look at the mosaic on the exterior wall of the church; seeing will be believing. The place of the mosaic was described by John as the wall of the church facing the Stadium; we can presume that this building was the supposed site of the combat of Nestor and Lyaios in the time of Galerius, and probably lay in the agora of Thessaloniki (currently under excavation).

The subject of this miracle, Marianos, was the eparch of the city, and so it must date from after the move of the prefecture from Sirmium in 441/2. One twelfth-century Byzantine writer said of this miracle that it took place not long after the construction of the church; but not much can be deduced from such a remark.

Marianos appears in the narrative as a senator of high birth and great riches, appointed to the prefecture by the decision of the emperor. He is portrayed as the ideal Christian administrator of justice, and a man who was very popular in the city. John stresses his qualities, so promoting popular support for Marianos, the privileged aristocrat, as well as for the Christian emperor who sent him to Thessaloniki. Sympathy is aroused because Marianos is, inexplicably, to be stricken with total paralysis. The onset of his disease was attributed to the work of the devil, who, failing to corrupt Marianos and tempt him from the virtuous execution of his duties, found the only way to harm him was through disease.

No local doctor could cure him, and his family prepared for his death. One of them suggested hanging around his neck an amulet with a parchment containing magical signs and Hebrew characters and even names of unknown angels. Marianos refused, preferring to save his soul rather than his body. He now dreamed that he saw a friend of his called Demetrios, a member of the imperial court at Constantinople, who told him to come to his house and to sleep there, promising that the glory of God would be revealed to him. Marianos on awakening despaired of such an impracticable suggestion, but one of his staff offered a possible interpretation: the Demetrios of his dream was not his friend in Constantinople, but the St Demetrios who dwelt both in the heavenly Jerusalem and at Thessaloniki.

Marianos was carried to the church of St Demetrios and admired the 'beauty of the house'—the language comes directly from one of the Psalms (Septuagint: 25, v.8)—and the fragrance nourishing the souls of the faithful as if in paradise. He was put down on the floor and prayed; a bed was arranged so that he might sleep in the church.

His miraculous cure came after a dream in which he spoke to St Demetrios. He recounted this dream when he woke up and the exact

18 This portrait of St Basil is taken from a manuscript where it appears at the head of the text of the eucharist. It shows an icon within an icon, with St Basil's portrait set on an altar below a ciborion. The image as a whole shows us how icons could be displayed in Byzantine churches.

moment of recovery coincided with his repetition of Demetrios' promise, made in the dream, that he would recover. He was now able to get up from his bed and to dress. He walked to the ciborion of the saint in the nave of the church and entered it. By treading in this holy space he demonstrated not only his cure (for he could now walk), but also his privileged relationship with the saint. His thanks for his recovery were finally marked by a donation to the church of gold and silver objects from his possessions and of a sum of money in gold coins. He also gave money to the poor and the sick.

The ciborion of the church of St Demetrios is an object which is often mentioned in the text of the *Miracles*; it is also depicted in the surviving mosaics (for example in Figures 23, 27, 29). It is a type of structure which was not normal in Byzantine churches, and which is special to this one. The ciborion was located in the main aisle of the church, about half-way down on the left side; its base was discovered during excavations after the fire of 1917. It was a tall hexagonal pavilion, made out of silver, which could be entered through decorated doors. Its shape is reminiscent of an Antique tomb, and it is not surprising that the citizens of Thessaloniki assumed that it was the tomb of Demetrios. But its original purpose and date are not documented, and the mystery is deepened when the writer, the archbishop of the city, indicates that although the ciborion was widely believed to lie over the remains of the body of Demetrios, he himself regards this assumption with scepticism. There was, as we shall find, some question whether any relics at all of the body of this saint did survive, and another chapter masks the embarrassment of the church by saying that it was not the practice of the city to display the bodies of saints, but instead to keep their relics hidden. The word ciborion appears more normally in Byzantine writings to refer to a canopy over the altar; icons were frequently to be placed within such a structure (as in the example in Figure 18). The ciborion of St Demetrios itself acted as a monumental container of icons.

The scene when Marianos entered the ciborion is hard to visualize. The brief description of the interior mentions some sort of furniture, perhaps a bed or a low table, but the word used to describe this is too imprecise to translate with certainty. However, the interior is represented on later Byzantine pendant reliquaries of St Demetrios (Figure 19) which show an effigy of the saint lying in his tomb, and these may suggest that in the earlier period too the interior of the ciborion seemed tomb-like. Perhaps 'couch' would be a suitable English translation for the furniture inside.

A second miracle is reported from this period for which John again has no eye-witness [1:2]. The narrative quite closely parallels the Marianos chapter, as in this case another aristocrat, probably an eparch, fell ill (with internal haemorrhage). No doctor was able to treat the disease and he tried wearing amulets, although he knew these were forbidden by the church. Finally he asked to be taken to the house of the protector of the city, by which his attendants worked out he must mean the church of St Demetrios. He was cured on entering the church, and

19 *This reliquary, probably made up (piecemeal) into its present form in the thirteenth century in Thessaloniki, helps one to visualize the descriptions of St Demetrios in his ciborion related in the Miracles. The three photographs show: (top left) the eleventh-century enamel of St George, now the back of the pendant, with its text: '(The owner) prays that you will be his strong defence in battles.' This is supplemented by a later text on the rim: 'annointed with your blood and myrrh' (referring to relics of St Demetrios); (top right) the front enamel (thirteenth-century? with a later inscription in Georgian), depicting St Demetrios lying in the ciborion, below a hanging lamp. This medallion can be opened to reveal (below) the relics and a gold effigy of the saint.*

gave thanks to God and to St Demetrios.

The next chronological event to be found in the text concerns the relics of the body of St Demetrios—or rather the embarrassing lack of them and how a good public face could be put on this by the church [1:5]. There are two stages of narrative: the earlier occurs in the reign of the emperor Justinian (527–65), and the later in the reign of Maurice (582–602). The account is constructed around a request, not precisely dated, from Maurice to archbishop Eusebios (the predecessor of John and his source for several miracles). Maurice asked for a relic of St Demetrios to help him in war. The archbishop had to refuse, with the excuse that even Justinian had been foiled in a similar request.

The attempt to find a relic for Justinian is described in some detail. The clergy descended into the crypt of the church and went off into an underground gallery in a procession, singing hymns as they moved forward and carrying lamps and incense. They started digging but were suddenly prevented by a flame and a voice which told them to stop. They did however manage to collect a special perfume from this spot, keeping some in the cathedral of Thessaloniki and sending a sample to Justinian, who is said to have received it with as much joy as if it had been the body of the saint. The moral of the story is, of course, that the body of the saint was not available for relic-seekers.

All the rest of the miracles recorded in *Book 1* belong to the time either of the archbishop Eusebios or of his successor John. The earliest of these seems to be the story about a sacristan of the church of St Demetrios called Onesiphoros and an event which took place early on in the career of Eusebios before he became bishop—that is before 586 [1:7]. (The fact that the whole ecclesiastical career of Eusebios was spent at Thessaloniki may suggest that he was born locally and grew up familiar with the cult of Demetrios.) As the guardian of the church, Onesiphoros had to maintain the ciborion, but he abused his position by habitually going inside and substituting small candles for any large ones which had been donated by visitors. Although he was troubled by dreams in which the saint appeared and warned him to stop the practice, he took no notice on the grounds that a sinner cannot be visited by saints in dreams and so what he saw was not Demetrios but a fantasy. But one night when someone donated some extra-large candles and had left the church after praying, Onesiphoros rushed into the ciborion in order to extinguish them and substitute smaller ones. Immediately a loud voice came from the silver couch of the saint inside the ciborion shouting, 'At it again?' The sacristan was propelled right out of the ciborion in terror and fell to the floor speechless and breathless. It was here that he was found by Eusebios to whom he confessed his story. The chapter offers a proof of the presence of the saint in his church.

The power of the saint is demonstrated in a different way in a miracle of around 586 [1:11]. Although an eparch is again the central figure, this one, unlike Marianos, is not portrayed as a paragon of virtue but as quite the opposite. His conceit led him to ridicule St Demetrios—he accused a group of citizens of malpractices (they seem to have been 'town councillors') and when they were prepared to swear their honesty in the name of St Demetrios, he declared that the saint must be in league with them. As a consequence he was struck down with a disease which could not be treated by doctors. He only had a remission from it when, after twelve months, he went to the church and confessed his sin and promised to recognize the power of the saint.

In the outbreak of plague in Thessaloniki in July 586 there was a communal dependence on religion [1:3]. People left their homes and moved into the churches, the most popular being that of St Demetrios, which soon filled up. The text argues for the power of the saint (but skates around the theological issues): this cannot be measured simply by claiming that he could cure anyone who stayed in the church—for a saint cannot necessarily change individual fate—but it can be seen through the fact that a greater proportion of those who stayed in the church survived the epidemic than of those who remained at home. The people believed that the saint visited the sick at night while they slept. One person saw Demetrios on his rounds marking only those he wished to save with the sign of the cross; the description of Demetrios which he gives—of a graceful man dressed like a consul as if charged by the emperor to give favours to the people—depends on the image conveyed by the icons in the church.

There is a whole cluster of miracles around the year 586, and this could be because the compiler consciously selected recent miracles for which 'reliable' eye-witnesses (in particular Eusebios) were available. But maybe the historical problems of the period, such as the incursions into the Balkans of the Slavonic tribes and the more distant pressures on the empire from the Persian advances towards Asia Minor, coupled with the collapse of so many traditional features of the empire in the second half of the sixth century, gave rise to traumas which were reflected in a growth in the occurrence, or at least in the reporting, of miracles.

The miracles connected with the very dangerous Avar and Slav siege of Thessaloniki datable to the week of 22–29 September 586 are related in three chapters of the text [1:13–15]. The role of St Demetrios seems to have changed from that of the earlier miracles; he now ranges in all parts of the city and he is described as a saint who can not only help in the troubles of life but can also act as an intercessor for the soul at the time of judgement after death. St Demetrios showed his powers in the city's defence by appearing in the form of a soldier on the walls and killing the first enemy to climb up. Maybe his appearance for the first time in military form marks the transformation of Demetrios from a civil saint into a military saint, his normal image in later centuries.

This military image of St Demetrios is brought out clearly in a story told by Eusebios [1:14]. This starts some days before the siege began, when Eusebios dreamed that he was sitting in the theatre of Thessaloniki, much to his embarrassment since churchmen were discouraged by the church from attending the theatre. Before he could leave, a voice spoke to him from the stage and Eusebios interpreted the words as a supernatural warning of impending tragedy. The weaknesses of the defences of the city during the siege are then fully described, including the depopulation which had resulted from the incidence of plague. Yet, it is related, the enemy retreated from the walls despite their strength. The only possible explanation that the citizens could offer was the intervention of supernatural help. This explanation was then happily confirmed when deserters from the enemy claimed that their army had left when they discovered the existence of a large force in the city and saw its commander: a man who dazzled them, mounted on a white horse and wearing a white cloak. To explain how the commander was dressed, the deserters pointed to those in Thessaloniki who were wearing the same uniform, a group in the army described as officers of consular rank (presumably the entourage of the prefect). The commander who dazzled the enemy was identified by the citizens as St Demetrios making a supernatural appearance in order to save the city. Although the description of the saint's dress corresponds with icons in the church, there are no representations in the mosaics of this period showing Demetrios mounted on a horse. This type of representation does, however, become frequent in later Byzantine art. It is hardly surprising that when Demetrios appeared as a warrior saint, he was visualized as a horseman; after all he was an aristocrat, and the rich in this society were assumed to go to war as cavalry.

The next chapter concerned with the siege forms a complementary proof that the end of the siege was due quite specifically to the intervention of St Demetrios [1:15]. Again the story revolves around a man 'of good birth' and around a dream (which occurred at dawn on the third day of the siege). The man was not named but referred to merely as an 'illoustrios', a word that indicates aristocratic rank, being a transliteration into Greek of the Latin 'illustris'. The aristocrat dreamed that he was standing in front of the narthex—the entrance hall—of the church of the saint when two men appeared, looking like bodyguards of the emperor. They asked one of the attendants in the church where his master was and they were directed to the ciborion. By now the observer, who had followed them, reckoned he was privileged with a vision of angels, and he stood at the ciborion to watch what happened. The attendant knocked at the door of the ciborion and announced visitors. The door opened to reveal the saint just inside. The observer fell to the floor at the sight of the saint, who appeared as 'on the more ancient icons' with rays of light gleaming from his face so that the observer was lit up by brightness. The angels then gave their message to St Demetrios: he should leave the doomed city at once and come to the master. They assured him that the fate of the city was settled and he was cast into gloom and despondency (as was the observer). Instead of departing with them, the saint gave them a message to take to God: since he had been ordered to live in Thessaloniki he could not leave at such a time of extreme danger; he would stay and if the citizens were saved, he would be saved too, or if they perished, he would die too.

The observer woke up and went around the walls announcing everywhere that St Demetrios was with them and so reviving the morale of the defenders. This dream is taken by John to be proof that the presence of St Demetrios was the cause of the survival of Thessaloniki in the face of its weaknesses and the enormous strength of the enemy. The implication is that this presence was virtually a physical one, and that his appearance was identical with the depictions in the church.

The motif of a visual appearance of the saint is repeated in the next episode, but this took place far away from the city. The siege of Thessaloniki was followed by another potential disaster—famine [1:8]. St Demetrios is seen on this occasion to have acted as miracle-maker on behalf of the whole community. He made an appearance to one Stephanos, the captain of a ship loaded with corn which he was delivering to the Queen of Cities (Constantinople). The miraculous appearance took place when the boat was off the island of Chios (on the eastern side of the Aegean Sea). The saint is said to have been dressed in the same way as on the icons. He told Stephanos to change course to Thessaloniki. Stephanos, who was in 'ecstasy' at seeing the saint on the ship and was therefore scarcely able to speak (the same state of mind as that of the 'illoustrios' who had the vision of St Demetrios in his ciborion during the siege), managed to object that he had heard that the city had been captured. The saint answered that it had been saved. St Demetrios walked on the sea in front of the ship to direct its course, and Stephanos persuaded other ships which he met to sail also to the city. Stephanos told his story when he arrived at Thessaloniki, taking an oath on its truth. In this case the rearrangement of the miracles into chronological order allows us to detect a development. Here for the first time the saint used his miraculous powers outside his home city, as he was later to do (around 610) when in the course of another famine he induced a second merchant to divert his cargo from Chios to Thessaloniki [1:9].

It seems there is a gap of some twenty years before John reports any other miracles. The next events, recorded in two related chapters [1:12 and 1:6], are centred on a fire in the church, which probably occurred in 604. During the annual festival of St Demetrios on 26 October, the whole population of the region had come to the city for the celebrations. It was a time of apparent respite from the Slav attacks which had begun in the 580s. Suddenly, during the night of the festival, the ciborion in the nave of the church caught fire (one suspects that the candles inside it were always a fire hazard) and was totally burnt down. Fortunately, when the alarm was raised, help was forthcoming from large numbers of people who were woken up and managed to extinguish the flames with water before the fire reached the wooden roof.

This left the clergy with a new problem. The church contained not only the melted silver of the ciborion but also all the precious ornaments put up for special decoration during the festival; now that it was dark and the church full of people, there was the obvious danger of looting. The solution came when the head of one of the departments of the prefecture, aware of the dilemma, decided the only way to clear the church was to invent a new alarm. He thought the most effective diversion would be to shout that there was a surprise attack on the city walls. His ruse was not only effective in clearing the church; it turned out that a vast Slav attack was indeed just beginning—and was now repulsed. Meanwhile the official helped the clergy to close the doors of the church and to recover the melted silver of the ciborion. The moral drawn by John is that St Demetrios started the fire as the only way to wake up a sufficient body of people to save the city, and that he put into the mind of the official the idea of shouting that the enemy was at the walls; the saint was therefore again responsible for the salvation of the city.

The outcome was inevitably the destruction of the famous ciborion and when the melted silver was examined, the residue was found to be insufficient to remake the whole object [1:6]. The practical difficulties and their eventual resolution are known to John through the direct witness of archbishop Eusebios. Eusebios was responsible for taking action and he decided that the best way to replace the lost amount of silver was to melt down and re-use the silver of a throne in the church (presumably a bishop's throne in the apse). He thought the greatest priority was to replace the ciborion immediately, because of the popular belief that it contained the tomb of the saint and because it was undoubtedly the outstanding ornament of the church.

But before Eusebios could carry out the work, a priest called Demetrios (whose duties in the church included the management of its possessions) had a dream in which the saint appeared. The priest immediately came to Eusebios and reported that the saint had forbidden him to melt down the throne. Eusebios had kept his plan secret and so persuaded himself that the priest was just guessing his intentions. A few days later, Eusebios, through lack of any alternative solution, was about to see the silversmith to commission the work on the throne when for a second time the priest Demetrios came to see him and reported another dream in which St Demetrios, described as sad in his mood, begged him not to melt down the throne. Eusebios was angry at the priest's demands, which he pointed out were utterly negative since they offered no alternative source of silver from which to renew the ciborion.

Some eighteen months later (taking the story to the year 606), Eusebios was still in despair at the lack of a solution to the problem of replacing the silver ciborion. He found the absence of this token offensive to his idea of the decorum of the church, a feeling which indicates the high value set on the artistic ornamentation of the building. He decided that his original solution was the only feasible one. Again the priest Demetrios had a dream in which the saint appeared, and for a third time he went to the archbishop. This time the message from St Demetrios was more positive, and gave an assurance that the saint's concern for his house and church was greater than that of the bishop. This satisfied the bishop that he need not take action at that time, and he told his staff to rely on the promise of the saint. Scarcely had he finished speaking when it was announced that a certain Menas was seeking an audience with him in private. When Menas saw the bishop, he told him that in return for the immense blessings he had received from St Demetrios, he had wanted for some time to donate part of his fortune to the church, but he had always been prevented by an inner voice which said the time had not yet come. But today it had changed its refrain and told him the time was right and that the gift should be in silver and not gold. He brought in seventy-five pounds of silver and said it was for the ciborion.

Later in the same evening another visitor to the bishop was announced; this was a man called John, one of the senior lawyers of the city. He said much the same as Menas, and donated forty pounds of silver for the ciborion. There were further donations, from men whose names were not preserved in the tradition, being known only to the archbishop. This is a formula of anonymous donation which is also found in the inscriptions on the mosaics in the church (there is an example in Figure 29). The ciborion was immediately remade, and it was this new work which existed in the church at the time of John.

Another miracle, which seems to have happened a few years later, brings even further into prominence the architectural and physical setting of the cult of St Demetrios [1:10]. It occurred in the reign of Phocas (602–10), perhaps in 608; the fact that Eusebios is not mentioned as the source of information suggests that by now John's period of office may have begun. A dream this time takes place against a background of widespread civil unrest in the empire in which Thessaloniki too participated. This dream is reported by a member of the family of the prefect, and so again reflects an aristocratic involvement in the cult of the saint. The dream occurs immediately on the man's arrival in Thessaloniki from the area of central Greece (Hellas) at a time when he is said to be still unfamiliar with the city. He dreamed he went to the church of St Demetrios, entered and prayed inside. On the left side of the nave he saw the ciborion, and this is described here in greater detail than anywhere else in the text: it was silver, hexagonal, with a circular roof, and surmounted by a globe and cross (this description fits closely with the mosaic representations in the church, particularly that in Figure 27). He asked those in the church to explain what the structure was, and was told that the tradition was that Demetrios was there. He asked to see inside and was directed to the attendant; the door was opened for him and he looked inside.

What he saw first was the same as any observer might, according to John: the couch. At its head, on a throne of gold and precious stones, sat St Demetrios, dressed, according to the text, in the same garments as on the icons. At the foot of the couch was a second throne of silver on which was seated a beautiful woman of noble appearance, modestly and simply dressed, looking at the saint. The sight deterred him from entering as he felt himself to be intruding upon a private audience. At this moment the woman made towards the door, but the saint grabbed her hand and led her to her throne, begging her not to leave the city, which had never had more need of her. She sat down again on her throne and Demetrios sat on his. The man in the dream felt he could not enter, and he made his devotions and 'proskynesis' outside. He then asked the attendant who the woman was, and was given the answer that he must be the only person in the city who did not know: she was Eutaxia (Good Order), installed by God with the saint who kept her in the church and prevented her from leaving the city.

At this point the dream ended. Both the visitor, since he did not know the local traditions, and the eparch with whom he was staying, were mystified by the content of the dream and they went for an explanation to a pious monk. He interpreted the dream as a sign that Thessaloniki would survive the present dangerous period, since St Demetrios had kept Eutaxia in the city.

One final miracle, described as 'recent' at the time of the compilation of the text [1:4], again incorporates the church of St Demetrios as the essential element in its setting. It records the healing of a soldier 'possessed by demons' who was so deranged that he could not even pray for his return to sanity. His companions took him to the church where they held him down on a bed. He slept, and in the morning he was calm and sane; he spoke to his fellow-soldiers in Greek (the text does not explain if beforehand he spoke some other language or local dialect or just gibberish). Since the soldier was surprised that he was in church when it was not a festival day, the reader is made aware of the benefits of entering church buildings at times of personal crisis.

The anonymous writer of *Book 2* seems to have compiled his text some time in the last years of the seventh century, more than half a century after the compilation of *Book 1*. The textual evidence suggests that the author of this second book was a citizen of Thessaloniki with a special devotion to St Demetrios, possibly an ecclesiastic and possibly an archbishop. Apparently he had access to written sources for the events of the last years of John's career, and his account is written chronologically. The literary style and format of the two books is therefore different; but the two have one significant common feature—they were written by and for citizens of Thessaloniki, and show a strong local patriotism. Even the chronological framework is seen in terms of the period of office of the local archbishop rather than those of the emperor and his provincial administrators.

Book 2 has a strong narrative bias, and so the aspects relevant to our argument have to be excerpted from this narrative. It starts with a combined Slav siege by land and sea during the lifetime of John, in about 615 [2:1]. The first miracle was seen in the fact that the enemy was very slow to organize its attack, giving time for mounting a defence. This respite was attributed to the intercession of St Demetrios with God on behalf of the city, although the text offers no evidence or sign to confirm this belief. When the attack finally came one dawn, the intervention of St Demetrios was again claimed. This time a reason for the belief is given. St Demetrios made an appearance dressed in a white mantle, in the same form as he took in the icons. He was seen by both Christians and Jews not only on the walls but also walking on the water. He is characterized as fighting together with the citizens and as responsible for the collapse of the Slav assault. A thanksgiving service for the repulse of the assault on the city by land and sea took place in the church of St Demetrios.

Another siege (lasting 33 days) belongs around 618 at a time when the city was full of refugees from all over the Balkans [1:2]. Archbishop John is portrayed as undertaking a major role in the raising of morale. He encouraged everyone to trust in help from God and St Demetrios and went out to meet the people on the walls, not therefore confining his activities to standard church occasions. One detects an element here of the special role of John in the events and the belief that he had a special relationship with Demetrios.

Three miracles in the course of this siege are mentioned. The first concerned the devastating effects of a stone on which the name of St Demetrios was inscribed. This stone was hurled at the enemy, and in its trajectory collided with a much larger stone thrown by the Slavs; the enemy stone was knocked backwards, and together both stones fell on to the enemy catapult and killed its operators. In this miracle Demetrios appears for the first time not as a person, but just as a written name; but this 'writing' has just as powerful an effect as if the saint

71

had come in human form. The second miracle is connected with an earthquake tremor, which struck without prior warning. The citizens cried out, 'Kyrie eleison', and the enemy rushed towards the walls, assuming extensive damage. To the surprise of all the walls were intact. Archbishop John claimed that this was the realization of a dream of his which promised salvation during the siege if the whole population shouted 'Kyrie eleison' with one voice. According to him the miracle proved the city was under the protection of God and St Demetrios. The third miracle occurred when the enemy attacked the city with a cloud of arrows as thick as a snowstorm; some of the arrows stuck in the walls with their heads reversed, pointing back towards the besiegers. This was seen as a miracle and the defenders were further convinced that St Demetrios was working on their side.

Another section of narrative is devoted to the events at the time of the death of archbishop John. John was still alive around the year 620 and dreaming of terrible earthquakes [2:3]. He prayed to God that such disasters would not happen in his lifetime and this prayer was granted; the series of earthquakes occurred about a month after his death. As a result of the tremors part of the city and walls collapsed; the citizens fled from their homes and lived outside the defences. But the nearby Slavs did not attack. St Demetrios is once more credited with the miraculous salvation of the city, for he made appearances as the guardian of the walls and gates, sometimes on horseback and in the company of other saints. The Slavs later confirmed that they were misled into believing that the city was intact and defended.

The earthquakes and the events which followed them form the pivotal chronological point for the study of the church of St Demetrios and its decoration. Soon after the earthquakes, the church was mysteriously burnt and the fire could not be extinguished despite the presence of willing people and equipment to fight it. The fire was of short duration, perhaps an hour, but the damage must have been relatively severe since the roof of the church was destroyed. Everyone was full of sorrow for the sins that must have led to this misfortune. One man, described as a true servant of St Demetrios and someone to whom the saint frequently appeared in visions, showed particular remorse, but soon had a dream in which the saint told him not to torment himself as in a short time the church would be fully restored to its past state. Indeed the writer says the restoration work was done and that the church was in its new state at the time of writing. Almost certainly a new ciborion would have been constructed after such a fire, possibly this time in marble, as implied by a later chapter [2:6]. The text is not specific about the date of this restoration. One of the manuscripts added a note that the restoration was 'in the time of the eparch Leo'; while this may be true, the information might be derived only from one of the inscriptions on the mosaics rather than from an independent tradition. Since the restoration did not involve substantial architectural alterations, it could have been done quickly. As we shall see, the work did include the commission of new mosaics, but those made before the fire were retained as they had not been seriously damaged.

The rest of *Book 2* records events after the time of John and belongs to the generation of the writer; the themes continue to be those of wars, sieges and famines. One siege [2:4] was provoked by the brutal treatment of a Slav chieftain called Perbound at the orders of the Byzantine emperor (perhaps between 675 and mid-676). The retaliatory attacks can be dated to the summer of 676 and went on for two years, with a brief assault on Thessaloniki in July 677. The narrative conveys a picture of a city which had managed now to come to terms with the Slavs and had established a kind of peaceful coexistence. This peace was terminated by the mistakes of an eparch who did not understand local conditions and who caused the emperor, remote in Constantinople, to act foolishly and to provoke the Slavs to active hostilities. Within the city the writer speaks of two groups (almost classes), the authorities and the citizens, and one can detect his hostility towards the former.

The miracles in this section consist of sightings of St Demetrios on the walls and the encouragement these gave to the defenders. He was seen on foot, staff in hand and his mantle on his shoulders. It is also suggested that through the intervention of St Demetrios other saints once more came to fight on the side of the defenders. The most spectacular miracle of the time concerned a mechanical siege-tower designed by one of the Slavs, who was given permission by his superiors to construct it against the wall of Thessaloniki. St Demetrios responded by slapping the inventor of the tower, who went mad before he could set it in operation. When he later recovered, this Slav inventor was allowed into Thessaloniki. He agreed that St Demetrios was the cause of his madness and was converted to Christianity.

Throughout this section all favourable events were attributed to the intervention and protection of the saint. Another case belongs some years after the incident of the siege machine, probably between 682 and 684. A scheme by two Bulgarian leaders, Kouver and Mavros, to take over Thessaloniki was foiled by an appearance of St Demetrios to the eparch Sisinnios [2:5]. This prefect was sent with the fleet to Thessaloniki by the emperor but had delayed further south on the island of Skiathos to wait for a favourable breeze. The appearance of St Demetrios three times in dreams persuaded him to set sail without waiting further and in fact the direction of the wind then changed. His arrival saved the city. The change in the direction of the wind as well as the insistence that Sisinnios should get to the city was seen as due to the miraculous management of St Demetrios.

The final miracle of *Book 2* is important for our purposes as it gives considerable information on the perceptions of the cult of St Demetrios. The passage is not easily dated and has sometimes been seen as a late addition to the text inserted by some other writer. Yet it is quite feasible as an episode of the late seventh century, and so is included here. A bishop called Kyprianos from the city of Thenai in North Africa (now the port of Henchir Tina in Tunisia, opposite the island of Cercina) was captured by Slavs in Greece while on his way by boat to Constantinople, and was made a slave. In answer to his prayers to God a handsome young soldier appeared and offered to help him to escape, provided he accepted that they must travel in silence. The young man said his name was Demetrios and that he was a soldier whose house was in the middle of Thessaloniki. To this city he would guide the bishop.

At the end of eight days' walking Kyprianos came in sight of Thessaloniki, and his companion disappeared. The bishop later tried to find him in the city to thank him; he asked around for the house of the soldier Demetrios, only to be told that the city was full of the homes of soldiers called Demetrios. In the end he was taken to the church of St Demetrios so that he could offer thanks to God for his salvation. He prostrated himself in gratitude and then arose and stretched out his hands in prayer. In front of him he noticed an icon of St Demetrios and immediately identified his saviour as the saint. Kyprianos told his story to the archbishop of Thessaloniki, who invited him to stay, but the visitor preferred to go back to the church and to stay there. He spent the winter in Thessaloniki, and then continued on his journey to Constantinople.

On Kyprianos' return to Africa, he pondered how to commemorate St Demetrios. He decided the right way to do this was to build a new church in his own region which was a copy of the church of St Demetrios in Thessaloniki. In his conception such a church must have a similar arrangement with columns, a ciborion and an ambo, but he did not know how to acquire the marble for them. St Demetrios appeared to him in a dream and told him that on the next day a boat would arrive with a cargo of marble purchased in Constantinople; it consisted of a ciborion and ambo intended for a church of St Victor but it could be used instead in a new church for him. Armed with this information, the bishop persuaded the captain of the ship to hand over the marble to him, and used it to build a church dedicated to St Demetrios at Thenai. This became a site of miraculous healings and in particular the oil from the lamps cured scorpion stings (a power which refers to one of the stories about the saint at the time of his death). In this case the power of the visual replica is so strong that it reproduces even the miraculous properties of its prototype.

Overall the second book of miracles is less useful for our purposes than the first. The strong narrative thread admits less discussion of the visual aspect of Thessaloniki and its cult places; while the miracles are treated in a more standardized, even monotonous way. The cult certainly flourished in this period, but perhaps also it was taken more for granted.

These anecdotal texts are richly evocative. They lead the modern reader directly into the life and obsessions of the citizens of Thessaloniki in the sixth and early seventh centuries. They are full of reflections of the ways that the visual environment affected people, but most obviously they give, as the title *Miracles* suggests, vivid illustrations of the working of one form of religious experience. We see miracles perceived as the revelation of the divine plan, and as an illustration of how far a saint can alter fate; we see miracles offering a prediction of the future or, as popularly understood, providing unexpected cures from illness. There is much in common here with the case of Theodore of Sykeon, but also significant differences. With Theodore the living holy man was believed to have the foresight to predict, for example, the identity of future emperors or the length of an emperor's reign. In Thessaloniki, we find the future foretold by St Demetrios, but by other means; long dead, he acted from the grave and made his appearances in visions or dreams. Likewise healing miracles show differences. In Sykeon these were done by a human intercessor between man and God. In Thessaloniki, the agency was himself a saint from the supernatural world, taking on the form of his icons. Miracles consistently demonstrated the power of good over evil or the power of Christian order over pagan disorder; but they did this in many different ways.

We can also find in these texts a multifaceted view of the patterns of social and political life in a provincial city. Violence was accepted as normal, and natural disasters and ill-health were frequent—all to be attributed to the punishment of God for sin. Political decisions and appointments were made elsewhere and remotely in the capital by an emperor whose policies might be open to criticism but whose constitutional authority was accepted without question. In the city, there are some indications of tensions between the rulers and the community as a whole; the eparch was an appointment by the emperor for a short term, and he was liable to be absent at key times, or inefficient when present. The permanent leader of the community was the archbishop. He was probably appointed by the patriarch of Constantinople (unless the Pope in Rome had powers in the election from a nominal ecclesiastical control over the region), yet seems to have been someone with local roots who might stay in office long enough to gain a strong communal loyalty. The archbishop, whatever he thought of individual eparchs, had in common with them a similar literary education.

The role of the archbishop and the successive eparchs in supporting and even promoting belief in the miraculous framework of Christian life is conspicuous in these texts. There is no support for the view that the cult of St Demetrios at this time is something which rises from the level of 'popular' religion and is remote from the members of the elite. Only on one issue might there be a distinction in the beliefs of the community: the writer of *Book 1*, archbishop John, implies that the view that the body of St Demetrios existed under the ciborion was a popular one which was not shared by him. It would be difficult to say whether his greater scepticism, offered in a public address, reflected the views of an elite, or was just professional clerical practicality. Of course it must be remembered that this story reflects only one stage of the development of the cult; how far the archbishop was a mouthpiece of the assumptions of his audience and how far he could manipulate belief is a question of some complexity, not easy to resolve. We cannot know whether the bishop and the aristocracy acted through credulity or cynicism in endorsing the cult of St Demetrios.

Within these rich evocations of the social and cultural life of Thessaloniki in the early Middle Ages, one element stands out: the importance of the physical and visual environment. What we call 'art' was essential for the working of this society in an obvious literal way—churches had of necessity to be constructed for the regular celebration of the liturgy and other services, and these buildings had to contain the fittings and materials for the practical functioning of the professional clergy and for the needs of the laity. Although the precise date of the building of the church of St Demetrios is not known (the lack of proof for the mid-fifth century accepted here has been mentioned before), and the early stages of the development of the cult of this saint cannot be easily discovered, yet the church quickly took a major part in the religious life of the city; so much so that there is only one passing reference in the text to the cathedral of the city. Although we would normally assume that the cathedral was the most important church in any city, in Thessaloniki at this time its identity and location (in contrast to the church of St Demetrios) cannot now be established with any certainty.

A visit to the church of St Demetrios was counted as a priority for anyone arriving in the city. On the outside of the church was a mosaic. This represented the miraculous healing of the paralysed eparch Marianos which was related as the first miracle in *Book 1*. Since his cure took place in the church, and was then commemorated with a pictorial record, it was clearly a mosaic later in date than any original decoration of the mid-fifth-century church. Inside the church was the ciborion, regarded literally as the tomb of the saint by the citizens, but more symbolically by the archbishop John. The ciborion was essential furniture in the church as a focal point for the personal devotions of the laity; the faithful went to the saint's home for prayer and lit candles in front of the ciborion. It was true that the saint could come to a citizen in a dream, but normally anyone would expect to go to the house of the saint, not expect him to come to them; those in need of healing went to the church to pray and sleep there. During the plague, protection was given by being inside the church; and the African bishop Kyprianos preferred to stay in the church during his stay in the city rather than with the archbishop of Thessaloniki.

Inside the ornate ciborion was the couch and beside it two icons, one of the saint and the other probably of the Virgin (although in 1:10 the woman is firmly identified as Eutaxia (Good Order); this identification may well be a moralizing invention to fit in with the account of the miracle). Elsewhere in the church there was a silver throne for the bishop when he participated in the rituals of the church. The text also refers in several different passages to icons (*eikones*), some of which are 'more ancient' [1:15]. These references are probably to both mosaics and panel paintings in the church. We cannot discover from the text when these works were made for the church or where exactly they were placed. Even the silver ciborion raises a number of basic problems. Did it date from the foundation of the church? Was it always a feature of the central nave on the left side? The text does, however, make clear the prominence of the rich laity as a source of patronage for the church—from this group came the donations of silver for the replacement of the ciborion after the fire of 604. Money also came into the church from a wider spectrum of society through the use of candles as ex-votos at the time of private devotions. The decoration of the church was a communal activity, which involved a movement of wealth from private purses into the church.

Such manufactured works, as the language of the text makes clear, served several purposes at the same time. One function was straightforward decoration, or rather the obedience to what was seen as the explicit Christian prescription that a place of worship should be beautiful. Twice [1:1, and 1:12] the justification for the aesthetic decoration of churches is made through the use of a noun taken from Psalm 25: 'Lord, I have loved the *beauty* of your house'. By this linguistic echo, the belief is implanted and confirmed in the minds of the audience that any church, the house of God, ought properly to look beautiful. A Christian was in duty bound therefore to approve of the spending of money on the decoration of churches. However, the interpretation given to the word 'beauty' by a Christian was different at various periods of history: already at the time of Theodore of Sykeon and these events in Thessaloniki beauty lay in an array of figural representations, and icons seemed normal in churches. But this particular idea was soon to be denied in Byzantium and then later re-affirmed; this will be described in the next two chapters, which will show for example that the word 'beauty' is used in the writing of the Constantinopolitan patriarch Photios in the ninth century in the same ways as in the seventh century. In other periods of Christian history also, the proper appearance of the church has been a recurrent issue; the radical rethinking at the time of the Reformation has led to the possibility in our time of totally diverse Christian perceptions of the 'ideal church', differing from the plain whitewashed structures of some Protestant groups to the decorative mazes of some of the churches of Rome and of the Orthodox communities.

Artists had an essential function in this society where so many buildings needed decoration and where people wanted icons around them at home and at prayer or in worship. But the works of art produced, although they may have received aesthetic approval from society, were not limited in their function to mere decoration. The ciborion, for example, although made from silver with special craftsmanship and containing icons, was regarded in various ways. It was a focus for prayers and worship. At the same time the structure and its decoration communicated messages about the existence of the saint and his appearance and hence his supposed historical life. It encouraged the believer to accept that he could gain a relationship with the saint and influence events. It made him believe that the saint once lived and died in Thessaloniki. It also made it possible for a citizen to recognize the saint if he made an appearance in a dream, in a vision, or in 'real life'. Its icons, as described in the dream where Eutaxia converses with St Demetrios, could be seen as a visual portrayal of hope at a time of crisis during civil war. The ciborion and its icons offered a place and the means for possible intercession with God.

The mosaic panel which, according to the text, depicted the miraculous healing of Marianos was also seen to have a more active role in the construction of the image of the saint than that of a mere 'document'. On the one hand it provided a simple record of the occurrence of the miracle; the mosaic was presumably a donation by the eparch Marianos, a member of the ruling elite of Constantinople, in order to commemorate his miraculous recovery and to thank the saint in the accepted aristocratic way. But its function did not stop there. It provided to anyone who might doubt it a concrete proof of the miraculous healing of Marianos and a clear indication that similar miracles might be expected in the future; and, in addition, it was in its own right a focus for men's prayers and a means by which those prayers were channelled towards God. It was a part of the decoration visible to the public, but also a promise of the benefits offered through a belief in the saint.

The evidence of the text of the *Miracles* can only show one side of society: how it behaved in public and what its hopes and fears were. But it does help to unravel how the community divided into groups, most obviously into the ruling aristocracy, the local aristocracy, the church hierarchy and the citizen body, which included foreigners, particularly Slavs, who had converted to Orthodox Christianity and so were acceptable in a Byzantine society. It shows how important the physical environment of Christianity was to the citizens, for when the plague came to Thessaloniki, the accepted refuges were the churches themselves, and especially the church of St Demetrios. The clergy, by its entitlement to be in the churches, would at such times be a conspicuously privileged group within society. The text also reveals a home-guard kind of defence of the city, with little reference to professional Byzantine soldiery resident in the city.

It is now time to re-enter the church of St Demetrios, not through the evidence of the *Miracles* but through the visual material itself which still survives. The modern visitor to Thessaloniki will find the building still one of the most popular churches in the city and some of the same mosaics which formed the environment of the audience of the *Miracles* can be seen inside. But the fabric of the church is substantially restored and rebuilt as a result of a vast fire in Thessaloniki in 1917 in the course of which the church was massively damaged (as visible in Figure 16). Unfortunately the restoration work was done inappropriately in stone, and not in brick in which the original church was constructed (Figure 15). At the time of the fire the church of St Demetrios had only recently been restored to Christian use after centuries of operation as an Islamic mosque (from 1492 up to 1912) during the period of Turkish Ottoman control of the city. During the fire, a number of the Byzantine mosaics were lost, and these panels can now only be reconstructed from photographs or watercolour copies made at the beginning of this century. The ciborion mentioned so often in the *Miracles* has also disappeared, though its location is still marked by its surviving hexagonal base.

In order to visualize the church beside the texts of the *Miracles*, it is easiest to recreate the decoration in two stages, the first at the time of *Book 1*, which was written by the archbishop John in the second decade of the seventh century and before the fire of about 620, and the second at the time of the writing of *Book 2* in the seventh century after the restoration of the church had been carried out.

For the earlier period we can start to look at the church from the point of view of the 'illoustrios', the 'aristocrat' who dreamed that he entered the building [1 : 15]. He first saw himself in front of the church, presumably in the courtyard to the west of the building, the place where at the beginning of services in the early Byzantine period the congregation would have assembled before entering the church in a procession behind the clergy. From here the 'illoustrios' entered the western entrance hall of the church—the narthex. (Figure 20 shows a plan of the building in 1907 and a section of the church as it was at this time is shown in Figure 21.) At this time the church must have had several entrance doors and from inside would have given an impression of great space and open access. No decoration from the period of the first book of the *Miracles* survives in the narthex but mosaics elsewhere in the church illustrate the 'beautification' of the text; we can look first at the west walls of both the north and the south aisles. The panel in the north aisle is the most fragmentary (Figure 22); all that survives is a piece of the left side. We can see two angels in the sky, one blowing a trumpet, with a standing figure of a saint with a gold halo below

20 This measured plan of the church of St Demetrios was made in 1907 when the building was still in use as a mosque and still intact before the fire. The Byzantine church was a wooden-roofed basilica with a nave and four aisles. The entrances in its west facade led from a courtyard into a narthex beyond which lay the nave and aisles. A transept at the east end of the church both increased the area available to the congregation around the sanctuary, and at the same time gave the church a symbolic cross-shaped ground plan. Galleries further enlarged the area available within the church.

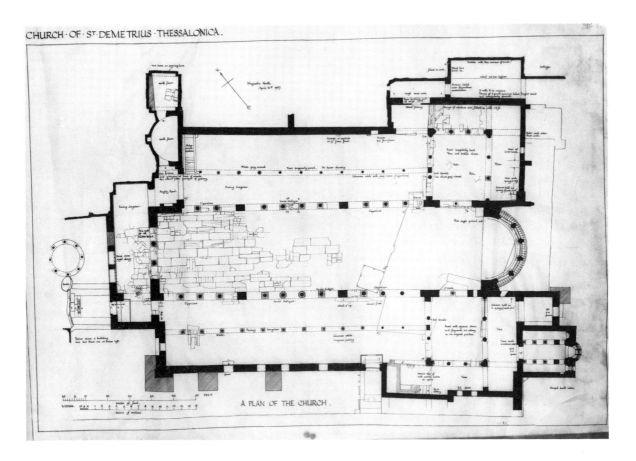

CHURCH · OF · ST · DEMETRIUS · THESSALONICA.

A PLAN OF THE CHURCH.

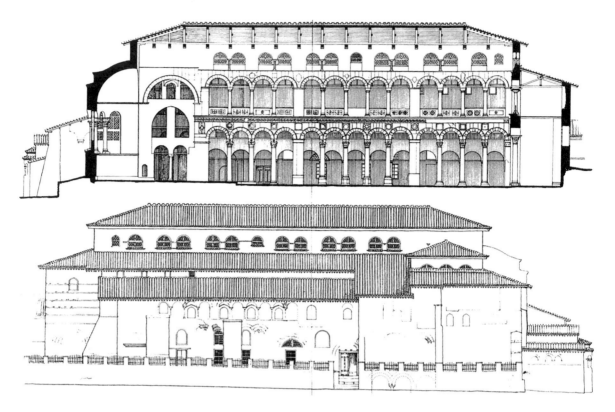

him. The saint is presumably St Demetrios and this would seem to be part of a scene in which he is accepted into Heaven; the suggestion has been made that the lost area shows his martyrdom. It is conceivable that the panel partly refers to the episode in prison when the saint is crowned by an angel.

Although the panel in the south aisle (Figure 23) has lost an area on the left side, it offers the best representation in the church of the saint as he appeared to the citizens at the time of the compilation of *Book 1*. Since this is the cult church of Demetrios and since the dress of the central figure corresponds with the descriptions of him in the *Miracles*, there can be no possible doubt that this is a representation of St Demetrios. This mosaic was not felt to need an identifying inscription. Demetrios was depicted at the centre of the original panel in the form of a young saint with a gold halo, with his hands represented in gold, and wearing a gold garment with a blue panel over the chest (a *tablion*) which marks it out as consular dress. His position is one of prayer, but it is different from the type of prostration which is ascribed to worshippers in the text; rather he is in the position taken by a priest who during the liturgy acts as an intercessor for the congregation. The association would not have been lost on the Byzantine spectator. The saint stands on a gold footstool and is in front of a small building with silver spiralling columns. This structure can only be a representation of his ciborion as it was described in the text and shows it as it was either before the fire of 604, or before the second fire of about 620. Through

21 This section of St Demetrios was also measured in 1907. All the vertical walls of the Byzantine church were faced in coloured marble, while marble columns with various types of capitals and masonry piers supported the galleries and the roofing system. The existence of the transept and several galleries implies that the designers of the church anticipated vast numbers of worshippers from the beginning, a confirmation of the importance of the cult of the saint.

an opening on the right is to be seen a vista of trees and plants in a landscape, and a pot on a column, probably a device, as often, to symbolize a spring; this setting may be intended to suggest a heavenly garden of paradise. The flat wall of the church is thereby contradicted by the illusion of space extending into the distance. This pictorial method helps to evoke the 'marginality' of a saint in normal life, for he is at the same time shown in the familiar setting of his church and in the heavenly paradise of the other world.

To the right of St Demetrios figures are represented who defer to him and have their hands respectfully hidden below the sleeves of their garments; such a gesture must also have reminded any spectator of the liturgy, because the sacred vessels and books are carried in this way to avoid direct contact of the human with the holy. A boy is dressed

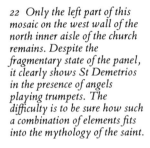

22 Only the left part of this mosaic on the west wall of the north inner aisle of the church remains. Despite the fragmentary state of the panel, it clearly shows St Demetrios in the presence of angels playing trumpets. The difficulty is to be sure how such a combination of elements fits into the mythology of the saint.

23 The mosaic on the west wall of the south inner aisle is far better preserved than Figure 22, but the left side is missing. This composition seems to be a record of some special donation or prayer, rather than a narrative illustration. St Demetrios is standing in front of his ciborion, receiving the prayers of citizens.

in a garment whose colouring suggests gold, and this may be a sign that he is a member of a rich family. He is propelled towards the saint by a larger figure who, though usually identified as a woman by those art historians who have discussed the panel, is surely male—a woman would wear a veil.

These two panels are not in prominent positions in the church, if prominence is to be defined as a position in the sanctuary area towards which the eyes of the congregation would be directed during services, or as one near the ciborion where so much of the action of the *Miracles* took place. However, they would be seen most obviously by someone leaving the church through the doors at the western end. The 'messages' of the panels are not simple to read. If the panel in the north aisle did show the martyrdom of the saint and his reception into Heaven, it would act as an authentication of the *Passions* of St Demetrios. The panel in the south aisle shows the saint both in his ciborion and in his other home in Heaven (the two places of abode are mentioned in the

Miracles), and conveys the promise of posthumous miracles and protection. Since there seems no direct correlation to be made between the context of these panels and the various episodes in the text, the message cannot be directly derived from the texts. It may be a generalized message that the protection of the saint will be given to children who are in some special way dedicated to him. Alternatively, it may be a more individual record of thanks for individual favours granted by the saint; if so, it might be compared with the mosaic panel of Marianos mentioned in the *Miracles*—the visual record commissioned by a grateful donor to commemorate his healing by the saint.

It might be easier to relate these two panels to the text of the *Miracles* if their date of production were known; but that date is as elusive as the detailed chronology of the stages of the construction of the church. The most useful date in the early history of the building, which can be argued fairly precisely from the *Miracles*, is the fire mentioned in *Book 2*. This fire broke out in about 620. A restoration of the church followed, mentioned though not dated in the text. Since a number of the earlier mosaics did survive in good condition in the building after that fire, and since the panel on the right side of the sanctuary which belongs to the restoration refers to topical events of the period around 620, the obvious deduction is that the restoration of the building should be dated to the 620s or very soon afterwards. This date for the restoration is accepted here, and so is the division of the mosaics in the church into two main periods, either before or after *c*. 620. This division of the mosaics of the church into two different periods of manufacture is nowhere clearer than in the cycle of mosaics in the north aisle which will soon be discussed; the interpretation of the dates of both periods even in this area is, however, still controversial.

The two panels on the west wall of the church can be grouped with others on the basis of style to the period before the fire of around 620. A comparison of the mosaic of St Demetrios on the west wall of the south aisle with that on the right of the sanctuary (Figures 23, 14) quickly points to the differences between the periods. In the later panel beside the sanctuary, the figure of the saint is broader, heavier and more stiffly drawn; the west wall panel shows a lighter and more impressionistic touch. But it is one thing to find differences between the various mosaics in the church and another to decide the exact date of the earlier works. A decision that the panels on the west wall date from before the fire of around 620 is a start, but further progress is difficult, even though the obvious solutions are straightforward. The panels could be attributed to the middle of the fifth century, when the church was founded, on the grounds that such a grand church can hardly have been devoid of mosaics at its foundation. Or they might be donations to the decoration of the church made soon after the foundation, with the development of the cult resulting in the feeling that the church needed extra decoration, especially from those who had benefited from the favours of the saint.

Another solution would suggest a renovation of the mosaics of the church after the fire in the time of Eusebios (probably in 604). Such a date might be compatible with the indications of style; but it is odd that no such decoration is mentioned in the text and the scenes do not, as might be expected, have any connection with the text compiled in this decade. Another, slightly different, approach, would argue that all the surviving mosaics of the church are separate and piecemeal additions to the building by a number of wealthy citizens over the years in response to the sort of miracles reported in the text; in other words they are offerings of a more magnificent kind than the candles offered to the saint in his ciborion, and depend on the existence of a rich elite prepared to show their devotion to the saint and through their actions to influence the growth of the cult.

The number of these possible solutions shows the impossibility of being precise over the dating of the earliest mosaics in the church; even the recent discovery in the amphitheatre of Dyrrachium (now Durrës in Albania) of mosaics similar in style and type—saints and donors—has not resolved the question, although these probably post-date the earth-quakes of 522. After this date the amphitheatre was likely to be unusable for its original functions, so that a part of it could be converted into a small chapel with tombs and mosaics (Figure 24). The lack of precise

24 Mosaics of the kind found in the church of St Demetrios were not unique to Thessaloniki, and similar types of composition have recently been discovered in the mosaics on the walls of the small chapel built into the amphitheatre in the city of Dyrrachium (in Albania), probably of the sixth century. This panel has St Stephen to the left (with his hands portrayed in gold tesserae like those of St Demetrios in Figure 23) and a representation of the Virgin Mary as Queen with attendant angels. The two small donor figures in the foreground closely resemble the portrayals of the citizens of Thessaloniki; perhaps a reflection of the fact that Dyrrachium and Thessaloniki were linked by a Roman road.

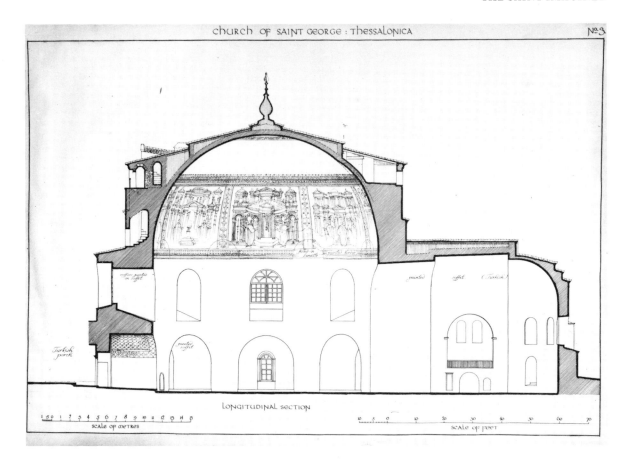

CHURCH OF SAINT GEORGE : THESSALONICA   Nº 3

LONGITUDINAL SECTION

SCALE OF METRES

SCALE OF FEET

25 *Within Thessaloniki the mosaics of St Demetrios have some features in common with those of the large circular church known locally as the Rotunda (or as the church of St George, although neither of these names was used in texts of the Byzantine period). This record was made in 1907 when the building was being used as a mosque by the Turkish community. The structure was originally built in the early fourth century by the Roman emperor Galerius—it was to be his mausoleum, but was never used for this purpose. Instead it was converted to act as a church (of unknown original dedication); an apse was added on the east side, and the dome was decorated with a set of Christian mosaics. This conversion and decoration probably dates from the middle of the fifth century.*

dating does not mean that the historical evidence of the mosaics is in any real way diminished; but it does show that a precise chronology must not be the only basis for interpretation. Whatever their exact date, for example, these mosaics can be set against other mosaics in the city, notably those in the Rotunda church.

The Rotunda was the building planned as the mausoleum of Galerius but never used as such; it was subsequently converted into a great centrally-planned church, most probably in the midde of the fifth century. Its mosaic decoration belongs to the time of the church conversion, and so can be attributed also to the middle of the fifth century. The vast cupola of this church was divided up into several registers of mosaics which encircled a central medallion of Christ. The best-preserved register shows groups of saintly figures set against rich architectural façades (Figures 25, 26). The likely interpretation of these figures is that they are popular early Christian saints arranged in a cycle of the liturgical year (their names and day of martyrdom are given in inscriptions). These mosaic figures, high up in the building, are works of great craftsmanship and the handling of the coloured glass tesserae used in their production aimed at a very realistic kind of portrayal—it might have seemed to the viewers on the floor that the saints high above them were almost alive in a heavenly realm of golden churches and palaces.

85

The comparison between these mosaics and the south aisle panel of St Demetrios points immediately to one fact: either the rendering of St Demetrios is a copy of the figures of these mosaics or his portrait type is invented according to the same principles. All the saints in the Rotunda fall into ideal generalized, saintly types, and none seem to be the established, individual, portrait types, which were subsequently used in later portrayals of the same saints. The artists of the mosaics in both churches transformed standard heroic portrait types of Late Antique art into ideal Christian saints. Whatever the precise date of the panel of St Demetrios, the comparison with the Rotunda suggests that his outward personality was an invention of art rather than history; his image was manufactured through pictorial means, using traditional artistic conventions. It was a construction of society, not a historical likeness. Of course this is not a reason for denying the historical existence of Demetrios. To take a comparative example, Alexander the Great did certainly exist in the fourth century BC, but the image of Alexander in art was a generalized social construction.

So far only a small number of mosaics inside the church of St Demetrios have been introduced and there are more to be considered. One area of the early mosaics was sadly destroyed in the fire of 1917, but they can be recreated through the watercolour copies and photographs made shortly before their destruction. These are the mosaics

26 The fifth-century mosaics of saints in the Rotunda at Thessaloniki are divided into a series of balanced panels; this one includes two saints (Leo and Philemon), identified by accompanying inscriptions which give their names and the dates of the annual festivals. They stand in a setting of magnificent church architecture, perhaps intended to signify Heaven.

which decorated the north aisle and which were therefore on the side of the church near the ciborion (Figures 27–29, 30). These mosaics are in a series of separately-framed panels of various lengths, perhaps set up piecemeal at various times—or more likely by a group of donors in co-operation at one time. Some of the panels are very similar in composition and all are similar in style to the panels on the western walls of the aisles; this can be taken as an indication of a similar date and method of production. Several panels are fairly simple variations of the scheme in the south aisle and show the saint framed in an architectural setting, with human worshippers beside him. Some of these compositions include written inscriptions which say that the picture conveys 'a prayer for a person whose name is known to God' (as in Figure 29). The same convention of anonymity was found in the *Miracles*, but it was not limited to Thessaloniki and is found widely in early Byzantine monuments. The text documents the practice as a social convention, but does not explain it.

Other panels in the north aisle are much more complicated in their compositions. One mosaic, for example, represents a whole group of figures, some human and some heavenly, distinguished by rank and hierarchy (Figure 27). Some figures are shown as portrait busts, others are much more prominent; the medallion icons show minor saints, while the full-length figures include St Theodore (if this military saint is correctly identified from his portrait type which was developing in this period; the same figure appears on the Sinai icon of the Virgin, possibly with St Demetrios, in Figure 12). St Demetrios, on the left, introduces some favoured individual to the enthroned Virgin and Child who are guarded by two archangels. On the far right, crouching below the right medallion, is a woman, perhaps the wife of the man with St Demetrios. No text explains the circumstances of the panel or tells us whether it commemorated an answer to prayers or even some miracle. The human figures, presumably the donors, are represented as tiny in the presence of the Virgin, but they no doubt came from

27 The longest cycle of mosaics in the church of St Demetrios (decorating the north inner aisle) was discovered in 1907 but almost entirely destroyed in the fire of 1917. The only records we have are a few photographs and watercolour copies, the best of which were made in 1907 by the British architect W.S. George. This watercolour shows a panel of the Virgin and Child enthroned, attended by angels; also present are several saints, some depicted in medallions, and representations of living human beings, like the donor figures elsewhere in the mosaics of this church and at Dyrrachium. On the right of this watercolour is the beginning of a separate mosaic sequence, the story of Maria and her family. This sequence opens with a scene of Maria and her mother in front of St Demetrios who is seated before his open ciborion.

the richer level of the society of Thessaloniki; they could after all afford to donate a mosaic to the church.

The longest (and most expensive) section of mosaics in the north aisle presents a sequence of episodes in the life of a child called Maria (starting on the right side of Figure 27 and ending on the right side of Figure 29). This identification depends both on the visual features—the repetition at four different ages of the same female figure, identified by a cross on her forehead—and on an inscription accompanying the series. The sequence opens (Figure 27) with a scene of the child in the arms of a woman, presumably her mother, being held towards St Demetrios who is seated in front of his ciborion and who raises one hand towards another saintly person in a medallion above him. This medallion figure is most likely Christ, although it is impossible to be certain about this since the mosaic was already largely destroyed when our records were made. The woman standing to the right is probably the Virgin Mary. The background story of the family is unknown, but the message is clear enough: the saint is well disposed towards the child and intercedes on her behalf to God. The ciborion is very carefully represented, to the extent that one can see many details of it, including the portrayal of bust saints on its doors. In the second scene (Figure 28) the child has grown larger but is still held in the arms of her mother. A prayer is being made to the Virgin, who is apparently turning to communicate with Christ and is attended by guardian angels. By the third scene (on

28 This watercolour continues the story of Maria, but the cycle is now disjointed in the central area, for the medallions of St Demetrios and two ecclesiastics are substitutions for the original mosaics at this point. This alteration was made about 620, and the two ecclesiastics are represented on other mosaics in the church made during that phase of restoration (see Figures 14, 31). This section of the mosaic illustrates two periods in the cult of St Demetrios.

*29 This third watercolour
shows the conclusion of the
story of Maria. The mosaics
are then terminated (right) by
another ex-voto panel showing
several donors in prayer in
front of St Demetrios: the text
reads 'a prayer for him whose
name God knows'. All the
figural mosaics in the north
inner aisle, except for the
inserted medallions, date from
before the fire of around 620,
probably from the sixth
century.*

the right of Figure 28) the child is of an age to walk, and both she and
her mother are offering candles to St Demetrios, probably in the interior
of the church. In the fourth and last scene (Figure 29), the grown child
together with her mother and father (?) and two other women
approaches St Demetrios and offers him two doves. The scene is set
in a garden, in which some art historians have seen a reference to the
garden of paradise.

The interpretation of such a cycle today without a related explanatory
text involves all sorts of difficulties. Not only are we confronted by
baffling ambiguities in the visual representations, but we lack any clues
as to how Byzantine audiences would have reacted to such complex
images. From the point of view of the modern spectator, the questions
that arise are clear enough. The child has lived through childhood, but
some feature of this childhood needed special commemoration. Is the
child especially devoted to the service of God and St Demetrios, and
specially blessed? Or is it a weakly child who finally dies in adolescence?
What is the reason for this apparent overwhelming concern for a female
child? Yet these may not be the appropriate questions; and the historian
must probably accept that whatever the private circumstances and emotions that lay behind these striking images, they are probably lost for
ever. It is more important to recognize that the text of the *Miracles*,
with its stress on the communal aspects of the saint's cult, and these
individual dedications both proclaim the power and ubiquity of St
Demetrios within the society of Thessaloniki already before 620. His
presence was more permanent than that of any human.

A different group of mosaics belongs to the restoration after the fire of around 620. These mosaics therefore relate to the opening chapters of *Book 2*, to the time of sieges and other disasters. The fire of around 620 damaged the mosaics of the north aisle—this is the simplest explanation of the condition of the upper parts of the various panels. The cycle of the childhood of Maria, for example, seems to have been damaged and repaired about this time. The mosaicists who worked on the area of the north aisle after the fire were cavalier in their treatment of it. They removed the previous composition which lay at the exact centre of the colonnade and inserted instead a new commemorative inscription of the restoration together with three medallion portraits showing St Demetrios in the centre between two unidentified ecclesiastics (Figures 28, 30). The inscription attributes the work of restoration to the time of an eparch Leo (presumably in office soon after 620). The two priestly portraits form a stylistic and iconographic link with other mosaics in the church, and especially with the panel which was described at the opening of this chapter (Figure 14). The figure on the right (to the saint's left), and therefore in Christian convention the less important of the

30 This photograph taken in 1907 is one of the best records of the state of the north inner aisle mosaics before their destruction. The photographer is standing in the nave of the church, very near to the site of St Demetrios' silver ciborion; the mosaics may have been specially placed to enhance the decoration of this sacred area.

two, is the same bishop who appears on the pier mosaic beside the sanctuary; there he is at the right hand of St Demetrios and is described as one of the founders after a sea attack on the city. With the information given in *Book 2* about the fire, the events leading up to it, and the subsequent restoration, the inscription on this panel becomes clearer: it refers to the sea attack of about 615, and by 'founders' is meant the restorers after the fire. This bishop cannot in this case be the archbishop John who was dead by the time of the fire, but must be some successor who kept up the tradition of special concern for the saint. The visual environment of the church was now dominated by portraits of an archbishop in the same way that the *Miracles* are dominated by Eusebios and John. The close relation between the higher clergy and the saint is now not only made visually explicit in the church, but as an icon the bishop becomes a possible image to whom prayers can be directed.

Who is the other person in the restored mosaics of the north aisle? He appears in the more prestigious position on the saint's right hand and he also reappears in a mosaic on the pier to the right of the altar sanctuary, but placed on the eastern side, and therefore visible from the apse area and transept but not from the body of the church (Figure 31). At first sight his garments suggest that he is a priest in his vestments, but a closer look reveals that he wears a strip of material (on which appears a cross) around his left shoulder. This is to be identified as the '*orarion*' or deacon's stole. The position of a deacon in the church hierarchy at this time was an important one. Although the priests of a city would be indispensable to the bishop for their part in carrying out sacred services, the second position after the bishop in prestige and authority in the diocese would be that of the archdeacon; he would be responsible for pastoral work, for the management of church property and for works of charity. So, although he was not ordained as a priest and could only act as an assistant in the liturgy, a deacon was far higher in civic authority than any of the ordinary clergy or staff of the church of St Demetrios.

The deacon here appears on the panel standing beside St Demetrios; the saint has his right arm around him and holds his left hand outstretched with the palm towards the spectator. An inscription accompanies the panel: 'Blessed martyr of Christ, friend of the city, take care of citizens and strangers'—very much a reflection of the civic role of the saint and of a deacon. The suggestion has been made that this deacon is the man who in *Book 2* was told by Demetrios that the church would be restored [2:3]; but there is hardly the evidence to support such an identification. It is more plausible to suppose that this deacon was the main assistant of the bishop at the time of the restoration and managed all the practical arrangements for bishop and eparch. He was able to make a visual record of his role, as did also the second-in-command of the monastery of St Catherine at Sinai in the sixth century who organized the mosaic decoration for the abbot and recorded his name in the apse mosaics.

Other mosaics set up after the fire of about 620 were also concentrated around the altar and liturgical area. The inclusion of other saints in this

scheme might seem at first sight to diminish the predominance of St Demetrios, but he had probably always been seen as part of a community of saints with access to a holy fellowship, and not simply as an individual. This was also the case on the ciborion where other saints were represented. On the west face of the right pier of the sanctuary of the church is a young saint inscribed with his name, St Sergios; another saint on the west face of the left pier, accompanied by two small human figures (posssibly, but not necessarily, children), may be St Demetrios or even perhaps St Bacchos, the other military saint who is often paired with Sergios. The military associations are not, however, underlined in the church, as the saints wear aristocratic civilian dress. All the mosaics after the fire consist of portrait icons of saints or donors and there are no narrative sections from this period. Moreover the new mosaics were mainly positioned around the sanctuary. This choice of position may reflect a specific wish to decorate the liturgical area of the church; but it could simply have been, more practically, that this was one area still relatively free for new icons. The effect was certainly to add to the availability of icons for prayer immediately in front of the altar. The new icons could immediately function as part of the ritual of the church.

We have considerable evidence that permits us to investigate closely many aspects of life in Thessaloniki in the sixth and seventh centuries, provided that we use images as well as texts. We can read what the people heard in sermons in the church of St Demetrios and we can also see much that they saw. The environment within which their beliefs and actions developed and within which their attitudes were formed is intelligible through all this evidence. There is information enabling us to understand how religion works in culture, integrating the community, the natural world and thought. We can appreciate in what ways icons established a saint, and how words confirmed and extended his powers. Through both, a category of Christian 'truth' was built up. The role of icons is more complex than that of the texts for they are at once both more concrete and more ambiguous. Their greater ambiguity is also a source of power over the observer. The texts record hearsay and oral witness and give these authority and refinement within a moral and morally-edifying system. The icons record miracles and other benefits, but they are not just mirrors of events. Once set up they become effective vessels in themselves, to which prayers can be directed and from which further benefits are guaranteed. They offer security in life. It is one thing for a bishop to give a sermon about the protective powers of St Demetrios; it is another to have before one a permanent image of the bishop shown in favour with the saint in front of which candles may be lit as part of a whole grid of prayer.

Whether St Demetrios actually lived and died in Thessaloniki around the year 300 is never doubted in the texts. Public confidence in his existence and powers had already been developed through the icons of the church and through his silver ciborion in the nave, believed by many to house his body and proved to all by his miracles to house his spirit. The visual decoration of the church was the effective proof

31 Some of the major mosaics in the church of St Demetrios are on the pier to the right of the sanctuary. Figure 14 illustrated the mosaic showing St Demetrios and the restorers of the church, while here the panel on the east face of the pier is shown. St Demetrios has his arm around a second ecclesiastic, the same man who appears in the mosaics of the second phase of the north inner aisle (see Figure 28).

not only of his appearance but of his historicity because the icons both record and promote miracles. When the sick came to the holy man St Theodore of Sykeon, they were in a high state of emotion at reaching his famed presence; they were miraculously healed after being ritually treated with holy oil or special words when in a state of 'ecstasy'. The necessary modulation of the emotions of the citizens of Thessaloniki into 'ecstasy' was achieved through the mystique of the church of St Demetrios and its decoration.

The power of saints is therefore documented in these two first chapters in different frameworks, though both were directed towards the miraculous and therefore the abnormal in life. In the case of St Theodore of Sykeon, the holy man was the personal mediator between men and God, though for himself the effective channel was likely to be through the icons. In Thessaloniki, where there was no holy man available and where a conventional type of bishop was able to control or influence social behaviour, the icons might provide a direct channel to the divine for the populace at large; or, perhaps more often, icons were an extension of the position and status of the bishop; he himself (or his predecessors) might be represented in the company of the saint. The result was that Thessaloniki no longer needed a living saint.

The conclusion that the promotion of the saint owed much to the activities of the bishops of Thessaloniki is a surprising one, but not one which can be explained away as the inevitable bias of writings produced by the ecclesiastical establishment. The building of the church and the first miracles are connected in the texts with the eparchs of the city, but by the end of the sixth century the leaders of the church dominate the life of Thessaloniki, and are soon themselves to be seen portrayed in mosaic on the walls of the church more effectively than the eparch is. Theodore of Sykeon was himself a bishop for a time, but he found this a source of administrative problems and a hindrance to his monastic ideals. Thessaloniki, to judge from the evidence of these texts and images, was well advanced by the seventh century as an environment where the aristocracy devoted much of its wealth not to subsidizing public entertainments or civic amenities, as in the period of Late Antiquity, but to enhancing the places of prayer and worship. Their acceptance that the interiors of churches must be seen to be richly embellished led to the covering of every part of the church of St Demetrios with figural icons and other decorations. The surrounding of the cult place of the saint with gold and silver works of art was soon to appear as more than mere ornament; because of the subjects depicted, all those who came to Thessaloniki found visible proof of the powers of the saint, and the promise of personal help. The visual evidence of this church shows how a haven of safety and peace became part of the special experience of this frontier region of the Byzantine empire perpetually facing the threat of foreign and pagan invasion. The presence of St Demetrios could encourage the citizens and convert the outsiders; the icons were the direct and ever-present witnesses of his powers.

3

ICONOCLASM:
THE IMPOSITION
OF CHANGE

At no time did the issue of the functioning of the visual in society receive more attention within Byzantium than during the period of Iconoclasm. For over a century after 726 successive rulers of the empire banned the manufacture and display of figurative icons in the Christian church and earned themselves the name of 'icon smashers'. This was the period of the most profound change in the visual environment which ever took place in the whole history of Byzantium. The imperial imposition of a ban on icons lasted from 726 initially up to 787; from 787 until 814, imperial policy was reversed and the doctrine was declared a heresy and, at least in theory, icons could be freely produced. A second phase of Iconoclasm was reimposed by the emperors from 814 until 843. Thereafter Iconoclasm was never officially to return. Official prescription, of course, was not always mirrored in practice. Even during the period when the icons were most strictly under ban, there is no doubt that access to them was not totally prevented; and there must have been 'underground' production of new works as well as the concealment of already existing works.

The concerted imperial attempt to set up a society without a figurative religious art did not succeed, and ultimately the parading of icons in public became even more conspicuous than during the period covered in the first two chapters. Yet the Islamic world which neighboured Byzantium enjoyed greater success in this respect, for during the period of Byzantine Iconoclasm Islam did develop an enduring style of art for the mosque which entirely lacked representations of the human figure. This chapter will look at the circumstances leading up to Iconoclasm, including the parallel and related Islamic experience, and then ask how the attempt to prohibit icons affected society and how the reaction to Iconoclasm was articulated.

The behaviour and attitudes of two communities, one rural and one provincial urban, have so far been illustrated. These might be thought to typify only the provinces or, at least, the mentality of the ordinary mass of people rather than the elites of Constantinople or the ruling imperial family. Yet we have already seen that Theodore of Sykeon was as widely popular on his three visits to Constantinople as he was at home in the villages of northern Asia Minor; and in Thessaloniki the cult of St Demetrios was conspicuously promoted by the prefects from aristocratic families who were appointed in the capital to one of the highest posts in the empire and by the archbishops who, even if reared locally, must have received advanced theological education in the capital from which they too were appointed. It remains to consider specifically how far emperors from the late seventh century to the middle of the ninth century were also deeply involved with the functions of religious art in such a society.

One emperor at the end of the seventh century was responsible for an act which sent shock-waves even through the neighbouring Islamic world. He changed the images on his gold coins. This act might sound trivial, but what was seen on coins was far from trivial in medieval society. Calculations for tax and for military and all regular annual salaries were assessed in gold, and the coins were regulated by the imperial civil service. Any new issue of the gold coin, the Byzantine *nomisma* or *solidus*, was seen by officials and at least the richer members of the empire soon after it was minted. It was the gold coins of Justinian II (685 to 695 and 705 to 711) which suddenly departed from all the traditional conventions and adopted a new and revolutionary scheme.

The most important element of the design on the normal issues of the coins of Constantinople during the preceding reigns had been the bust of the reigning emperor, occupying the place of honour on the front (technically 'obverse') side; the only symbols used on the reverse side in recent reigns had been the cross, a Victory in profile or a frontal angel. The first two issues of Justinian II continued these traditional schemes, with great attention being paid to a well-designed portrait head of the new emperor; on his accession he is first represented beardless, but this is soon changed to show him with a small beard. For the rest of his reign his effigy is bearded.

The great break with tradition came in the third issue of the coins of Justinian II, probably to be dated to the early 690s. Instead of seeing the portrait of the emperor on the obverse, Byzantine subjects were confronted with an icon of Christ, who was not, however, directly named on the coin (Figure 32). It was a bust portrait, like some of the holy figures in the seventh-century mosaics of the north aisle at St Demetrios (Figures 27, 28, 29, 30). Christ looked out towards the observer and had long hair and a beard; there was a cross shown behind his head. This portrait type must have been acceptable, at least in imperial circles, as an authentic record of Christ, but we do not know what predisposed the acceptance of this type. The usual suggestion is that a specific icon was being copied and that the coin was inspired by the famous representation of Christ which at the time decorated the ceremonial entrance-gate to the palace, the so-called Chalke Gate. However this is only one possibility among many. It has also been suggested, for example, that the coin was copying a classical model, the

32 In the course of the first reign of the emperor Justinian II (685–695), new gold coins were minted which departed from previous conventions and introduced several innovations. Instead of a portrait of the emperor on the obverse, a head of Christ appeared; the emperor, holding a cross, was now delegated to the reverse side, implying he was of lesser rank. Christ is depicted on these coins with long hair and full beard. Two examples of this coin are shown; the example from the British Museum (right), for which we have both reverse and obverse, is damaged.

fifth-century BC statue of Zeus at Olympia (by Pheidias of Athens)—a traditional model for 'divinity' throughout the period of antiquity. It may even be that the coin had no direct source and that Justinian was trying to establish a new, orthodox representation of Christ.

On the reverse of this new coin the emperor was depicted as a standing figure holding a cross attached to a stepped plinth. The emperor wears a *loros*, and this dress also marks a change of practice from the coins of the preceding reigns. The sixth-century emperors were usually represented wearing armour, but this representation went out of fashion in the seventh century. The emperor Heraclios introduced the *chlamys* decorated with the *tablion*; this is a civil garment very like that worn by St Demetrios in the mosaic icons in Thessaloniki (the long garment is the chlamys, and the ornamental patch over the chest the tablion). Justinian II chose instead to be seen on the coinage in a garment which had specific connections with the celebrations of Easter. The *loros*, a very long jewelled robe, seems to have derived from the traditional dress of the Roman consul. When the emperor took over the powers of this office, which was phased out as a separate appointment in 539, he retained the option of wearing this garment on particular occasions. One such ritual occasion was at the ceremonies of Easter, when a parallel might be made between the *loros* and the winding-sheet of Christ. The emperor, it can be conjectured, chose to be depicted in this same garment on his new coins, since (as at Easter) he was there in the 'presence' of Christ. The relation between the two sovereigns (the heavenly and the earthly) is made explicit in the inscriptions on the coins: Christ is King of Kings (Rex Regnantium), and Justinian II is the slave of Christ

(Servus Christi). The special relationship between emperor and Christ expressed in the poetry of Corippus in the sixth century is now highlighted even further and put into the most direct visual statement in the coins of Justinian II.

Justinian II was deposed in 695 as a result of a military coup by the general of the 'theme' of Hellas, the commander of central Greece—one of the new military units known as themes which were gradually replacing the old Roman provinces. When Justinian was deposed, he was mutilated as a symbolic sign for all to see that he was unfit to rule society; his nose was slit and he was exiled to the Crimea (Cherson). Mutilations had usually deterred further imperial ambitions, but not in the case of Justinian II. The summer of 705 saw his return to power. The coins of the intermediate emperors, during his years of exile while he was making military preparations for his return, had dropped the portrayal of Christ in preference for the traditional designs. Justinian II immediately re-issued his innovative coinage, but with a major variation: the portrait type of Christ was changed (Figure 33). Christ is now shown not as a full-bearded 'Pantocrator' (Ruler of all), but as a young man with short curly hair, and virtually beardless. The first new issues bear a portrait of Justinian II on the reverse, now accompanied by the inscription 'Peace' (*Pax*) within his orb; later a second design on the reverse showed the emperor together with his young son and heir as well as a new coin inscription: 'Long Life!' (*multos annos*), a phrase drawn from the traditional acclamations shouted to the emperor at public ceremonies.

Why was the portrait type of Christ changed? No Byzantine writer of the period refers to the change. Some art historians, primarily arguing from representations of Christ on liturgical vessels in precious metals, have supposed that each of these two types was limited to one region of the empire. This would mean that the artists of Constantinople consistently chose to represent Christ as Pantocrator fully bearded; while the artists of other parts of the empire chose the virtually beardless image. Such attempts to explain the development of Byzantine art in terms of separate regional 'schools', as if neither patrons, artists nor objects freely travelled in the period, are obviously too simple to explain such distinctions as are found on these coins issued under Justinian II. As an explanation, it sidesteps questions of the associations and functions of portraits of Christ.

The key innovation made in the coinage in the reign of Justinian II was a design with the representation of Christ. It has been suggested that the idea for such a portrait on the coins was at least stimulated by a decision of the so-called Quinisext Council and ought to be linked with it. This was one of several church councils which dominate the intellectual thinking of the Byzantine period, of which the purpose was to assemble the bishops of the whole church in order to decide on questions of doctrine or discipline So long as every episcopal see was represented, the council could be designated a General or Oecumenical Council, and its decisions, drawn up in the form of a list of decisions called canons, were binding on all Christians. A council where only

33 *When Justinian II re-established himself on the throne after a period of exile, a new set of gold coins was produced for his second reign (705–711). On this new issue Christ is depicted with a thin beard and curled hair, in contrast to his portrayal on the coins of Justinian's first reign. In this example, the reverse side shows the emperor with his son and designated heir (Tiberios).*

98

a limited number of bishops was present had no real constitutional validity in the wider church. Justinian II organized a Council that was intended to be Oecumenical during his first reign, but in fact not all sees were properly represented: the Pope in particular failed to send a properly constituted delegation. Not a legitimate Oecumenical Council, therefore, the meeting was known as the Quinisext Council ('fifth and sixth')—a title which interprets the role of the meeting as a continuation of two earlier Oecumenical Councils (the Fifth of 553 and the Sixth of 680/1). Neither of these earlier meetings had produced a list of canons and Justinian convened the Quinisext in order to rectify this omission. 102 canons were produced. Technically the absence from the Quinisext Council of representatives of all the bishoprics of the Christian world meant that the decisions were not binding; but whether or not they were accepted at the time as legitimate canons, they represent current theological concerns, and happen to coincide with the time of the new coinage.

The canons of the council are a concise record of the discussions held, and of the ideas which seemed acceptable to those present, both bishops and emperor. One particular canon may be the basis for the coin innovation and this will be quoted in full; but in order to understand it fully the reader must bear in mind the conventions of expression in Byzantine theological thought, which are a peculiar combination of the language of the New Testament and technical terms from philosophy. Christ is often called the Lamb, as in the New Testament and in the sacrifice of the eucharist; and the Bible is the Law. The canon sets out a new rule. It records that in some icons Christ is shown only in a symbolic form as a lamb (a surviving example of this convention is on the mid-sixth-century ivory throne of Maximian in Ravenna where the central figure of St John the Baptist on the front holds a disc on which a lamb is depicted; see Figure 34). This symbol is to be banned in future, and Christ must be shown in human form. Such a representation will be more effective than the symbol in conveying the fact that God took on human form and then was put to death on the cross. It is therefore a canon which expresses the belief of the assembled elite in the didactic and emotional power of figurative art; its effect is to encourage the expansion of the representation of Christ as a man in art. The canon was formulated as follows:

CANON 82

In some venerable icons, a lamb is depicted towards which the Baptist points a finger. This image has been accepted as a symbol of grace, a prediction through the Old Testament of our true Lamb, Christ the Lord. While accepting the ancient symbols and shadows as signs and clues of the truth to be given to the Church, we give preference to the Grace and Truth which we have received as the New Testament. So, in order that the perfect should be represented before the eyes of all people, for example in paintings, we ordain that from now on Christ our Lord, the Lamb who took upon Himself the sins of the world, be portrayed in images in His human form, and no longer in the form of the lamb. Through His figure we perceive the depth of the humiliation of God the Word and are led to remember His life in the flesh, His suffer-

34 *The central ivory panel of the mid-sixth-century throne made for Maximian, archbishop of Ravenna, has a figure of John the Baptist at its centre, prominently displaying a disc with a representation of Christ in the form of a lamb. The Quinisext Council of the Church, which met in Constantinople in 692, was critical of exactly this sort of traditional scheme, maintaining that the use of the symbol of the lamb in art obscured the truth of the New Testament. The argument was that since Christ as the Lamb of God came to earth in human form, representations of him in art must also show him in human form in order to conform to Christian belief. This theological debate on the correct nature of images in Christian art dates from the period of the new coin designs for Justinian II, only a few years before the banning of all figural icons by the iconoclasts.*

ing and His saving death, and the redemption which comes from it for the world.

Was this canon the cause of the coin innovation? Unfortunately we can only date the issue of the coins very roughly and cannot indeed be certain whether it comes before or after the decision of the Council. It is equally easy therefore to argue the opposite case—that the striking of the coin led to the discussion and formulation of the canon! This does seem the more unlikely sequence of events, but one thing is certain: the evidence of both the canon and the coins shows that at this time there was imperial and ecclesiastical debate about the ways and propriety of representing Christ. The topical questions of the time were whether icons which showed Christ in human form should be made and exhibited more prominently than previously, and whether it was desirable to avoid symbols because these were unnecessary, if not actually ineffective ways of influencing the Christian public in its beliefs and loyalty to the Byzantine concept of empire. The new coins with their message would have circulated widely, although in fact their power as specific propaganda was limited, for they were only seen by those who handled gold denominations (or the rarer silver coins); the copper coinage remained traditional.

These coins of Justinian II and the deliberations of the bishops in the Quinisext Council illustrate a concern with using the visual in a Christian society. In the Quinisext Council the bishops from all the provincial cities under the presidency of the emperor discussed the role of art. What they recommended, and what was put into practice, was the public display of icons of Christ in order to further the acceptance of the message of Christianity for the redemption of the individual believer, and to make belief easier. In other words, the church believed that pictures of a visible Christ made religious education more effective. There is, however, no record of any discussion on the possible implications for prayer and worship of having such icons displayed in the liturgical atmosphere of a church.

The Council drew up another canon (no 73) concerning representations of the cross and decreed (not for the first time in a church council) that the cross ought not to be represented on the pavements of churches on which people would tread, but only where proper veneration (*proskynesis*) could be given to it as a sign of salvation. What this canon again does not tell us is whether any broader attention was given to the way art functioned. Yet the evidence we have already seen demonstrates how an icon was not simply a teaching aid in a book or a 'work of art'. The icons in the church of St Demetrios both established the powers of Christian saints and were a focus of prayers, acting as a channel leading to the company of saints in heaven who could confer benefits on the inhabitants of the temporal world. When the Quinisext Council endorsed the manufacture of figurative icons of Christ in preference to indirect symbols, it did more than encourage the expansion of art, including probably the new coins of Justinian. It intensified the devotional practices of the whole church, and increased the range of objects in front of which prayers and contact with saints could be made.

The outlook of the Byzantine empire was permanently changed in the course of the seventh century as a new culture and society established itself first in the regions of the Middle East beside Byzantium and then within some of the territories of the empire. For centuries thereafter the various Islamic empires formed a hostile military threat to Byzantium, and in 1453 Constantinople finally fell to the Ottoman Turks. In the early stages of Islam, its society went through many of the same discussions about religious art as did Byzantium and it is useful to look at the Islamic response to the problems. Furthermore Islam also developed into Iconoclasm and so offers evidence of parallel, if not connected, thinking.

The great Arab expansion began a few years after the death of Mohammed in 632; within ten years Persia had fallen under Muslim control to be followed by the Middle Eastern provinces of the Byzantine empire. Christians in these regions found themselves living under 'heretical' rulers, who had ambitions to take over all of Christendom and convert it to Islam. Each side regarded the other as a group of religious heretics; the eighth-century theologian John of Damascus, who went as a monk to the monastery of Mar Saba, listed Islam as the 101st Christian heresy. However, the Arab caliphs of the seventh century, from the Umayyad dynasty, took over many of the external characteristics of the former rulers of the conquered regions. When criticized for their 'Byzantinization' of power, these caliphs had an answer: 'Damascus is full of Greeks, and so the caliph must behave and look like a Byzantine emperor to express his power'. Obviously, therefore, the new Islamic rulers paid close attention to Byzantine behaviour and to the methods of influencing society employed by Byzantine emperors.

In the early years of the Arab empire in the seventh century, the new rulers struck coins resembling those Byzantine or Persian coins already in circulation in the Islamic territories (as in Figure 35). Attention was then applied to the development of a new monetary system. In designing the new Islamic coins, the procedure of the Arab designers was to study coins in circulation elsewhere and adapt them to their own needs. Byzantine coins were first of all adapted by eliminating any conspicuous Christian elements in the models, such as, for example, crosses (as in Figure 36). After a period of such adaptations more momentous changes in the designs came in the course of the caliphate of 'Abd al-Malik (685–705) whose capital was at Damascus. He experimented with new designs and ultimately changed the denominations of his coinage.

The first Arab-Byzantine coinage was in copper, but 'Abd al-Malik struck coins in gold for a time before finally returning to copper for his reformed currency. His experiments with the gold dinar included a coin which used a Persian model for the obverse—a portrait of the Sassanid king Chosroes was adapted into an ideal portrait of the caliph with professions of Koranic faith written in the border (Figure 35). The reverse of this coin was derived from a Byzantine model, but instead of a cross being depicted an equivalent Islamic symbol is used, the ceremonial lance of Mohammed set within an arch of honour or a

mihrab, representing the power of the caliph. The inscriptions on this coin read: 'Chief of Believers', 'Caliph of Allah', and (probably) 'May Allah assist'. Another issue of this group (Figure 36) represented portraits of the dynasty of the ruling caliph on the obverse, a design that must be a copy of coins such as those of Heraclios which have a group dynastic portrait; the reverse seems to show the sceptre of Mohammed on a plinth, an adaptation of the Byzantine scheme of the cross on steps. The inscriptions in Arabic on the reverse are professions of the Islamic faith in the words of the Koran: 'In the name of God. There is no God but God. Mohammed is the prophet of God'. Another coin (Figure 36) showed the caliph with a sword on the obverse, and on the reverse a sceptre on a plinth, if that is the correct interpretation of the Islamic adaptation of its model, a cross on a plinth.

36 Other coin types of 'Abd al-Malik were more direct adaptations of purely Byzantine models. In one case (left) the model showed Heraclios or one of his successors grouped with their dynastic heirs: the ruling caliph and his dynasty appear on the obverse and a relic on the reverse, in this case what is probably a sceptre of Mohammed, instead of a Christian cross. In the other case (right), the model was a coin, probably of Justinian II from the beginning of his reign, showing the emperor holding a cross on the obverse and with a cross on a plinth on the reverse; on the Islamic coins the caliph holds a sword and there is a sceptre on a plinth on the reverse.

37 'Abd al-Malik's
experiments in coin design
ended with his final solution:
Koranic texts on both sides of
the coins and no images at all.

These experiments came to an end in 695–6 when not only were
the denominations and weights of coins rethought, but the designs were
changed to the system which has survived up to the twentieth century.
In the new system the designs of the coins were entirely non-figurative:
their content was limited to words, to professions of faith and Koranic
verses on the mission of the Prophet (Figure 37). It is difficult not to
see this system as the logical outcome of the religion of Islam. In Islam
the word of God is sent down to mankind; to find that the coins and
the places of worship of this religion give privilege to words seems only
appropriate. In Christianity, where God takes on human form, the
development of an art which shows God in human form seems equally
appropriate.

A closer look at the stages through which the Islamic coins passed
and at how the Arabs responded to these changes will help to explain
why this culture must be considered in parallel with Byzantium before
we can confront the period of Iconoclasm itself. There is some evidence
that the coins showing the caliph 'Abd al-Malik with a sword (Figure
36) met with opposition from his subjects; the effigy was, according
to later Islamic writers, 'reproved' by the Arab religious leaders at
Medina. This is one of the hints which point to the existence of opposition to images of the Byzantine kind in Islam—although there is no
explicit prohibition in the Koran. Occasional examples of the removal
or destruction of pictures by Arabs can be found in the sources relating
to the seventh century, from soon after the conquest of the Middle East
onwards. But the reasons for opposition to such images are not the issue
here; the fact is that from the middle of the 690s figural images were
never again found on Islamic coins, despite their initial appearance for
some years before.

Neither Islamic nor Byzantine coins of this period are precisely dated
and this causes difficulties in deciding the interactions between the
cultures. The most convincing interpretation of the course of events
is that Islam adopted the rules of visual representation of Byzantium.

The production of the first coin issues of 'Abd al-Malik after he came
to the throne in 685 did not offer any real complications. It was just
a matter of deleting the obvious Christian elements of the Byzantine
coins that were taken as models. The smoothness of the operation was
completely disrupted with the appearance of the revolutionary coins
of Justinian II with the bust of Christ which appeared on the scene in
about 692. The design was radically offensive to Islamic belief and the

coin designers were forced to react to find an image with a different meaning. Their solution was to produce the issue with the standing caliph with the sword on the obverse and the sceptre on a plinth on the reverse. Their model for the caliph would have been the portrait of Justinian II holding the cross on the reverse of the new Byzantine coin; the sceptre which they had used on earlier issues as a substitute for the cross on a stepped plinth now corresponds to the face of Christ on the new Byzantine coins. In other words, Byzantium made the innovation which forced the caliph to sponsor his own new designs, but these, in turn, met with the disapproval of his subjects. Islamic opposition to the image of the caliph forced the final innovation and the creation of a coinage with no figures at all, but instead religious slogans in Arabic script. Islam ended this 'war of images' between the two empires by changing the rules of signification.

The Islamic coins are only part of a wider change in the use of visual symbols in Arab society. The creation of a new visual identity which differed from that of Christianity is a feature of the reigns of 'Abd al-Malik and his son 'Abd al-Walid I (705–715) and is documented not only in coins but also in their major monumental structures. The decoration of both the Dome of the Rock at Jerusalem (688–92) and the Great Mosque at Damascus (finished about 706) appears to have consisted of mosaics, carried out by contract with Byzantine artists, whose schemes were non-figurative. The mosaics include intricate designs derived from Antique and Byzantine decorative motifs, landscapes with similar traditional elements and building types familiar from Roman art, and also Koranic texts and other symbols. A few years later (in 723/4) one Islamic ruler even tried to ban figurative images in the Christian churches in his empire: the 'iconoclast edict' of Yazid II at Damascus is documented in historical texts and evident in churches of the region where images of human figures (and even animals) have been obliterated. One example of this Islamic iconoclasm is found in the surviving floor mosaic pavement of Ma'in in Jordan, manufactured in 719–20, and then later 'adjusted' by the removal of the figures.

Byzantine Iconoclasm cannot be studied without remembering the parallels from the neighbouring empire of Islam, a society superimposed over part of the previous territories of Byzantium. The experiments in coins reveal something about the visual grammar of the time. It is not likely that the correlations between the designs of the Byzantine and Islamic coins reflect a one-sided situation of a new culture following an older one; the Byzantine decision to mint coins which contained the image of Christ could have been partly intended as an act of provocation towards Islam, since the fact that the coins circulated into the Arab empire must have been well known. Whether or not this was an intentional 'war of images', the nature of the Islamic reaction to the expansion of Byzantine figurative art at the end of the seventh century must be remembered in considering the outbreak of Iconoclasm in Byzantium itself and the consequent changes in its religious life and man-made environment.

The evidence of the coins of Justinian II and the church pronouncements of his time introduce us to the nature of the Byzantine use of religious art and how this reflects conceptions of power and mediation with God on the eve of Iconoclasm. The immediate successors of Justinian abandoned his precedent and dropped the representation of Christ on their coins, a decision which may betray an element of public concern over the design. But this concern is greatly overshadowed by the total ban on religious images imposed by the emperor Leo III (717–41), inaugurating a century of violent debate and change.

Many of the apparently obvious questions about Iconoclasm, such as its genesis, motivation, scope and consequences, are battlegrounds of disagreement amongst historians. The concern of this book is not to enter into these disagreements in any detail, but rather to examine the period of upheaval for the light it throws on the role of the visual in Byzantine society more generally. However, even such a broad approach cannot entirely ignore the controversies among modern scholars, for these controversies necessarily influence the view we take of the primary texts and images that provide the contemporary evidence for Iconoclasm. So in the first instance (after looking at the circumstances of Iconoclasm and Byzantine explanations of it) we shall consider in what ways the subject has been treated in recent literature and what recent theories have been proposed to explain it. Two particular Byzantine texts will then be examined, both of which are polemical attacks on iconoclasts and iconoclast thinking. One is a biography of a monk said to have been martyred for his support of the veneration of icons, and the other purports to describe the arguments of an anti-iconoclast synod. Between them they offer some introduction to the ways of thinking which formed the basis for decisions which had to be made by all members of society about their public behaviour and beliefs. Unfortunately, the disappearance of virtually all the texts written on the iconoclast side, as a result of later censorship, limits the choice of literature that can be analysed.

Just as vandalism or hooliganism would not be thought to a commentator today to have been 'explained' when the events involved were described or when a dictionary definition was given ('vandalism is to destroy the beautiful or venerable'), so an explanation of Iconoclasm must go beyond a description of it as 'breaking or destroying images, especially those set up as objects of veneration'. Certainly eighth- and ninth-century iconoclasm involved the smashing of images and those participating in the destruction believed deeply that the act of destruction was their duty; but it cannot be supposed that such beliefs and actions were all that Byzantine Iconoclasm was about. The underlying question is how such beliefs came about, and what the iconoclastic protest was meant to achieve.

The two first chapters of this book have focused on some aspects of Byzantine society which, though not necessarily entirely new in the late sixth and seventh centuries, were confirmed by popular assent in that period. For example, we saw in Sykeon how the monastic holy man gained a surprisingly central role in society through his various powers, particularly the ability to overturn the natural world and with the help of the supernatural to achieve miracles; in Thessaloniki miracles were achieved through the spiritual presence of a benevolent saint. We have seen the power of images and their place in the order of the things of the church. We have seen a society in which the bishop as head of the church was the pivot around whom the community gained its unity. Such features of seventh-century society cannot have been limited to Sykeon and Thessaloniki, and both the texts that have been summarized indicate how the sphere of influence of St Theodore and St Demetrios expanded outside their home region. The beliefs and conditions of the period promoted a general extension of confidence in the power of God and the saints which gradually affected assumptions about how human affairs were decided. One senses the growth of a kind of determinism in the way success in war, or other kinds of good or bad fortune, are attributed not to human endeavour but to divine will and favour or disfavour. Even in the capital of Constantinople, when the emperor Leo III repulsed the Arab attack from the walls in 717, the patriarch attributed the victory entirely to the Virgin. Associated with this grow- ing trust in the power of the divine (and its visual manifestations) we can detect a decrease in the power of the imperial administrators and army officers in the provinces, and indeed of the emperor everywhere— at least as perceived by his subjects. This change of balance is certainly suggested by the criticisms of individual emperors and officials voiced in both the texts studied so far, and it forms the background to the attitudes which emerge in the succeeding period of Iconoclasm.

The spark which lit the flame of Iconoclasm in Byzantium was the order of the emperor Leo III in 726 to remove the icon of Christ from the Chalke Gate, the main entrance into the Great Palace (a panel which may have resembled the icon of Christ on Sinai, Figure 3). It is this image which has been suggested as the model of the representation of Christ which appeared on the coins of the first reign of Justinian II (Figure 32). The figure of Christ was apparently painted on a panel and fixed on to the gate together with other representations, notably of emperors. The icon was taken down and destroyed; possibly a cross was erected in its place, as certainly happened in December 814 when a similar series of events took place. The extent to which icons were destroyed following 726 is not documented in the extant sources, but there was a distinct intensification of activities in the course of the next reign when Constantine V (741–75) succeeded his father. He called a church Council in 753–4 to gain official recognition of Iconoclasm as the orthodox belief of the Byzantine church and state.

It was some years later, in 768/9, that Iconoclasm struck even the church of St Sophia in Constantinople. Some of what happened in St Sophia is known not only from texts but also from visible traces in the church. The iconoclasts cut out a set of sixth-century mosaic portraits of Christ and saints in medallions in one of the private rooms of the patriarchal palace which is directly accessible from the gallery of the church. They replaced each portrait with a cross and picked out and obscured the inscriptions which had named the saints represented (Figure 38). This was a room which Theodore of Sykeon must have

visited when he was received by the patriarch in Constantinople; the saint would have seen the mosaic portraits which then decorated it. The iconoclast changes were carried out in such a way that the original design which he saw may still be traced today (Figure 39).

Iconoclasm lapsed from 787, when the Council of Nicaea condemned the doctrine as a heresy, until 814, when the emperor Leo V (813–20) reimposed it. During these years there are several references to the manufacture of figurative icons, but in the charged atmosphere of the time, many potential sponsors of art must have been cautious and unwilling to make too obvious a public demonstration of support for the veneration of icons. Even when Iconoclasm finally came to an end in 843, the possibility of another relapse must have been considered, and apart from a firm imperial statement of policy with the display of a mosaic icon of Christ on the Chalke Gate of the palace, the restoration of icons in the ninth century was a slow process.

The texts and surviving visual material which show the activities of the Iconoclasts over these years make it obvious that the removal of icons involved their replacement with other forms of visual representation, such as crosses or other non-figurative symbols. The aim of

38 Some of the acts of Iconoclasm in Constantinople are still visible, unaltered since the eighth century, as in this example in a room in the patriarchal palace attached to the church of St Sophia. From textual evidence, iconoclasts are known to have destroyed icons in this part of the building in 768/769, and the decoration which has survived shows clearly the changes that were made: a set of sixth-century portrait medallions of saints were systematically cut out and replaced with crosses.

iconoclast substitutions was positively to prescribe the sort of religious art which was allowable in the Christian church; it was not a negative movement, a desire to eliminate all art from the church. Like the discussions at the Quinisext Council in the reign of Justinian II, it continued the debate on how to represent Christ and the saints. The decisions of the Iconoclasts, like those of that Council, impinged on all aspects of religious behaviour.

All Christians agreed that idolatry was forbidden. They had, most obviously, to come to terms with the Second Commandment: 'You shall not make for yourself any idol or any likeness of anything that is in Heaven above or on the earth below or in the waters beneath the earth. You shall not adore them nor worship them; for I am the Lord your God, a jealous God' (*Exodus*: 20, v.4). This is a literal translation of the Greek Septuagint text in which the term *proskynesis* is used for 'adore' and the term *latreusis* for 'worship'. Both words had a common currency in Byzantine Greek and a certain lack of precision as a result. The use of these words in the Bible, we may be sure, had led to individual, isolated outbreaks of image-smashing before the main period of Byzantine Iconoclasm.

It was much more difficult, of course, for the church to reach general agreement about what precisely idolatry was: a question which both the supporters and the opponents of Iconoclasm had to attempt to answer. The traditional method of reaching a proper orthodox decision was to look at what previous authority said, yet this method was open to an obvious abuse—the altering or the faking of the texts adduced! On the occasion of the pro-iconoclast Council of 754 it was subsequently alleged that the iconoclasts made use of loose sheets of parchment on which doctored extracts of the writings of previous authorities were assembled. In order to forestall such criticism, whole books of the Church Fathers were produced at the anti-iconoclast Council of Nicaea in 787. The procedure used at Nicaea is, of course, not foolproof either, as whole books can be faked too.

However, both Councils made the assumption that written testimony from the past overrides spoken arguments. The same kinds of questions were put to the test by both sides in these debates. Could God be portrayed at all? If so, was his image to be conveyed only through the eucharist, or through the cross or other symbol, or through portraits of Christ? Could images work miracles, despite the earthly materials from which they were made? The only difference, in Byzantine eyes, between iconoclasts and iconophiles (lovers of icons) lay in the answers they provided to this set of questions.

The modern observer may formulate the conflict in rather different terms. Indeed many of the divergences in modern interpretations derive from disagreements about the formulation of what the conflict was about. From the viewpoint of today a new formation of society can be distinguished: once the emperor commanded that figural images of Christ, the Virgin Mary and the saints could not be placed in public churches or even kept in private, then Byzantine society was polarized into two groups—the convinced iconoclasts, the icon smashers, and the

convinced iconophiles, the icon lovers. Each group had different attitudes about prayer, worship and the way to salvation, and therefore about modes of everyday behaviour and conduct. What is more difficult to understand from a distance is what caused people to align with one side or the other, or how rapidly, when imperial policy changed, the previously convinced were able to adapt to new circumstances.

These polarities do not seem to have represented two simple opposing social categories, such as, for example, the aristocracy against the populace, the monks against the secular clergy, the church against the laity or the army against civilians. All members of Byzantine society, whether in the capital or the provinces and whether in town or countryside, were inevitably involved in the conflict. Iconoclasm had a political as well as a religious dimension. It was imposed by, and therefore was a test of, imperial authority. Yet the analysis is complicated by the interweaving of the secular and the religious in Byzantium. The emperor saw his power partly in religious terms, and was prepared to interfere with the organization and even the teaching of the church. Iconoclasm, therefore, can appear to us as a trial of religious strength between imperial and ecclesiastical power and as a particular crisis when a dynasty of strong emperors were prepared to force their policy through. These emperors could argue that it was they, not the church, who made laws, and that the church should support them. An emperor could even claim that he was able to mediate with God from a superior level to that of a priest.

The most straightforward kind of commentary on the events is to take at face value the 'facts' of narrative history and to see the events in terms of personalities: to say, for example, that the first iconoclast emperor, Leo III, changed the policy towards icons because of deep personal beliefs about correct forms of art and worship. Or taking a somewhat broader view than this highly individualistic perspective, the point could be reformulated to suggest that Leo III supported one side of a traditional debate within the Christian church about the legitimacy of certain kinds of images and was influenced by one party within the current church hierarchy. Or again emphasis could be laid on the regional background of Leo III who grew up, apparently, in Syria, and therefore had personal knowledge of Islamic and Semitic prejudices towards the figurative arts and might have sympathized with them.

The treatment of Iconoclasm as the history of individuals and their personal reactions has led to much careful investigation of the events leading up to the removal of the icon of Christ from the public façade of the imperial palace in 726. But which events are to be directly connected with the decision? It has been suggested that a volcanic eruption around the island of Thera (Santorini) in the southern Aegean Sea stimulated Leo III's first iconoclast action. This natural disaster occurred just before 726 and in Byzantine writing at the time it was attributed to the sins of the empire. Leo certainly is reported as believing that the eruption was a sign of God's anger towards him and that his attack on icons would appease that anger. On this sort of interpretation Iconoclasm becomes a concession to one superstition which in turn

39 A detailed look at one of the altered medallions in the patriarchal palace shows how the artists used by the iconoclasts achieved their results. They cut out all the tesserae of the figure inside each medallion, and inserted the mosaic crosses on a new plaster bed. Below the medallion, where the name of each saint had been written in mosaic letters, the disturbed surface discloses that the tesserae were just cut out one by one and then replaced with white limestone cubes which matched the colour of the ground. This obliterated the name, but failed to conceal the fact that the alterations had been made.

offended another superstition—that of reliance on the supposedly miraculous powers of icons. In more general terms this view of Iconoclasm sees it as a straightforward reaction of the ruling elite towards popular beliefs about icons; it was a measure to stop abuses and offensive practices which were reflections of the credulity of the people.

All these explanations must face the obvious objections. It is hardly justifiable, for example, to assume a simple opposition between the 'oriental' piety associated with Leo's Syrian origin on the one hand and Western forms of 'Hellenic' piety on the other—that is, a crude division between the non-figurative East and the figurative West. For not only does this kind of division (which was vehemently argued in scholarship in the early years of the twentieth century) now seem excessively schematic; it also raises a range of further problems. On what geographical boundary, for example, is the division between West and East supposed to lie? Is it reasonable to claim Syria for the 'East', while leaving Constantinople as 'Western'?

Similarly, the division of the beliefs of society into a polarity of popular and intellectual can scarcely be justified. It is true that in periods of limited literacy written source material might inevitably seem biased towards the views and attitudes of the elite. Yet the texts and visual materials we have so far used are not entirely centred on the upper ranks of Byzantine society. Texts and images had an audience. The *Life of Theodore of Sykeon*, for example, aimed to influence both monks and the public. Its author, a rural monk in Asia Minor, must have taken into account what he believed to be the generally-held beliefs of his intended audience. In the same way publicly delivered sermons (even if published in written form to impress other theological 'professionals') are certain to point to some of the conventional attitudes and beliefs of the church congregation in general. It is noteworthy, then, that the main divergence expressed in the *Miracles of St Demetrios* between the beliefs of the educated bishop and those of the community at large concerns the vexed question of the significance of the ciborion—was it a shrine for the relic of the saint or a symbol of his presence in the church? We might see this as a disagreement between a literal-minded and a metaphysical attitude, but we cannot assume that this was a universal division or that (for example) the literal belief about the ciborion was held by no member of the Byzantine elite. Like the division into East and West, the opposition between elite and popular beliefs is too crude a tool with which to handle the outbreak of Byzantine Iconoclasm and its causes.

A different approach to the complexities of this period is represented by a broader 'structural' view of Iconoclasm and the conditions preceding it. This kind of analysis is not necessarily of a type ever developed by the participants themselves, who may well have conceived their actions in terms of personal conviction and circumstances. It attempts rather to go beyond these individual explanations by asking what general conditions in society led to iconoclast actions and encouraged wide acceptance of a hostile attitude to images. One such view (though formulated in various ways by its different proponents) suggests that

Iconoclasm represents a response to the rise of Islam and the Arab empire and to the consequent changes in Middle Eastern culture which this caused. It is a view which is mirrored by some Byzantine writers themselves, who (framing it more personally) cast Leo III in the guise of a traitor and Arab sympathizer.

The rise of Islam meant the appearance of a new monotheistic religion in the east Mediterranean which challenged the 'truth' of Christianity as well as the temporal power of Byzantium; it was a new threat which forced Christianity on to the defensive and forced it to review its values. Intellectually there was an overlap between the two religions, particularly in their shared belief in the divine inspiration of biblical texts. Both Muslims and Christians, for example, as well as the Jews, were bound by the Ten Commandments. But interpretations of the text differed from religion to religion. This was strikingly the case with the Old Testament prohibition of idolatry, for while Christianity traditionally allowed figural representations in religious art, the Islamic faith from the end of the seventh century did not. Christian Iconoclasm is thus seen as part of a 'reformation' in Byzantine Christianity stimulated by the threat of a new religion. Christianity accommodated itself to Islam (and even stole its thunder) by also banning figural images. A similar transition is evident in Judaism, which from at least the third century had allowed figural representations, but also at this stage tightened up.

The obvious merit of this type of explanation, which appeals to the influence of Islam, is that it accepts that there was a relationship between two similar movements, in neighbouring countries, at the same time. But the definition of that relationship is more complicated than it might at first sight appear. The various Christian groups in the Middle East did not in fact form a combined front against Islam, but disagreed among themselves about questions of dogma. So, for example, some Christians in Syria and Asia Minor came out on the side of prohibition of figural images in agreement with the two predominantly Semitic religions, Judaism and Islam, some time before the main movement in Constantinople. They even went so far as to criticize Christianity for becoming a corruption of Christ's true religion. Given this diversity, it seems that an interpretation of Iconoclasm as a straightforward and co-ordinated reaction to Islam is almost as much an over-simplification as the other explanations we have considered.

The explanations for the outbreak of Iconoclasm so far described are sometimes untenable, sometimes only partially relevant. What occurred throughout the Byzantine world from the late sixth century was a prolonged period of disturbance, caused partly by external attacks and partly by internal changes. Iconoclasm was a part and also a symptom of this disturbance and can only be fully understood against such a background. For the majority of society in the seventh century their relation to the visual had come to seem part of normal existence: icons were a necessary part of Christian life. When Iconoclasm was imposed by the emperor, it had a massive impact, both as a reaction to the previous conventions and as part of a continuing disturbance. It intensified and accelerated the areas of change that had emerged in the previous century.

The new circumstances of the period before Iconoclasm are implicit in the texts looked at so far, but have not yet been made explicit. Not all of them are novel to the period; some were marginal features of earlier society which then became publicly acceptable norms. The rise of the holy man and the development of monastic life, the growth in the power of the long-serving bishop and of his role in fostering and manipulating community spirit, and the production of icons are all three features of the Byzantine empire by the time of Justinian I in the mid-sixth century; but these tendencies become more prominent a feature of life in the conditions of the next two hundred years. At the same time Byzantium faced major invasions from the Persian empire; from the vast numbers of nomadic tribes arriving in the Balkans, pressing into Greece and attacking Constantinople and setting up their new Slavonic and Bulgarian settlements; and finally from the expanding Arab empire.

The long-reigning emperor Heraclios in the first half of the seventh century had some success against the Persian threat. He managed to recover the relics of the Holy Cross which the Persian army had removed after the capture of Jerusalem in May 614 and transferred to their capital of Ctesiphon; he returned them to the church of the Holy Sepulchre in Jerusalem on 21 March 630. Heraclios destroyed the threat of Persia, and emphasized the new power of his reign by taking for himself the formal imperial title of *'Basileus'* ('King'), a title previously used in the Byzantine empire only to refer to God. In the event the belief in a victorious empire under Heraclios and his dynasty had no substance, for the main beneficiary of the collapse of Persia was found to be the Arab caliphate. In the seventh century Byzantium found itself continuously hemmed in by foreign powers who were all conspicuous for their religious convictions: the occupying nomadic tribes in the Balkans, mostly Slavonic, were pagan, and probably the most promising group for missionary activity; the Persians were long-established Zoroastrians; and the Arabs were Islamic. The last religion was the closest in its beliefs to Byzantium, and so the most aggressive threat.

In addition to these external threats in the East, the Western Roman empire was passing out of the sphere of control of Constantinople. The loss was not at first, however, admitted by the Byzantine emperor, as is most graphically illustrated by the decision of Constans II (641–668) to transfer his official residence to the west. He left Constantinople in 662 and by 663 had set up his new capital in Sicily at Syracuse, a change which pleased neither the Byzantine court nor the inhabitants of Italy on whom he imposed heavier taxation. His assassins of 668 might be described as more in touch with the realities of the time. The political organization of the West was in a process of change. No Byzantine emperor after Constans II was to exert any control there in person and in this vacuum the authority of the Popes grew (a development which had gained momentum since the time of Gregory the Great, Pope from 590 to 604).

Constantinople itself was in a state of crisis both because of enemy sieges and because of internal struggles. The reigns of the emperors at the end of the seventh century and early eighth century were generally short and unstable. The years after the assassination of Justinian II in 711 were times of disruption, ended only by Leo III's seizure of power in 717. Some of the signs of the troubles of this time immediately before 717 are to be found in religious matters. One emperor, for example, attacked church orthodoxy as established in the Sixth Council of 680–1 and, to mark his disagreement with its main decisions, he took down the visual representation of the Council which had been placed in a vestibule of the palace (in the centre of the city), and put up images of himself and the patriarch Sergios (who was one of the theologians anathematized at the Council). In the next reign, the Council was again declared representative of correct belief, and to show the reversal of opinion a new picture of the Council was made and the images of the previous emperor and Sergios destroyed. Such acts show how the apparent consensus of faith which was imposed on the Byzantine world under Justinian I in the sixth century was now open to challenge from both inside and outside the church hierarchy.

There were also conspicuous physical differences in the environment. Plagues and wars had caused demographic decline and the reduced population of the empire meant a change in the nature of urban and rural life. Although many 'cities' survived the disasters of the late sixth and seventh centuries, their character changed. This is clear enough in the picture that has emerged of life in Thessaloniki, one of the largest cities of the empire in the medieval period. It has become an administrative centre and local refuge. Its new personality lies in its walls—the physical protection of the inhabitants of the whole region—and in its saint and his icons—their spiritual protection. Within the remaining cities, the amenities built in Late Antiquity or earlier were falling out of use. Theatres and hippodromes, the principal cultural centres of Late Antiquity, were in decline (if not totally abandoned), especially outside Constantinople. In part they could not be structurally maintained or financially supported, but in part also the church directed a long campaign against their use; bishop Eusebios of Thessaloniki was not the first or the only churchman to keep out of places of public entertainment and the Quinisext Council (canon 25) expressly forbade clerics to go to the hippodrome.

The background to Iconoclasm, then, is one of wide-ranging changes in the Byzantine world. The previous certainties were collapsing, and with that collapse came also new uncertainties about the status of images in Byzantine society. Iconoclasm is in part a symptom of general disruption; but it also has a more positive political dimension. The decision to prohibit icons was a decision of the emperor; it was a statement by the emperor that he held the position of supremacy in mediating between God and men and that he was the source of all decisions. Bishops, monks and icons themselves were no longer to be the dominant force we have seen them becoming in the texts we have looked at so far; they were to come under the control, and if necessary the ban, of the emperor. So paradoxically (although a symptom of disruption) Iconoclasm also represented a reassertion of imperial authority and an attempt to find once more stability and certainty in a changing world. That stability was to lie in the word of the emperor.

Iconoclasm started with the public removal of the image of Christ from the gate of the palace in 726 and thereafter there were a number of lulls and reintensifications in the attacks on icons. The imperial action of 726 was subsequently followed up with a firm stance against the church in order to bring it into line with the new doctrine. In 730 the patriarch of Constantinople, Germanos, still a firm opponent of Iconoclasm, was expelled from office; he was replaced with a compliant successor. The transition was carried out constitutionally by the emperor convening a small council (on 17 January 730) at which the highest secular and ecclesiastical dignitaries were asked to subscribe to an edict ordering the destruction of all holy icons. When Germanos refused to sign, he was immediately deposed (but allowed to retire without persecution to his private estate), and replaced on 22 January by a former assistant. The rest of the participants in the council assented and the decree became official and legally valid. There is no doubt that there were active churchmen among the participants in Iconoclasm.

A major church Council took place in the next reign, in 754, under the emperor Constantine V (741–75), the son of Leo III. The purpose of this Council was to establish the imperial policy of Iconoclasm as the orthodox belief of the church. It covered a greater range of doctrinal matters and problems than the small meeting of 730. In practical matters, for example, it dealt with such questions as the prevention of indiscriminate vandalism; it seems that candles and incense had been destroyed as well as icons, and this was to be avoided. From our point of view such acts, like the desecration of relics which also occurred, are hardly surprising as extensions of the unacceptable face of idolatry into related areas. The attention to detail in this Council can be seen to have the effect of increasing the control of the emperor over church doctrine and regulations.

Persecutions of monks are also recorded after this Council and are a feature of the reign of Constantine V. In the 760s we read of various violent acts, such as the martyrdom in 765 of a holy man, St Stephen the Younger; the ridiculing of monks by making them parade in the Hippodrome of Constantinople, each holding a woman by the hand; and the secularization of a number of important monasteries in the capital. Monks who did not comply with imperial commands, or who had not managed to flee to the safe areas out of effective imperial control (the areas which monks thought safe were parts of the northern Black Sea and southern Asia Minor, Cyprus, and Italy), were threatened with imprisonment, torture or execution.

Iconoclasm was declared a Christian heresy after the death of Leo IV (775–80), during the regency of his widow Eirene for their son. The Council of Nicaea in 787 declared the production and the veneration of icons to be true doctrine. We must assume that from that time until the recurrence of Iconoclasm in 814 a number of new icons were produced. Since they have not survived there is little certainty about their appearance, but we may guess that artists mostly derived their styles of work from the art of the period before Iconoclasm which still survived, or from the small number of works made under Iconoclasm itself (both for iconoclasts and, one supposes, for dissident iconophiles). To judge from texts the subjects of icons after 787 were much as before Iconoclasm—predominantly portrait icons of saints.

The second period of Iconoclasm began with a small council of similar type to that of 730, called by the emperor, which decided once again in favour of Iconoclasm. Leo V (813–20) requested the patriarch Nicephoros to remove portable icons from the churches in order to prevent an unacceptable degree of adoration. A few days later in December 814 the image of Christ, replaced on the Chalke Gate soon after 787, was again removed, and again replaced with a cross; the patriarch too was replaced with an iconoclast successor. According to a contemporary source, Leo perceived a connection between Iconoclasm and long, successful imperial reigns; the people of Constantinople are also said to have made the connection. In this period, therefore, the motivation for the outbreak of Iconoclasm is complicated by the associations of the previous regime, but theological arguments on the subject followed the well-worn, traditional lines.

The final restoration of icons took place with a council in 843, and the circumstances have the appearance of a re-run of the ending of the first period; the negotiations took place under another woman, Theodora, the widow of the iconoclast emperor Theophilos (829–42), while acting as regent for their son Michael III. It is not clear on the basis of the thin documentation whether the support for icons should be directly linked to the presence of women as regents. It is no doubt significant, however, that the ending of Iconoclasm is linked both times with the lack of an adult male emperor on the throne and the consequent sharing of power among the elite of Constantinople. If Iconoclasm is to be seen as the positive assertion of imperial authority, it is not surprising that it should end when strong imperial authority was lacking.

The narrative of the period of Iconoclasm reflects a period of strong imperial direction. The military achievements of the main emperors were signal. The Arab threat was repulsed in the eighth century and, when the centre of Islamic rule had shifted east from Damascus to Baghdad, more congenial relations were established between Byzantium and Islam, particularly under the emperor Theophilos. The end of Iconoclasm coincided with a position of rivalry rather than hostility between the empires, so that one of the conditions present at the outbreak of Iconoclasm had dissolved. The situation in the Balkans was also more stable. Persecutions of monks still occurred under Theophilos, but the intensity of opposition to icons was sufficiently weak for communities of iconophile monks to manage to survive with their icons. Iconoclasm for a time changed society; but when, after that, Byzantium settled down into a new period of stability, the church, the monks and the icons themselves managed to retain in an altered world some of their powers of the period before Iconoclasm.

This explanation of Iconoclasm, that it was a result and a symptom of a society under radical readaptation to a changing world, a disturbance which reflected in particular a reassertion of central imperial authority and a new belief of what was allowable in Christian art, now needs to be looked at in the light of contemporary evidence. Two texts will be considered as sources for the perceptions of the Byzantines themselves. Both texts are, inevitably, written by supporters of icons.

The *Life of St Stephen the Younger* tells of the life of a monk who was commemorated as a martyr in the cause of the veneration of icons (Figure 94 shows how he was visualized in Cyprus in the late twelfth century, holding an icon of the Virgin). He died in the 760s after spending most of his life as a monk on the mountain of Auxentios on the Asiatic side of the Sea of Marmara. He received numerous visitors from Constantinople there, including army officers and numbers of aristocratic women. His cell contained also two figural icons.

The framework of his *Life* is a biography presented in chronological order and superficially rich in historical information about the period of Iconoclasm. However, the selection of material was clearly influenced by the writer's desire to denigrate the cause of Iconoclasm, and for this reason the text might be a dangerous source for neutral history; it is however of great value for our understanding of the mentality of an iconophile writer. What is striking about the text is the way it sets the issue of the destruction of visual images within the context of other oppositions in society. As a monk Stephen was not simply a supporter of the use of icons, but was on the losing side in any confrontation with the emperor; monks more than any other group fall into the category of institutionalized subversion. The text shows clearly how society at the time was marked by the activities of bitter dissidents; the situations described reveal an atmosphere of conflict. The *Life* will be used here as a means of reaching an understanding of the wider implications for society of the removal of an accepted way of life in which icons had become an essential catalyst.

The *Life* was written 42 years after the death of the saint, in 807 if the chronicler Theophanes correctly dates his death to 20 November 765. Its composition belongs to the period of relaxation of Iconoclasm, although there is reference in the text to the fact that sympathizers with that cause still existed. The text, known through a number of manuscripts, was written by Stephen, a deacon of the church of St Sophia at Constantinople, and addressed to a priest Epiphanios, the abbot of a monastery on the mountain of St Auxentios. The character of this monastery is hard to determine and the monastic organization of the mountain in the early ninth century is not clear, but any monks would doubtless have had a strong interest in the commemoration of their local saint. The monastery of St Auxentios itself, where St Stephen had lived, was destroyed by Constantine V for its opposition to imperial decree.

The career of St Stephen the Younger is portrayed in the *Life* as follows. He was born in 714. His mother attributed his conception to the miraculous intervention of the icon of the Virgin of the Vlachernai Monastery in Constantinople, for she conceived when she had prayed there after years of apparent sterility. She thankfully dedicated her son to the Theotokos (Mother of God) of the Vlachernai. Stephen was a child when the 'impious tyrant Leo III the Syrian' told his subjects that it was forbidden to venerate images, when the patriarch Germanos (715–730) was deposed and became a monk, and when Leo destroyed the Chalke image of Christ and executed (on the advice of his new patriarch) the pious women who tried to prevent the destruction of the image. No doubt in reaction to these events, Stephen was taken by his parents to Mt Auxentios in Bithynia. This place was already famous as the home of a fifth-century hermit, St Auxentios, who had lived in a cave on the mountain; under his leadership lived a group of other solitaries, although technically they were never officially constituted as a monastic community. The position formerly accorded to Auxentios was now in the time of Stephen accredited to a hermit called John. This hermit accepted Stephen as a monk at the age of eighteen.

When John died, Stephen was regarded as his successor and a community of twelve monks was established in a new officially-constituted monastery. In time Stephen retired to his own retreat at the top of the mountain where he wore iron chains on his body as a test of his Christian endurance; it was this sight which attracted numerous visitors from all round. But by this time the reign of the second iconoclast emperor had begun, who ruled with the co-operation of a compliant patriarch. This 'satanic' couple, the emperor Constantine V and the patriarch Constantine II, convened a council against the holy images and set out on a systematic destruction of icons. The arguments of this council were, according to Stephen's biographer, deeply flawed: mounting a traditional iconophile defence, he claims that in worshipping icons men worshipped not the image, but the prototype, not the portrait of Christ, but the 'reality' of Christ behind the image.

In the aftermath of the council of 754, monks flocked to Stephen for advice, and he told them that Satan had divided the church into two. The iconophiles, he claimed, were being mocked by heretics on the order of the lion's cub, a reference to Constantine, the son of the emperor Leo ('lion' in Greek). He advised the monks to go into exile in safe places both in and outside the empire. Meanwhile, Constantine had covered over the decoration of the life of Christ in the church of the Vlachernai and called the icons 'pagan idols'; this church had of course particular significance in the life-story of Stephen.

The emperor sent a mission to Stephen requesting him to sign the acts of the council; when he and his monks refused they were kept under guard. While the emperor was absent at the wars, a smear campaign was conducted against Stephen, and stepped up when Constantine V returned to the capital. Finally the monastery was set on fire and Stephen escorted to another monastery near Constantinople. He still refused to sign the acts of the council and he denounced its decisions. During his stay in the new monastery he demonstrated his holy powers by healing the abbot (presumably an iconoclast sympathizer); but this did not prevent his being sent into exile on one of the islands of the Sea of Marmara. He installed himself in a cave, and was soon joined by his relations and monks from St Auxentios.

At this point in the narrative a few miracles of healing by the saint are mentioned. It seems that a precondition of a cure from Stephen was a declaration of belief in images, and in one case, when a soldier was healed, he had to kiss an icon as part of the process of the cure. In due course the saint was recalled from exile and brought to the emperor's presence. A theological disputation between the two about the image of Christ is described, which resulted in Stephen being thrown into prison—in the company of 342 other monks! He spent eleven months in prison and his only food was bread and water brought to him by the wife of one of the guards, who sympathized with his cause.

The climax of the *Life* comes when the emperor is inflamed by reports that Stephen has transformed the prison into a monastery. These reports were brought to the emperor while he was celebrating the wicked pagan festival of the Broumalia with his adulterous third wife! His fellow revellers went to the prison to drag Stephen away from his would-be monastery. This led directly to the saint's death, for he was killed by a blow to the head in a scuffle that ensued in the street, and was then stoned by a mob. The date is given here as elsewhere in the text by reference to the age of Stephen—he died on 28 November in his 53rd year.

Much of the narrative of the *Life* resembles a carefully contrived piece of pseudo-history. The actual chronology of events is concealed, and the precision offered for the date of Stephen's death may itself have had an ulterior motive. The date of 767 implied by the *Life* fits ideally with the view of Stephen as an iconophile martyr and serves to exculpate him from the suspicion that he might have been put to death as a result of his involvement in a major conspiracy against the emperor in 765. By contrast the *Chronicle* of Theophanes, compiled a few years after the *Life*, places his death in 765, and so implies a possible link with the conspiracy.

A number of recurrent themes emerge from the narrative and the terms in which it is presented. Firstly there is great emphasis on imperial authority. The emperor is a dictator who will stop at nothing in his persecution of a harmless monk, who is portrayed both as a saint and as necessarily correct in his beliefs; and it is the emperor who is seen as the source of all iconoclast action. One may doubt the accuracy of the portrayal of the character of Constantine here, but the tone of the text strongly supports any interpretation of Iconoclasm which sees it in part as a reassertion of imperial authority.

A second point of interest in the text concerns the relationship between the two main participants. The *Life* teems with binary oppositions between the iconoclast emperor and the iconophile monk. Constantine is an aggressive dictator, Stephen a powerless monk. Constantine is a man of action, Stephen is passive. Constantine has not one wife, but three; Stephen has no sexual relations. Constantine does not just eat, but stuffs food down himself; Stephen is abstinent and lives on bread and water for eleven months. Constantine does not just laugh, he guffaws; Stephen lives in tears. Constantine likes a background of music from stringed instruments; Stephen chants hymns. The climax of these contrasts comes when the saint dies while the emperor is feasting at the pagan festival of the Broumalia (one of the festivals specifically banned in canon 62 of the Quinisext Council). The profane and sacred ways of life are seen as opposites, and the attempt is made to connect anything profane with heresy. The emphasis on all these oppositions is more than a literary device; it shows how the dispute about icons was associated with a number of other alignments and contrasts.

A third pointer to the areas of conflict during the iconoclast period comes from the description of dress. Clothing appears as an index of spiritual life and the identifying sign of the monk's habit features in several episodes in the saint's career. When a monk was stripped of his distinctive clothing the iconoclasts believed that he was at the same time transformed into an ordinary citizen. Attacks on monks included the burning of their beards and the removal of their black habits. The visual importance of dress has already been observed in the perception of St Theodore of Sykeon. Yet there may be another element here. When the writer suggests that the removal of the outward signs of a monk's dress will also remove his character *as a monk*, we are reminded of the confusion on the part of both sides in the iconoclast controversy as to the status of images: was there, or was there not, something inherently holy in the painted image of a saint? Did the signifier have the properties associated with the signified? It is interesting to note that such issues were not restricted to the perception of icons, but found a focus also in other areas of external display.

The *Life of St Stephen the Younger* transmits a version of the Iconoclasm of the eighth century as a series of perceived oppositions in society, at a time of strong imperial authority and control. But it does not answer the question why Byzantines might opt for one side or another. In the case of monks, their adoption of the iconophile side followed the seventh-century perception of icons as a channel for intercession with God. But why should anyone in Byzantium after more than a century of propaganda for the power of icons, articulated by monks and the clergy, join the iconoclast party? This touches on the problem of how an individual can suddenly change apparently fundamental religious beliefs. Although some examples of changing sides might superficially be taken as opportunism—conformity with imperial authority as a means of furthering social ambitions—or as provoked by the fear of becoming a dissident, taking this decision must have depended on the whole range of circumstances of the time. Times of social and political disturbance and change send their shock waves through previously stable religious beliefs.

★   ★   ★   ★

A second text which brings out the place of icons in the perceptions of the period is a historically bizarre document that dates from the end of the conflict. It is set out as the formulation of an enormous church council which took place in Islamic-occupied Jerusalem; its authors describe themselves as the loyal subjects of a pious and orthodox emperor.

It records their irrefutable case for the veneration of icons and it is addressed to the attention of a notorious iconoclast emperor and persecutor of iconophiles. The original letter, so our copy claims, was sent to the emperor headed with a painted portrait icon of the Virgin and Child. All the evidence is that the *Letter* is a careful Byzantine fake from the years around 843 at the end of Iconoclasm and that the 'original letter' never existed.

The text is now known from two manuscripts, one dating from the ninth century and the other from the twelfth. It certainly existed in the wording in which we find it by the ninth century. The only modern edition of the text was produced in 1864. It will be treated in some detail because it has never been introduced into the study of Iconoclasm and it is central to the argument of the perception of icons in Byzantium.

In outline the *Letter of the Patriarchs of Alexandria, Antioch and Jerusalem to the Emperor Theophilos in the year 836* argues the case for icons in a preface and fifteen sections, of which the longest is a list of famous miraculous icons. The council it purports to record met in the church of the Holy Sepulchre in Jerusalem in April 836, and its authority depended on the size of its membership: three patriarchs, 185 bishops, 17 abbots and 1153 monks. The first seven sections argue the case in favour of icons from the point of view of church history, starting with the incarnation of Christ on earth known from the writings of the Gospels and from pictorial representations of his life. The Christian community was put under the care of God's chosen emperors, helped by priests; church councils confirmed their combined decisions. Constantine the Great was the central figure in the definition of correct practice and belief; he put an image of Christ on his coins and icons in his churches, and the Church Fathers justified his acts. Icons had in any case already existed from the beginning of Christianity, and their veneration had been implied by the Old Testament from the time of Moses. A list of icons, some of which date from the time of Christ, proves both their historical existence and their miraculous powers. The final seven sections of the *Letter* are in general less theological. They state first that a distinction is to be drawn between 'images' and 'idols', but point out that this is in fact a dead issue, already eliminated by the early church. More centrally these chapters argue that Iconoclasm is a heresy; orthodox emperors must imitate models like the fourth-century emperors Constantine and Theodosios. Specific incidents in recent years prove, it is claimed, that God disapproves of Iconoclasm; to declare his anger at the banning of images God has sent all the miseries of human life which are deserved by human error and sin. The text closes with a prayer for divine favour for the emperor Theophilos.

This text opens up many possibilities for study. It reveals no doubt a great talent for wishful thinking; yet within it is a core of assumptions through which we can approach the world of the ninth-century writer and his audience. Some of these can be explored briefly here.

In the first half of the text, the largely theological sections, the most important material for us is less the logic in favour of the production and veneration of icons than the specific examples chosen to illustrate

40 The reproduction of multiple copies of icons must have been a feature of the years leading up to Iconoclasm and in later centuries the needs of the Orthodox church must have called for the production of far greater numbers of icons for churches, monasteries and homes. This representation of a Russian artist's workshop in the seventeenth century suggests the mass production of icons of the Virgin and Child, a reflection of the fact that the failure of Iconoclasm led ultimately to the excessive, if theologically legitimate, production of icons.

the case. One such example concerned the use of representational art by Constantine the Great: he produced, it is claimed, a coin (nomisma) on which he put not only the cross which appeared to him as a sign in the sky, but also a representation of Christ in human form together with himself. The text explains the message of this combined representation as demonstrating the concord between the ruler of Heaven and the ruler of earth. In fact, this example is a fiction; no such coin was ever minted by Constantine. But, as a fiction, it reveals the importance of the appeal to tradition, and to earlier Christian emperors, as part of the arguments against Iconoclasm.

The text moves on to record the decoration of churches with icons, and insists that the apostles, before they wrote the Gospels, had already painted churches with pictures and mosaics showing Christ in human form

and the narrative of his life on earth. Again, of course, this is pure fiction; but again it reveals the strength of the example of the past within the controversy over icons. The practice of the apostles formed, we may suppose, even more convincing a case than that of Constantine (the early church is seen as being as prolific in producing icons as Russia became in the seventeenth century; Figure 40).

The nucleus of the *Letter* is the list of twelve images which are quoted as the practical visual proof of the existence of icons going back to the time of Christ and sanctioned by him as well as by their divine powers. Many of these were famous images in the ninth century and most, it seems, existed then or had done in recent memory—even though the stories told of their miracles and genesis were often sheer invention. Much more convincing than the supposed artistic activity of the apostles, these were the essential, visible witnesses of God's approval for the production and veneration of icons by true Christians. They formed the best evidence that the authors of this letter could find for belief in the power of images. For this reason the list is summarized here, retaining the order of the text and outlining as far as possible the reasons for the inclusion of each image. Later we shall discuss the force of such examples within the arguments against Iconoclasm.

1 The image of Christ at Edessa on a soudarion (cloth)

This image was an imprint of the face of Christ on a cloth, taken by one of the apostles to the ruler (toparch) of the city of Edessa in Syria, who received baptism into Christianity. It is described as still at Edessa at the time of the *Letter*, and compared with a royal sceptre, in that the signs and miracles associated with it demonstrated the grace of Christ towards the city. Its production was miraculous, recording the appearance of Christ while on earth.

A miracle enacted by this image some centuries later at the time of the Persian advance under Chosroes is also recorded. The city of Edessa was under siege and the walls were set on fire by the enemy. When the orthodox bishop, named Eulalios, saw that the citizens were expecting disaster, he went in procession around the walls with the *soudarion*. The result was spectacular: a miraculous wind which blew the flames towards the enemy and consumed the besiegers instead of the citizens.

The most striking feature of this image is that it was made directly from the body of Christ. Although in the ninth century it existed primarily as a visual image, the story of its creation stresses the physical contact with the holy body. Moreover, for the iconophile case, it provided superb ammunition: for Christ himself created this image, thus confirming his approval of the display of his portraits.

This particular image was, in fact, famous for many centuries. It entered history in the sixth century, and was soon to be described as the image on the *mandylion*, a term for the cloth that was used in Byzantium in preference to the earlier title of *soudarion*. It enjoyed such popularity that it seems to have become normal for every Byzantine church to include a replica of it in some form (as in Cyprus in the twelfth century; Figure 41). By the tenth century imperial favour had brought the original object to Constantinople, where it was lodged in a chapel of the palace. The *mandylion* was finally acquired by the French during the Crusader occupation of the city in the thirteenth century and taken to the Sainte Chapelle in Paris. It seems almost certain that it was lost during the French Revolution, although attempts have been made (without success) to identify it with the well known 'Turin Shroud'.

2 The image of the Virgin at Lydda

The apostles Peter and John were said to have built with their own hands a church at Lydda (or Diospolis) in Palestine and to have dedicated it to the Mother of God. They prayed to the Virgin to come to its dedication. She answered their prayer with a miracle: her form was found imprinted on one of the columns of the church.

Later, in the fourth century, the pagan emperor Julian (361–3) sent two Jewish painters to investigate this image. They found the form of the Virgin on one of the columns, a full-length figure wearing a purple garment and ornaments, and so life-like as to seem to be able to see and talk. They tried with their tools to take it off the column but however deeply they cut into the marble, the image (we are told) remained as clear as before, if not more so.

This story not only provides an example of a figural image in a church in the time of the apostles, but more strikingly it demonstrates the power of the image to resist attack, even when confronted with the scepticism of a pagan emperor and his Jewish assistants. Again no artist was involved, but the Virgin herself created the image.

41 For the iconophiles the existence of a group of images supposed to be miraculously produced, and not the manufacture of mere artists, naturally formed a key argument against the iconoclast claim that figural images were not endorsed by God. Of these images 'not made by human hands', one of the most famous was the mandylion *of Edessa—it was thought to be the direct imprint of the face of the living Christ on a cloth. In the tenth century, after Iconoclasm, the image was brought to the Great Palace in Constantinople, and a painted copy of it was included as a standard image in any church decoration. This rendering comes from a twelfth-century church on Cyprus.*

3 The icon of the Virgin painted by St Luke

The third icon listed is an icon of the Virgin supposedly painted from life by St Luke, in order to leave a record of the Virgin's form for posterity. She was delighted with his work and exclaimed when she saw it, 'My grace will be with it'.

The origin of this icon differs from that of the first two. It was not formed by the Virgin herself, but by a human painter in the person of St Luke. However, a close connection with the divine is retained, for the Virgin is said to have sat for the painting and to have approved it. This at once serves to legitimate the activity of human icon-painters. Moreover the role of Luke as painter is not without significance. As a writer of inspired scripture he was recognized by all Christians as a vessel of the word of God; he could hardly lose that status when he turned to painting. Painting could also be the 'Word of God'.

The belief that St Luke was also a painter became common and at least one icon kept in Constantinople was later attributed to his hand. Even today this notion still flourishes. Yet it probably originated no earlier than the period of Iconoclasm, when the status of painting was most seriously called into question. In fact the text of the *Letter* contains one of the earliest references to St Luke as a painter.

4 A miraculous image of the Virgin at Lydda

After St Peter had cured a paralytic man called Ainea, the grateful patient was said to have built a church with his own hands at Lydda, dedicated to the Virgin. He was helped by seventy disciples of Christ, and the church was near to completion when the Jews and the pagans tried to obtain it for themselves. To settle the dispute they asked the local governor to arbitrate. He said he would lock up the building, seal the doors for three days and guard it. Then it would be reopened and given to those who could point to a sign of their faith inside. At the end of the three days the doors were opened and in the western part of the church was found a female figure, three cubits in height, wearing purple, and inscribed with the following letters: MARIA, THE MOTHER OF THE KING, CHRIST OF NAZARETH.

The governor asked whose image and inscription it was, and the Jews and pagans had no option but to give the church to the disciples. Numerous miracles were attributed to the image—devils driven out, the sick cured, and lepers healed.

This story demonstrates the constructive power of images in propagating the Christian faith. It reveals indeed an early Christian community being dependent on an image of the Virgin for its public identification; the only way, that is, that the governor could distinguish the Christians from the Jews and pagans was by means of a visible symbol which incorporated both words and image. It thus implicitly makes the claim that Christians of the ninth century should display their faith through icons.

5 A mosaic icon of the Virgin and Child on Cyprus

This image was a mosaic in a village in the south of the island of Cyprus in a church dedicated to the Virgin; the mosaic was a representation of the Virgin and Child. One day an Arab shot an arrow into the mosaic striking the knee of the Virgin on which the Child in her arms was seated; immediately blood flowed out in a stream pouring down to her feet. The icon was still in the church at the time of writing the text.

This story stresses the clash between an Arab and an image. As in the last example it is an icon which forms the identifying mark of Christianity and defends the faith against its opponents. Here, however, the opponent goes so far as to attack the image, suggesting (in the terms of the iconophiles) a parallel between iconoclasts and the enemies of Christianity.

This is one of three icons in the list which are said to have bled when wounded. The assumption made that an icon could bleed, like a human body, raises again the issue of the relationship between the image on the icon and its prototype. Although the iconophiles sometimes made a point of distinguishing between the materials of the image and the holy figure represented through them, here the two are conflated. The inanimate image, by bleeding, shows that it contains the properties of the prototype.

6 A mosaic icon of the Nativity at Bethlehem

On the western façade of the church of the Mother of God at Bethlehem, Helena, the mother of Constantine the Great, set up a mosaic of the Nativity on which was to be seen the Virgin holding the Child in her arms and the adoration of Christ by the Magi. When the Persians invaded Byzantium and Syria and burnt down Jerusalem in the seventh century, taking the patriarch Zacharias prisoner and killing Christians, they came eventually to Bethlehem. Here they saw the representations of the Magi on the front of the church, and because these were shown as Persians and astrologers, they respected the figures as if they were alive; with respect and love for their ancestors, they left the church unharmed. As a result the ancient church was still in existence with its mosaic at the time of the writing of this text.

Once again the image in this story appears as a supernatural defender of Christianity, keeping the church safe from the Persians. Yet here the context is different. The icon is associated not with scriptural characters, but with the renowned Helena—the mother of the first Christian emperor and a woman reputed to have found the True Cross of Christ. The patronage of icons is thus linked to a heroine of the early history of Byzantium.

Part of this story is historical. Jerusalem did fall in 614; but there is no reason to connect Helena with any decoration of the church of the Mother of God (now called the church of the Nativity) as it was in the seventh century. The church then standing on the site was built almost two centuries after the death of Helena around 330.

7 The image of the Virgin at Alexandria

A prefect of Alexandria customarily mocked and insulted a holy icon of the Mother of God which was in the courtyard of the Great Church of that city. One day when he was alone there and fully awake (that is, not in a dream), the Virgin herself appeared to him, accompanied, he claimed, by two eunuchs. They held his hands and feet and stretched them and she tore apart his limbs with her holy finger; his arms came apart at his elbows and his feet at his ankles, just as leaves fall from a fig tree.

The next paragraph of the text probably refers to the same icon. Another man, who had likewise abused the icon of the Virgin, once found himself pursued by soldiers and went for asylum to the holy icon of the Virgin. The icon of the Virgin, in the sight of all, turned away from him and so delivered him for slaughter like a traitor.

The point of these stories is straightforward: the Virgin protects her own icons and is no doubt waiting to wreak terrible vengeance on the iconoclasts.

8 An icon of Christ

A man maliciously threw a stone at a holy icon of Christ. Straightaway a dove flew out of his mouth and a crow flew in; that is, the man now had inside him a black devil instead of the holy spirit and he experienced darkness instead of light—he went blind.

Once more vengeance is taken upon an iconoclast, this time we must assume by Christ himself.

9 An icon of Christ at Berytus

A Jew stabbed the icon of Christ at Berytus in its side with his spear—like the Jews at the time of the Crucifixion—and a stream of blood gushed forth. Since then this blood has caused many miraculous healings of the blind and lame and of those with other diseases.

This story is one of the most popular stories of a miraculous icon and is found in other texts. Its inclusion in this list serves to raise once again the issue of the relationship between image and prototype.

10 The Holy Well in St Sophia at Constantinople

The church of St Sophia at Constantinople contained among its relics the well-head on which Christ supposedly sat when he talked to the Samaritan woman. Beside this was an icon of Christ. A Jew stabbed the figure of Christ on the icon in the heart with a knife whereupon streams of blood spurted out so that his face and clothes were spattered. In alarm he threw the icon into the well, but thereupon all the water in the well turned red. Scared that he would be taken for a murderer because of the blood on his clothes, the Jew confessed what he had done. The icon was recovered from the well, but it still had the dagger in the chest of Christ and blood still poured out. The Jew was converted to Christianity by his experience.

This story combines several of the themes that have already emerged from this list. It justifies the use of icons by appealing to their closeness to Christ, their supernatural qualities, the dangers of attacking them and their efficacy in gaining converts. This last element was no doubt meant to suggest to the iconoclast that it was not too late to change his mind.

In this story the text has moved to Constantinople. The incident was famous among the legends of St Sophia, though later the icon was described as representing the Virgin and Child. The version here is the earliest known.

11 An icon of Christ from the patriarchal palace of St Sophia at Constantinople

This story is of the miraculous rescue of an icon from iconoclast Constantinople and its subsequent powers. The icon was of Christ and was kept in the patriarchal palace next to St Sophia until the outbreak of Iconoclasm under Leo III. Then the patriarch Germanos took the icon out of his palace and put it in the sea, saying, 'Lord, Lord, save yourself and us who are being destroyed.' The icon floated all the way from Constantinople over the sea to Rome, and despite the salty water stayed dry and upright, just as Christ did when walking on the water. Pope Gregory received the icon, as if he were Simeon receiving the Christ Child at the time of the Presentation, and placed the icon in the church of St Peter. At the time of writing the *Letter* there were still said to be traces of salt at the bottom of the panel. The icon in Rome caused miraculous healings, especially of the blind and paralysed.

This story emphasizes that icons were more than pieces of wood. Although this icon did not bleed, it was likened by other means to the person of Christ—it walked on the water and was received into the temple.

The mention of names allows the period to which the story refers to be dated between 726 and 730, but what exactly gave rise to the story is more obscure. This account is the earliest version of a story which became very popular.

12 The icon of St Andrew on Lemnos

The last item is an icon of a saint on the Aegean island of Lemnos. This was a portrait icon of the apostle St Andrew in a church dedicated to him in the south part of the island; it was placed in the ciborion over the altar in the sanctuary (like the icon of Figure 18). One of the priests under the influence of madness brought on by a wicked demon mutilated the right eye of the portrait of St Andrew with the knife designed for dividing the bread of the eucharist. The priest immediately suffered divine retribution, and his own right eye jumped out of its socket and stuck into the gouged-out hole in the icon.

The miracle described here claims instant divine protection for an icon. This kind of mutilation was a notorious feature of the iconoclast period and the last iconoclast patriarch, John the Grammarian, is recorded as removing the eyes of an icon which he found in the monastery in which he was detained after the end of Iconoclasm in 843. The story suggests very sharply that those who indulge in activities of this kind will be visited by divine retribution.

The list of twelve images in the *Letter* is followed by a final section of extravagant defence of the church, which had fought to establish the difference between idolatry and veneration. Iconoclasm is characterized as another heresy against which orthodoxy had to battle—like Arianism, the major dispute about the nature of Christ which exercised the early church. Emperors are named who supported monks and decorated churches. The emperor Theodosios I (379–95) is chosen as an example and an object attributed to his patronage forms the subject of one story recalled in the text. This was a liturgical paten, the dish used in the eucharist to hold the bread, and this special one was decorated with the Communion of the Apostles, as were two which have survived from the sixth century (Figures 7–9). Under the iconoclast patriarch Antony (821–837), the dish was used by Theodore, a priest of the church of the Holy Apostles in Constantinople, to hold his signed agreement of support for Iconoclasm during his election as a bishop. The patriarch was required to prove his beliefs by stamping on the paten, which he readily did. Divine retribution soon came to both iconoclasts: Theodore died prematurely and the patriarch suffered a long wasting illness.

More ninth-century stories against Iconoclasm are narrated, of equal vividness and vehemence. Their particular interest for our argument is that they form written parallels with the visual evidence to be introduced in which iconoclasts are caricatured and pilloried.

One of these narratives again concerns the iconoclast patriarch Antony (821–37), and happened under the emperor Michael II (820–29), the father of Theophilos, to whom the *Letter* is addressed. The emperor had recommended a friend and relation of his called Michael for election as the archbishop of Ephesus. Michael was reluctant to accept the nomination as he was not, apparently, a convinced iconoclast. On the morning before the planned ceremony, which was to be performed by the iconoclast patriarch Antony (821–837), the bishop-elect had a vision: he entered into the sanctuary of the church of St Sophia accompanied by an angel who promised to reveal the true relation between the patriarch and God. The angel called out from under the altar a black Ethiopian of ghastly appearance, his right hand completely withered like that of a skeleton, and his left arm trembling and bloody. The Ethiopian came up to Michael to anoint him; he sprinkled Michael's face with blood and made the form of the cross on his head in the shape of an X, and he spoke the words of God taken from Psalm II, verse 7: 'You are my son; today I have begotten you.' The angel explained to Michael that the Ethiopian was his Father and his Patriarch. Michael decided to put off his election, as it was obvious that the figure represented the devil. The text gives parallels for this sort of vision from fourth-century Alexandria in which a black Ethiopian danced on and a donkey kicked an altar, both taken as signs of the Arians, in order to emphasize the kind of heresy that Iconoclasm was supposed to be.

A second piece of anti-iconoclast polemic is the story of a vision seen by the iconophile patriarch Nicephoros (806–15) who was expelled from office with the second outbreak of Iconoclasm in 815. The vision foretold the replacement of Nicephoros by the iconoclast Theodotos

(815–821) through symbols. Nicephoros saw an olive tree covered with fruit growing in the ambo in the nave of St Sophia. The tree filled the church with its branches up to the dome. An enormous black Ethiopian with an axe appeared from the imperial box on the right side of the church and cut down the tree. A woman, shining like the sun, was seen standing inside the sanctuary, wailing and tearing her garments in misery. Another Ethiopian appeared from the sacred well of the church and he, together with the emperor (at this date Leo V, 813–20), went to the altar and stood on it. This Ethiopian was a giant and as tall as the high ciborion over the altar. The Ethiopian danced on the altar, spat towards Heaven and shouted words of blasphemy; the emperor, surrounded by a troop of soldiers in black uniforms, joined in. The emperor also made the court, generals and people join this devil in insulting the Virgin Mary. The vision ended at this point, and an interpretation of it is given: the healthy olive tree growing in the house of God represented the orthodox iconophile patriarch Nicephoros, one Ethiopian represented the iconoclast patriarch Theodotos, the weeping woman tearing the garments of orthodoxy represented the Church of Christ, and the insults represented the blasphemy of the impious iconoclasts.

To complete the text, a list of the signs which are sent by God when he wants to communicate his anger is given: these are plagues, earthquakes, shipwrecks, floods, sudden deaths, civil wars, barbarian invasions, fires in churches, the desolation of villages and cities, and people taken into captivity or slavery or put to death. The implication is that the period of Iconoclasm is marked by all of these and the way to stop such punishments is to venerate the representation of Christ.

Finally the text makes reference to the picture of the Virgin and Child painted at the beginning of the 'original copy' of the *Letter*. This image, it claims, says all there is to be said about the value of art; it embodies without words the entire contents of the letter and so demonstrates the iconophile case. At the very end, a prayer to the Virgin and all the saints is offered on behalf of Theophilos for peace and a long life.

★ ★ ★ ★

One question which needs to be considered before assessing the broader evidence of the *Life of St Stephen* and the *Letter* for the understanding of Iconoclasm is the list of the twelve images and the basis of its selection. The idea that miraculous icons could form a justification for the iconophile case was not novel and had been exploited at the Council of Nicaea in 787. In the fourth session (4 October), the Berytus icon stabbed by a Jew (item 9 in our list) was brought into the discussion. One question, then, is whether the *Letter* contains a carefully selected set of twelve images. This does not seem to be the case. The choice of nine from the regions of the oriental patriarchs points to inclusion on the basis of local knowledge. Even so a selection has been made, for some of the miraculous images of these regions mentioned elsewhere are omitted; one might also have expected some of the famous images of Asia Minor to merit a notice, such as the Virgin of Sozopolis to which Theodore of Sykeon made a special visit, or the famous icon of Christ of Camuliana, found in Cappadocia in the sixth century and soon afterwards brought to Constantinople. The latter was, like the *mandylion* of Edessa, thought to have been produced miraculously and 'not made by human hands', and therefore would have been an exploitable icon for the argument. The list does no more than represent the tip of the iceberg of this kind of material, which must have been a large component in the arguments of the iconophiles in the ninth-century period.

Among the material of this kind, one particularly important image still exists, which shows how the iconophiles operated in embroidering their case. The image in question is one of the few from the western parts of the empire and is in Thessaloniki, in the small church now dedicated to Hosios David. It is an apse mosaic of Christ, to which a Byzantine text attached a legend of miraculous origins and miraculous powers (Figure 42). The style of the mosaic is similar to that of the earliest mosaics in St Demetrios (as Figure 23), and so it is most likely that it was produced in the sixth century. It shows a central figure of Christ, depicted as a young man without a beard, who sits within a shining circle of light (or *mandorla*) surrounded by the four signs of the Evangelist. In the landscape around him are two astonished witnesses of his appearance—from their point of view this was a vision of God. The image is full of symbols and the text held by Christ helps in understanding its meanings.

Our knowledge of the Byzantine beliefs about this mosaic comes from *The Edifying Narrative of the Image of Christ of the Monastery of the Latomos*. This account claims no end of miraculous connections— that the mosaic was being manufactured at the beginning of the fourth century (secretly during the persecutions of Galerius) as a representation of the Virgin, but overnight it miraculously changed into an image of the young Christ; the mosaic was next hidden from view during Iconoclasm and all knowledge of its existence forgotten; another miracle was its sudden re-appearance from under its concealing cover in the reign of Leo V (813–20) in answer to the prayers of a monk. This mosaic of the Byzantine church of the Latomos shows just how the list of images in the *Letter* could be developed. It was visible in Thessaloniki at the end of the Iconoclasm, and was a work of the period after the middle of the fifth century, yet a legendary history could be invented, to claim that it was an image of great antiquity produced without human agency in Roman times. This was the case for its legitimacy as an image. Furthermore its story shows how an image was able to resist iconoclast attacks, and how its power could be recognized by a pious iconophile monk. This surviving image shows therefore the kind of evidence which did exist at the time of the creation of the *Letter*, and how the iconophile arguments were universally understood through the empire.

Even though the list of images in the *Letter* does not seem to be a carefully selected repertory of the best cases, its message is effective

42 *This mosaic of the young Christ in the church of the Latomos at Thessaloniki (now dedicated to a local saint, Hosios David) must date to the same period as the first mosaics in the church of St Demetrios. During Iconoclasm it was concealed under a plaster covering and completely hidden from sight. Its rediscovery during an earthquake (in the last years of the period of Iconoclasm) was declared to be a miracle, and the image of Christ was itself claimed as a miraculous one, 'not made by human hands'.*

enough. We see that icons were taken as the best evidence of the appearance of Christ and the Virgin, because they were supposed to have been produced from the life. We see icons taken as proof of the existence of Christ and other saints. We see icons which directly refute the beliefs of Jews, Muslims, pagans, and other enemies of Christ. We see that images will prevail over the attacks of the iconoclasts. We see that, like the saints, images can do miracles. Without images, only heresy and disaster can prevail. With images normality and prosperity are promised.

The method of argument in the *Letter* is simple but follows a pattern. The veneration of icons is no different from the veneration of God. To attack icons is to attack God, to attack the church and to attack the monastic way of life. Iconoclasm is a heresy and the inspiration of the devil, comparable with the Arian heresy which Constantine the Great had to face and overcome. The attitude of mind in the *Letter* is similar to that of the earlier *Life of St Stephen the Younger*, and the texts were perhaps not very remote in place of composition and intended audience. The polarities which both texts delineate in society are the same.

The violence and vividness of the stories against Iconoclasts might be taken as indications that the two texts demonstrate the 'popular' thinking of Byzantium and are in contrast with the dryness of official theology. This explanation might well seem to account for their style, full of personal attacks on iconoclasts and of fictitious and invented evidence, but such an interpretation of their content has little to support it, just as our consideration of Thessaloniki before Iconoclasm did not encourage the idea of such a clear division in the thinking of society. At the end of Iconoclasm there is also visual material to take into account in considering the issue. Three illustrated psalters have survived from the ninth century, and the best preserved of them is the Khludov Psalter, now in Moscow (Figures 43–45). These books contain the Psalms in the arrangement of the Septuagint, the Greek translation of the Hebrew Old Testament used in Byzantium. A set of rubrics records the chanted refrains which accompanied their recitation and the terms of these accord with the liturgy of the church of St Sophia in Constantinople. Unless these refrains were used elsewhere at the time of production (a controversial point), the proper conclusion is that the Khludov Psalter was made for the clergy of St Sophia and probably in the patriarchal palace. The manuscript and its illustrations would therefore represent not the outlook of a 'popular' mind but of the cream of the Byzantine clergy. The pictures in these manuscripts show just the same modes of thinking as the texts.

Within the enormous cycle of pictures in the Khludov Psalter such motifs as an Ethiopian, and allegorical fruit-bearing trees, can be found and these are directly comparable with the verbal imagery of the *Letter*. The three miniatures described here can be taken as examples of the way the images in these manuscripts are constructed and used.

Look at the representation of the Crucifixion of Christ and the two thieves on folio 45 verso (Figure 43). The three victims are shown dead, with the sun and the moon in the sky on each side of Christ, a motif that is frequently included to refer to the eclipse mentioned as coinciding with the Crucifixion in the Gospels. A large group on the right consists of onlookers, including the soldiers; separate from these are other figures who are discussing the scene with each other. There is no reference in the psalm to the Crucifixion, but the exact verse illustrated by the picture is indicated by a small blue arrow pointing to one passage (Psalm 45, v. 7) which says: 'Nations may be in turmoil and thrones totter.' The Crucifixion is chosen to illustrate this text, but the meaning of the whole image has to be deduced from the inclusion of the particular figures and the inscriptions beside them. The words, now hard to read, mention 'Hellenes' and 'Dionysios'. The figure on the right, holding his writings, must be the philosopher Dionysios, 'the Pseudo-Areopagite', who is also mentioned as an authority in the *Letter*. Byzantines believed this writer to be a pagan (the meaning of 'Hellene') who was converted by St Paul at Athens and who became the first Bishop of Athens, known as Dionysios the Areopagite; but modern scholarship dates the writings of this author to the fifth or sixth centuries and calls him Dionysios the Pseudo-Areopagite in order to distinguish him. His work of mystical theology was influential on the Byzantine church throughout its history (and on the Catholic church). The reason for

43 The paintings in the margins of the manuscript of the Khludov Psalter (which contains the Psalms in the order of the Septuagint) illustrate particular passages in the Greek text, on which they form a commentary. Out of the several hundred pictures, a number openly pillory the iconoclasts, as this one here. Particular individuals are shown in caricature, and their error is criticized through biblical parallels.

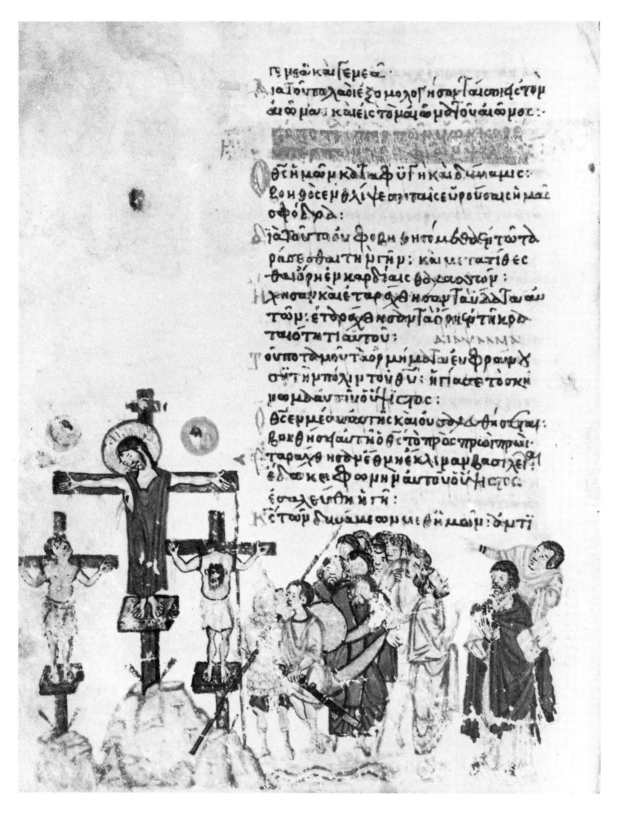

his inclusion in this particular icon is a passage in his writings where he observes and interprets an eclipse to a follower (shown here pointing at the scene): 'An unknown God suffers in the flesh.' The meaning of the picture is therefore that the eclipse proves that Christ suffered in the flesh on the cross, whereas iconoclasts denied the reality of the incarnation when they refused to accept the possibility of imaging Christ. Among the spectators in the picture are two emperors wearing the *loros*, but without crowns. These are presumably iconoclasts whose 'thrones have tottered'.

The illustration on folio 51 verso is more directly pointed (Figure 44). The blue arrow indicates the text illustrated as Psalm 51, v. 9: 'See the man who relied not on the help of God, but trusted in the abundance of his riches and strengthened himself in wickedness.' This verse is illustrated with two parallel cases of the triumph of the virtuous over the corrupt, one example biblical and the other topical. The persons involved are identified through inscriptions. The haloed figure in the top scene is St Peter triumphing over Simon Magus who (in *Acts*, 8) had tried to buy the power given by God to do miracles. Simon is trampled on the ground and has dropped all his money. The haloed figure of the pair below, wearing the bishop's *omophorion*, is identified as the patriarch Nicephoros, who was expelled as an iconophile in 815, and he tramples underfoot the last iconoclast patriarch John the Grammarian. John, visually caricatured with wild black hair, is described in the inscription as the second Simon and iconoclast. Coins are on the ground all around him. The visual imagery here depends on types of binary opposition very similar to those in the written texts, and Nicephoros is taken as the type of the orthodox and apostolic iconophile.

Another representation of the Crucifixion on folio 67 recto demonstrates the opportunities of this kind of illustration (Figure 45). Two scenes are shown to gloss the text of Psalm 68, v. 22: 'They gave me gall to eat, and when I was thirsty they gave me vinegar to drink.' In the picture of the Crucifixion one of the soldiers is seen offering Christ a sponge soaked in vinegar. Below are two iconoclasts (the figure in front clearly John the Grammarian) explicitly described as mixing water and lime for the portrait; they are whitewashing an icon of Christ. Such a visual statement of the parallel between the iconoclasts and those who crucified Christ is direct and powerful.

Comparisons between these texts and images concerned with the refutation of Iconoclasm do show a close similarity of thinking. But the productions do not work in identical ways. No doubt the *Letter* and the psalters come from a similar circle, most probably from the patriarchate in the years just after Iconoclasm; but they are devised to achieve different effects. The *Letter* is made to resemble an official church document to be studied in the library or read out as a record at later councils. The psalters were commonly-used service books, arranged for everyday use, though hardly technically necessary for a clergy that knew the Psalms off by heart. They could be displayed, or studied in private meditation. The images in the psalters were, as the *Letter* says about

44 In this miniature from the Khludov Psalter, the contrast of good and evil is made visually: the purity of the iconophiles (in the person of the patriarch Nicephoros) is set against the corruptions of the iconoclasts (in the person of the patriarch John the Grammarian). A New Testament event is deduced out of the Old Testament text, and current Byzantine circumstances paralleled with the Passion of Christ. The interpretation of the pictures is made even more specific by the inclusion of verbal slogans written beside the figures.

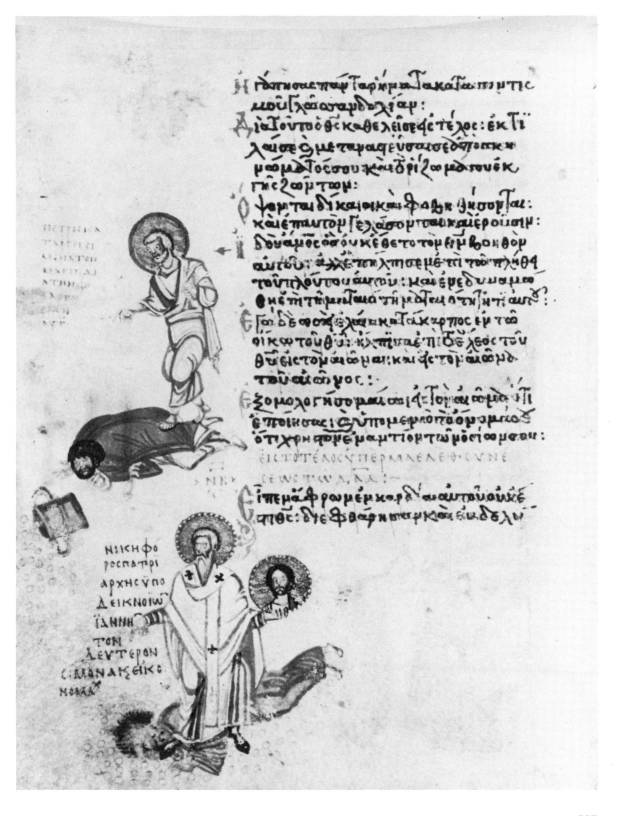

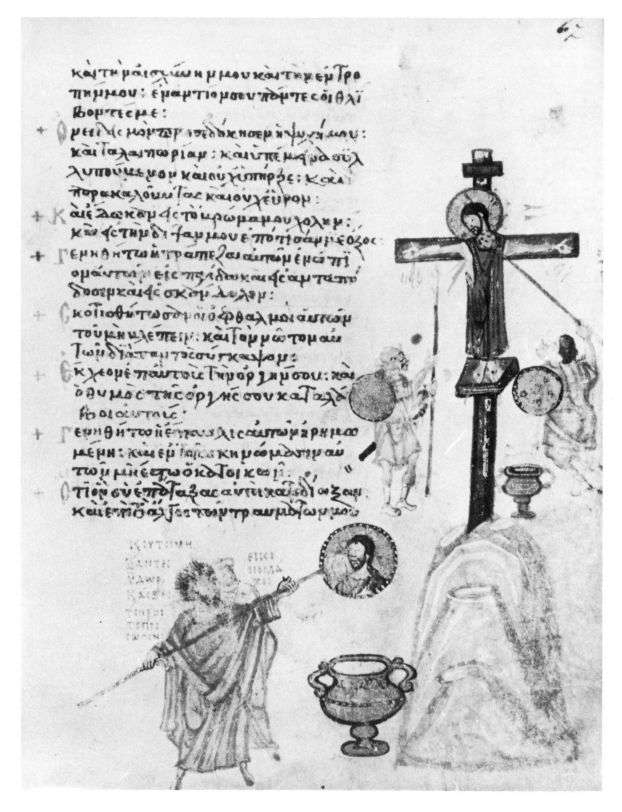

Khludov Psalter art is used to
insinuate that the iconoclasts
are identical in their sins with
those who crucified Christ:
patriarch John the
Grammarian is shown using a
pot of whitewash to obliterate
an icon of Christ, and this act
of desecration is conflated with
the execution of Christ on the
cross.*

the image of the Virgin at its head, instant proof of the iconophile case; care was taken to increase their possible connotations beyond mere illustration of a text. This is the propaganda of a group that is currently 'in'. It was more likely to confirm the ideas of the convinced or to frighten the waverers than to convert the convinced iconoclast to the view that images were essential for salvation.

The final question on the subject of Iconoclasm must be how these texts and images from its final years help us to see the conflict between iconoclasts and iconophiles. Can we through them find expressions of the tensions which arose in a time of change and adjustment?

When Iconoclasm broke out, for much of society life was unthinkable without icons, holy men or the ways of support offered by the church. These were accessible and intelligible to the public and contrasted with the remoteness of the emperor, whether in his palaces or on campaign. From their viewpoint, the emperors found that the common reliance on icons and on the growing number of church and monastic institutions was diminishing their own power and control; they may well have felt hemmed in and threatened by the growth of irrational and superstitious practices. In this sense, their policy was to reform society and to make it return to a simpler state, closer, as it might have been, to Islamic ways. Yet all the material we have suggests that the acceptance—or need—for these visual or religious supports was too ingrained to be eradicated. The iconoclast emperors and their supporting establishment appear to be in the minority. Although Byzantine society had been in a state of gradual change, it resisted what it believed to be revolutionary innovation and the denial of the past.

The material presented here throws light on how tradition was manipulated in this society. Both sides in the conflict assumed that the justification of their views must lie in an appeal to past tradition and precedent. The iconoclast emperors tried to make new changes in society and to public belief; they looked back to the Old Testament for religious justification for the prohibition of images, and they tried to turn back the clock to a time before the expansion of icons and proliferation of monks. The iconophiles resisted change and appealed to the traditions which they knew from the time preceding Iconoclasm, but they also had to manufacture an old kind of certainty. Hence the necessity to invent and manipulate a church history which had from the beginning included both icons and statements on the orthodoxy of their veneration. The period before Iconoclasm invented miraculous images and found icons 'not made by human hands', but only the iconophiles developed a justification for them.

Although the iconoclasts failed to produce the outward signs which they wanted of a new kind of society, Byzantium after the middle of the ninth century was a different empire within a changed world, and no European country has ever forgotten the Byzantine attempt to change the nature of the Christian religion and Christian worship. The arguments and the texts adduced by Byzantine iconoclasts reappeared in the polemics of the long-drawn-out Reformation of Western Christendom between the fourteenth and seventeenth centuries; attacks on images in churches were likewise a feature of this time. To make a historical comparison between the two movements has its value, but also its difficulties. There do seem to be parallels between the two periods, and these may help to give insights into the processes of thought that appear to be common to both. In England, for example, the structure of events under Henry VIII (reigned 1509–47) has some similarities with Byzantine iconoclasm: we find the will of a monarch imposed from above on his subjects, calls for a return to the practices and values of primitive Christianity, attacks on images and attacks on monks (which resulted in the Dissolution of the Monasteries), and, as a consequence of all these actions, the reduction in the power of bishops and the higher clergy.

But while some of the outward signs of the Reformation movement are familiar to the student of Byzantine Iconoclasm, the circumstances which led to the Reformation in England are not exactly to be paralleled in medieval Byzantium. Henry VIII was not seen as a divinely-appointed ruler with consequent power over the church in the way that the Byzantine emperor was always perceived. Moreover, Henry VIII's desire to obtain the wealth of the disestablished monasteries is not paralleled in the behaviour of the iconoclast emperors in Byzantium. There is no evidence in the case of Byzantium that the church was being challenged by the rise of an educated laity. Yet despite the difficulties of relating the two periods for the purposes of historical explanation, perhaps something is to be learned from the different outcomes of the events. The success of the Reformation led to change in the church's role within the state, and this was one factor in the further development of Western Europe. The failure of Iconoclasm may be a reason why conservatism and resistance to intellectual change remained a feature of Byzantium.

Iconoclasm as a conflict about the allowable ways of using religious art has been seen here as only a symptom of much wider change in the situation of Byzantium. But by focusing on this art and the attitudes expressed towards it, the power of traditionalism in this culture is given a meaning, as are the resulting problems of attempting to reconcile the new with the past.

4

AFTER ICONOCLASM:
THE ILLUSION
OF TRADITION

WITH the ending of the ban on images, Byzantium found itself in new circumstances. The empire was materially more prosperous and better established as a political power in the eastern Mediterranean with the threat of invasions much reduced, and the Christian church was in a position to consider its future conduct and attitudes. It was no simple matter of just replacing images in public places as if nothing had happened, and as if religious attitudes and behaviour would again be identical with those of the period before the iconoclast emperors changed society. The perceptions of those living in the new situation of the ninth century were likely to show an ambivalent mixture of the traditional and of adjustment to the new, conscious or unconscious.

The end of Iconoclasm was soon to be marked visually in Constantinople by the placing, once more, of an icon of Christ on the Chalke Gate of the imperial palace. It was a mosaic and showed Christ as a full-length standing figure. This was a conspicuous public statement of a change in imperial policy and it gave permission for the replacement of figural images elsewhere. Since we can no longer observe this image on the palace—because, like so many other major works of art of Byzantium, it has disappeared—the closest we can come to the imperial restoration of figurative art is in the gold coinage. Not only were the established schemes of the iconoclast reigns rejected, they were rejected in the most decisive way possible. At some date in the period between 843 and 856, while Theodora, the widow of Theophilos, was regent for her son Michael III (842–67), the gold nomisma appeared with a bust of Christ struck on the obverse (Figure 46). From now on Byzantine coins always in some form showed Christ, the Virgin, or a saint.

The new coins had a bust of Christ with long hair and beard on the obverse and bust portraits of the emperor Michael and his mother Theodora on the reverse (Figure 46). It is obvious that the model for the image of Christ is the coinage minted by Justinian II in the 690s

(Figure 32). We cannot of course know how this coin would have been read by the inhabitants of the Byzantine empire at the time. Maybe it appeared not as a revival of the coin of Justinian II but as a throwback even to the time of Constantine the Great, for the *Letter of the Oriental Patriarchs* had claimed the existence of such a coin under Constantine.

The reappearance of figurative art on the walls of public churches appears to have been more gradual than on the coins, though the chance survivals of evidence makes complete certainty on this point impossible. The mosaics in the church of the monastery of Hyacinthos in Nicaea (the church of the Koimesis, destroyed 1922) are an example of simply changing the clock back. A new set of figurative mosaics in the apse of this sixth- or seventh-century church was made probably quite soon after 843 (although the inscription on the mosaics does not record an exact date, only the name of the donor responsible, Naucratios). The history of these mosaics and the procedure of the artist who was employed in the ninth century to reintroduce figural images removed during Iconoclasm can easily be deduced from photographs (Figure 47). The lines of alteration in the surface of the mosaic demonstrate that it passed through three consecutive periods. The first decoration of the apse, presumably at the time of the dedication of the church, was a mosaic representation of the Virgin and Child; on the arch in front of the apse and over the altar were figures of archangels. All these mosaic figures were torn out at some moment during Iconoclasm, while leaving the plain gold ground in position. A new mosaic showing a large plain cross was fixed into the empty space in the apse.

After 843 the mosaics were altered again and the original subject matter was exactly replaced. This suggests that either the restorers, like us, deduced the original scheme from the remnants, or that some other kind of record had been kept—it can hardly be sheer coincidence of thought that produced a restoration of the exact pre-iconoclast scheme. As in the case of the coins, this mosaic restoration marked an attempt to make a straight return to the old traditions.

The end of Iconoclasm superficially offered the possibility of a return to the past, but this was of course impossible. However, some of the changes in what was acceptable in behaviour and belief did mean the re-establishment of patterns acceptable over a century earlier, while the boundaries of what was allowed in religion were largely redefined along previous lines. Most obviously approval was once again given to the promotion of image-making and the monastic life. The course of these changes and restorations in the ninth century can be illustrated by looking at one individual who rose to the top of the church hierarchy and was at the forefront of the readjustment of society to the new circumstances—the patriarch Photios. In his patronage of the arts he reflects the impetus given to the cult of the Virgin with the failure of Iconoclasm. To focus in this chapter on the career of one individual is not to argue that his personality 'caused' the developments of the ninth century, but rather that the period can be well illuminated through him.

46 The restoration of images in 843 was in practice publicized in Byzantium through the fact that icons reappeared in churches and at such places as the entrance facade of the Great Palace. At the same time the official imperial policy of support for the use of figural icons was easily communicated throughout the empire through the medium of coins. Various messages could be conveyed by the careful choice of designs: the portrait type of Christ was copied from the coins of the first reign of Justinian II (see Figure 32), and once more was placed on the obverse. On the reverse, bust images of the imperial family (Michael III and the regent, his mother Theodora) conformed to the designs of the emperors of the iconoclast period.

The career of Photios has always fascinated modern scholars of Byzantium; he was a learned intellectual who first rose high in the civil administration, and then moved on to become the head of the church. To some of his contemporaries his career was more a matter for disapproval; one writer, a chronicler (Symeon) living at the end of the ninth century, gives a very colourful picture of Photios. He is described as the son of a foreigner who raped a nun; a boy who spent his childhood in pagan studies and sold his soul to a Jewish magician in return for renouncing the sign of the cross. Especially striking as an inverse characterization of Photios is the picture painted of his personal rival, the monk Ignatios, whom Photios replaced as patriarch when Ignatios was dismissed from the office. In contrast to Photios the life of Ignatios

143

described in his biography is one of acceptable monastic piety: he spent the years of Iconoclasm on his knees praying and in tears. Although we might now interpret this to mean that he was passive and cautious, the biographer sees in Ignatios the honourable alternative to the ambition of Photios and to his inappropriate, partly secular, career.

Photios himself as patriarch of Constantinople used art to convey a stereotype of Ignatios at a time when his own position in office had become insecure. In about 867, Photios, assisted by Gregory Asbestas, bishop of Syracuse, produced a book with illustrations which recorded seven acts of a council against Ignatios, with one picture placed at the head of each act. The first showed Ignatios being dragged and beaten; its inscription was 'The Devil'. The second showed him being spat on and pulled about: 'The origin of evil'. The third showed him being deposed from the patriarchal throne: 'The son of perdition'. The fourth showed him being fettered and banished: 'The greed of Simon the Magus'. The fifth showed him as a prisoner: 'He who raises himself above God and above worship'. The sixth showed his condemnation: 'The abomination of desolation'. The seventh picture showed him being dragged along for execution: 'The Antichrist'. This visual way of conveying abuse had paradoxically been developed in the church under the stimulus of Iconoclasm, and is similar to that in the Khludov Psalter (which some have attributed to the commission of Photios).

Photios was apparently born into an aristocratic family (his uncle was Tarasios, the patriarch under whom the icons were restored in 787), which had been established in Constantinople for some generations, though to outward appearance he looked 'oriental'. He was born around 810 and died in about 893. He became a leading member of the imperial administration in Constantinople, working closely with the regent Bardas, and one of his duties was to go as an ambassador to the Arab court (possibly in 855). His career changed abruptly in 858 as a result of the action of the patriarch Ignatios who excommunicated Bardas (because of Bardas' affair with his own daughter-in-law) and was in retaliation himself deposed. Photios was persuaded to take over the job. On 20 December 858 Photios was a layman; on Christmas Day he was enthroned as patriarch of Constantinople after a week of ecclesiastical promotions. His career in the church was not smooth. He was himself deposed in September 867 and replaced by Ignatios until 877, when Ignatios died; Photios returned from 877 to 886, when he was again edged out (in these years after 877 Photios may have been responsible for organizing the portrayal of Ignatios in mosaic on the wall of St Sophia; see Figure 48). These decisions about the appointment of the patriarch were made by the imperial court, and must be taken as an indication of the nature of imperial control over the church after Iconoclasm.

The learning of Photios is documented in his literary productions, as well as in his mandarin prose style full of allusions to the literature of the past, both classical and Christian, and with convoluted grammar and vocabulary. He wrote the *Lexicon* (a thesaurus of useful words for prose writers, but judging from the small number of manuscripts in

48 A portrait of Ignatios, probably made just after his death, allows us to see a ninth-century Byzantine rendering of one of the key figures of the church of Constantinople in the years immediately following Iconoclasm. The first three patriarchs after 843 were Methodios, Ignatios and Photios, and each one had to decide what his policy would be on how icons should be used. This mosaic of Ignatios in the church of St Sophia may have been set up during the final part of Photios' period of office. Ignatios is represented as a saint, and his 'official' portrait takes into account his historical appearance—the lack of a beard is noticeable on a man who was a monk as well as patriarch; it underlines the fact that he was a eunuch.

which this is known it was not found widely useful), the *Bibliotheca* (a vast record of his reading in a format we would call the 'book review'), the *Amphilochia* (some 300 chapters on a variety of topics, many theological), around 250 published *Letters*, and nineteen *Sermons*.

The writing of Photios particularly helpful for our purposes is one of his sermons (no XVII). This is known in the form in which Photios prepared it for publication and which circulated quite widely in Byzantium, although this may not record the exact words in which it was originally delivered. The sermon was given on Easter Saturday, 29 March 867, from the ambo in the centre of the nave of St Sophia in the presence of the joint emperors Michael III and Basil I (the ambo, now removed, stood in the nave under the central dome of the church; see Figure 49). The title records the special occasion of the sermon: this was the day of inauguration of the image of the Mother of God. There can be little doubt (since the recent archaeological investigation of this part of the church) that this image was the mosaic of the Virgin and Child, accompanied by the archangels Michael and Gabriel, which still decorates the apse and sanctuary vault of St Sophia (Figures 50–53). Both text and image can therefore be studied side by side.

The mosaic was the first monumental icon on the walls of the church since the end of Iconoclasm, and it therefore represented an official view stated openly for the first time of the correct environment for worship and prayer in the main church of the Byzantine empire. From this time it was normal for the major churches of the Byzantine world to be decorated with mosaic pictures; other churches also received some figural decoration whose type and refinement depended on the funds available. Icons were again available to assist the Christian in mediation between earth and Heaven.

The new mosaic in the apse of St Sophia was framed with a short inscription in verse, presumably written by Photios (this was on the face of the conch of the apse but only the last letters remain in place; see Figure 50):

The icons which the heretics threw down from here, pious emperors have set up again.

This text implies that in the period before Iconoclasm the apse of St Sophia was decorated with figurative icons. All our knowledge of the church suggests, on the contrary, that it had never before been embellished with such pictures, but was decorated only with ornamental designs and great numbers of representations of the cross. Therefore, although Photios expresses an intention to return to the conventions of the previous age before the arrival in power of the iconoclasts, this claim was in fact historically untrue. Perhaps Photios was deliberately misleading the public. More likely he was reflecting the assumption, unquestioned at the time, that the decoration of the church before the advent of Iconoclasm must have been figural.

At first sight Photios' sermon no XVII ('On the Inauguration of the Image of the Virgin') is opaque, convoluted and on occasion unintelligible. The combination of his literary style and the expressions of

49 The church of St Sophia in Constantinople was the largest and most important church of the Byzantine empire, and the major arena in which Orthodox belief on the use of the visual arts was developed and expressed. Some effort of imagination is needed to visualize how it would have looked during the Byzantine period. The present building was constructed for Justinian I between 532 and 537 and remained in use as a church until the Turkish conquest of the city in 1453 (although from 1204 until 1261, when the Crusaders occupied the city, it was adapted for use as a latin cathedral). It was converted into a mosque in 1453, and remained in active Islamic use until the 1930s, when it was made a museum. This history accounts for the various Turkish fittings to be seen in this view from the west gallery looking towards the apse: the mihrab in the apse which indicated the direction of Mecca from Istanbul, the mimbar to the right of the apse, various special enclosures in the nave and aisles, and the large placards with Koranic texts. In the Byzantine period this view would have included a large ambo in the nave under the dome, and the sanctuary arrangements around the altar and its ciborion.

Byzantine theology has resulted in a piece of writing which might be taken to typify the views of Byzantium held by such writers as Edward Gibbon ('the triumph of barbarism and religion'). Like much Byzantine literature, the sermon is full of quotations, imitations and repetitions. Its theology depends as much on the allusion to inspired scripture as on argument; the choice, arrangement and use of biblical texts and writings of Church Fathers could be analyzed in detail, and much could be made of the sources of Photios' thought (for example, in the case of his ideas on art, the eighth-century writings of John of Damascus); but the value of the sermon for us lies in its public expression of attitudes in the years after the final failure of the iconoclast movement.

During his address Photios had in front of him an Easter audience consisting of two emperors, the court, the clergy and the congregation of the cathedral church; this audience explains the particular formality of the speech, its highly worked presentation and its pointed deference to the emperors. Photios did not start directly with the theme of the image but worked it in with another event of this Holy Week, the

50 This view shows the situation and present condition of the ninth-century mosaic in the apse of St Sophia. Only a few letters of the inscription which ran around the face of the apse between the figures of the archangels and the enthroned Virgin and Child are still to be seen; this text recorded the triumph of piety over heresy, marked visually by the new figural image after Iconoclasm. A fragment of mosaic on the left marks the original existence of an image on this side of the vault—this must have been a figure of the archangel Michael matching that of Gabriel to the right.

acceptance into the church of new members, in this case a group of
former heretics. They had just been converted from their deviant belief
about the way of deciding the correct day for the celebration of Easter:
the sect of the Tessaraskaidekatitai (from the Greek for 'fourteen') or,
to use the Latin form, the Quartodecimans, believed, among other
things, that Easter should be celebrated according to Jewish rules for
the Passover and on the fourteenth day of the first lunar month, whether
or not it was a Sunday.

The topical issues were carefully interwoven by Photios into a statement of theology about images, and references to the festival of Easter.
The summary which follows tries to bring out the thought which lies
in the sermon, and because it is short may give an artificial tightness
to what Photios said. The sections of the modern edited text are given
beside the summary in brackets.

*Sermon XVII: of the Most-Blessed Photios, Patriarch of Constan-
tinople, delivered from the ambo of the Great Church on Holy Saturday,
in the presence of the Christ-Loving Emperors, when the form of the
Theotokos, the Mother of God, had been depicted and uncovered.*

[1] An Easter sermon requires the greatest oratory, because the events commemorated show the power of piety, and how impiety can drag even emperors
down to hell, if they introduce innovations. Today under pious emperors and
with their help orthodox theology prevails. Even former heretics have recan-
ted; a group of people dressed in white, who were received into the orthodox
church yesterday, will soon enter. These Quartodecimans were under the influence of the Jews, and fell into numerous errors; they will now increase the
membership of the Catholic church.

[2] This heresy is not irrelevant to the theme of this sermon, which is also
a celebration of orthodoxy. Piety has set up a sign to mark its victory over
the anti-Christian impiety of the part-barbarian and bastard tribes who took
over the throne of Byzantium; these shameful emperors are now universally
deplored. Today we have a loved pair of pious emperors, father and son, both
shining in royal purple. Their orthodoxy is the cause of what we see today:
the representation of the Virgin. This welcomes us, not with an offering of
wine, but with a beautiful sight through which the thinking part of our soul,
nourished through our eyes and helped in its growth towards the divine love
of orthodoxy, achieves the most exact vision of truth. So the grace of the Virgin
delights us, comforts us and strengthens us through her icons. A Virgin with
a Child reclining in her arms for our salvation is a Christian mystery. She
is both mother and virgin at the same time, but no shame to either condition.
Through art we see a lifelike imitation of her. She looks with affection at the
child, yet her expression is detached and distant towards the emotionless and
supernatural child. She looks as if she might speak if someone were to ask
how she could be both virgin and mother, for the painting makes her lips
seem of real flesh, pressed together and still as in the sacraments; it is as if
this is the stillness and the beauty of the original.

[3] Look at the beauty and brightness of which the church had been deprived.
That was the action of an insolent Jewish hand, an act of hatred; this representation is a gift of divine love, as is the veneration of the holy icons. The destruction of icons comes from uncontrolled and foul hatred. Those people stripped

the church, the bride of Christ, of her ornaments, and wounded and scarred her, and wanted to leave her naked, unsightly and wounded—imitating Jewish madness. The church, though she still bears on her body the scars of the wounds received in dishonour from their Isaurian and heretical belief, now regains her ancient beauty and sheds the mockery of her insane insulters. If one called today the beginning and the day of Orthodoxy, this would be the right description; for, even if a short time has passed since the iconoclast heresy has been extinguished and orthodox doctrine has lit the world through the command of emperors and God, this ornament is the beginning of orthodoxy for me, the achievement of the same God-loving reign.

[4] This famous and sacred church looked sad with her visual mysteries scraped off before she had received this new pictorial representation; she gave faint light to those who entered her and the face of orthodoxy appeared gloomy. Now sadness is cast off and she is richly ornamented again in her bridal garment.

[5] We too with happiness and joy celebrate the restoration of the church and our deliverance from our enemies; Easter is the most appropriate festival for the restoration of the image, for Christ conquers death and the image of the Virgin rises out of the depths of oblivion and raises with her the likenesses of the saints. Christ was born in the flesh, and is carried in the arms of his mother. This is seen, proved and demonstrated by icons; the observer sees for himself and believes. No one can disapprove of teaching through icons— unless he has rejected the message of the Gospels. Just as speech is transmitted through hearing, so a form is imprinted on the tablets of the soul through the sight and it conveys to those whose understanding is not perverted by heresy a representation of knowledge. The stories of martyrs are contained in books, but paintings offer a much more vivid record. Take those martyrs who were burned alive; their sufferings are known through writing and through pictures, but those who see the pictures are more likely to imitate the martyrs than those to whom the stories are simply read. Similarly in the case of the Virgin and Child, seeing rather than hearing will allow anyone better to understand the great mystery of the incarnation. The memory is most effective when acting through the sight.

[6] Only an iconoclast who scorns the veneration of images can reject the truth of Christian writings. Only the iconophile can believe the writings. People either accept both icons and writings or accept neither. The iconoclasts fell into heresy and impiety. Now, in front of our eyes, is a motionless depiction in art of the Virgin carrying the Creator in her arms as a child; we see in painting exactly what is described in writings and visions—an intercessor for our salvation, a teacher of reverence, a grace for eyes and the mind, through which the divine love in us is lifted to the intelligible beauty of truth.

[7] It is time to finish speaking, and to continue the service. I ask forgiveness for my inadequacies from the Word and Bridegroom and Wisdom of the Father, in which name this church of St Sophia is dedicated. Grant to those whom you have made emperors on earth to consecrate the remainder of the church with holy images; as they are the eyes of the universe, protect them like the pupil of an eye, keep them above any evil, make them seem terrible to their foes and keep them, as well as us, worthy of your endless and blessed kingdom. Yours is the power and the honour and the veneration of the Trinity, now and for ever and for all ages.

Amen.

★ ★ ★ ★

The importance of the sermon is that it is the most sophisticated public statement on the role of the visual in Byzantium after the final failure of Iconoclasm had become evident. The expression of the arguments in the text is convoluted, but it is nevertheless possible to identify the most important strands of thought and those which provide an underlying link between the different sections of the sermon. Particularly noticeable are the series of binary contrasts that recur throughout the text: Iconoclasm is equated with heresy, innovation, 'foreign-ness' and impiety and contrasted with the right-thinking of the iconophiles who embrace orthodoxy, tradition, the proper custom of Constantinople and true piety.

Exactly the same contrasts were drawn in the brief inscription which accompanied the image of the Virgin and Child in the apse of St Sophia inaugurated on the day of the sermon. It too speaks of the replacement of heretical emperors by pious emperors, and of images cast down and now restored. The implication is that the church is turning the clock back to the time before innovation changed its decoration. Paradoxically all our evidence from the archaeological examination of the apse is, as has been mentioned before, that this icon of the Virgin was the first figurative image ever placed in that area and that the church as built and decorated in the sixth century under Justinian had no such representation here. Whatever Photios' understanding of the history of the decoration in St Sophia, it was, as we shall see, consistent with the rhetoric of the sermon to describe the icon as restoration rather than innovation. For innovation is here seen to be the equivalent of impiety.

Throughout the sermon icons and figural images are seen by Photios as the representatives of orthodoxy, and as declarations of the ending of a period of wrong belief and heresy. This is the relevance of the mention of the imminent arrival into St Sophia of the group of Quartodecimans and the reference to their presence in St Sophia on the previous day. Good Friday was the traditional day for the ceremony of baptism and for acceptance of new members into the church community. In the case of the Quartodecimans a ceremony would have taken place in the baptistery, but they would not have been required to be rebaptized, simply to be anointed with oil and to swear allegiance to orthodox belief. The Quartodecimans could be quoted as an example of the return to the church of large numbers of heretics coinciding with the end of Iconoclasm. By extension the veneration of icons was to be taken as the symbol of right-thinking Christianity, a position confirmed as official by the presence of the emperors in St Sophia on this occasion.

A strong contrast is also drawn in the sermon between the 'foreign' and traditional Byzantine practice. The heresy of the Quartodecimans, for example, is tarred with the brush of being 'Jewish'. Likewise Iconoclasm itself is characterized as Jewish madness and so comparable to the Jewish attacks on Christ himself; this is the exact point made visually in the Khludov Psalter (Figure 45). In other respects Iconoclasm is seen as geographically alien from Byzantium, stemming from the distant region of Isauria in South Asia Minor, where Leo III was thought to have been born [Section 3]. In the mind of Photios the word 'Isauria' itself has become synonymous with evil. A clear opposition to such foreign influence is found in the persons of the current emperors, present to witness the inauguration of the icon. They, at last, it is claimed, are orthodox rulers and no longer 'foreign intruders'—a technically inappropriate sentiment, since neither in fact belonged to the traditional Constantinopolitan aristocracy.

Photios shares the 'traditional' expectation that the interior of a church would be beautified as a mark of honour to God. This expectation arose from a visualization of God as an emperor in Heaven, and therefore to be seen in a setting even more luxurious than that of the Byzantine emperor on earth. Such a view of Heaven as mirroring the local political system and social hierarchies has already been met in the seventh-century texts. Although Theodore of Sykeon might be called puritanical in his way of living, he still accepted that the churches in his monastery should contain paintings and the richest possible vessels for use in the services. This tradition is taken by Photios as the correct orthodox one, and so a church without icons is offensive to his aesthetic and religious senses. The consequences of such a view are apparent today to any modern visitor to an Orthodox church, furnished throughout with tiers of icons to suit the expectations of its congregation. Without visual embellishment, the church would lack its power.

Icons are further justified as an important means of teaching Christian doctrine and conduct. Photios argues that visual aids are essential for teaching the facts of Christian history, and for the encouragement of the imitation of past deeds of Christian bravery and perseverance. Such a justification for the didactic uses of art had several precedents, and was stated both in the writings of the early church Fathers and in the Western church, notably by Pope Gregory the Great. The standard argument had been that imagery was 'silent script' and a means of instruction or edification for the illiterate. At the Council of Nicaea in 787 the value of icons was accepted in a wider way; they encouraged the more frequent veneration of Christ and the saints and the imitation of their ways. Photios is influenced by such iconophile statements to accept the widest value for art. His view is that every spectator will benefit from exposure to art, and he does not distinguish between the response of the literate and that of the illiterate, partly perhaps because he assumes that a normal way of learning about church history is from listening, not reading. His view of art gives it an integral place in society; the visual is a more vivid medium than writing, and more likely to help a Christian to see and understand the nature of heaven and the 'other world'. Anyone who rejects icons is likely to reject the inspired scriptures. The implication is that because the iconoclasts lacked icons they could not see Christian truth or copy the good deeds of the early Christians.

Art was not, however, seen by Photios as merely didactic. A beautiful image provided a focus for prayer in times of good fortune or crisis and could, by its very beauty, convince the spectator that prayer would be effective. Just such an image was that of the Virgin and Child in St Sophia, which gave delight and comfort and strength to the spec-

51 *The fact that the apse of St Sophia is so far above any viewer and has a relatively small surface area needs to be taken into account in any consideration of the apse mosaic as an artistic production and how a Byzantine audience might have responded to it. Its size and its distance from the viewer might have encouraged the characterization of the image as 'lifelike', for the eye may have supplied what the critical language of the time suggested. The apse composition overall incorporates various conceptions of sanctity, both, for example, that of the majesty of the Virgin (the dominant element in the earlier mosaic at Dyrrachium; see Figure 24) and also that of the caring intercessor implied through the image of a loving mother with a restless child.*

tator, and impressed upon him (by its aesthetic and 'ordered' qualities) a belief in the divine order of the Christian world as a whole. The aesthetic qualities of art, he says, predispose the mind to accept the order of the universe.

Throughout the speech the focus of the argument is the mosaic of the Virgin and Child then being inaugurated. This image provides visible proof that Iconoclasm is over and marks a turning point in the history of the church—just as the turning points in the *Life of Theodore of Sykeon* were marked by the appearance of icons. With its own 'resurrection' (occurring appropriately enough at Easter time), the image heralds also the 'resurrection' into the church of the visual forms of the saints, in this case Michael and Gabriel on the arches in front of the apse (Figures 50, 53). In addition the Virgin and Child raise two other issues for Photios. First he alludes to the complications inherent in the position of Mary as both virgin and mother, but this leads on to a second statement involving his views on art. He describes the portrait as lifelike, meaning that the Virgin looked to the spectator to be a real person, with the lips seeming like real flesh, not like the materials of a work of art. Photios does not say, of course, that this is a true portrait of Mary as she was in life. But he does seem to say that an icon can be more than just an imitation of its model; it almost incorporates the model.

To the modern observer, despite Photios' remarks, the image of the Virgin and Child does not immediately seem lifelike (Figures 51, 52). Indeed some modern art historians have (perhaps rather crudely) characterized it as abstract in style. But before making sweeping judgements on this issue, we should consider the position of the Byzantine artist. He was no doubt expected to depict the subject in a form that accorded with the perceptions of his audience, but this scene of Virgin and Child was not simply a representation of two holy figures but also the encapsulation of an absolute religious truth, to be directly imprinted on the mind of the spectator. What is it, in these circumstances, to be lifelike?

LEFT 52 *Photographs of the apse mosaic in St Sophia taken from a scaffolding show us details of the mosaic which could never have been seen by the Byzantine viewer. This one records how the face of the Virgin was depicted, the colour gradations in the tesserae and the flow of their setting lines across the cheeks being used to convey the contours of the face.*

RIGHT 53 *This photograph of the archangel Gabriel in the vault on the right of the conch in St Sophia gives, as in all photographs of representations on curving surfaces, a distorted version of the original (a factor that has to be taken into account in modern characterizations of Byzantine art). Gabriel is holding a staff and orb.*

In seeking an answer to this question the Byzantine artist was already confronted with a considerable variety of traditional solutions—from the stiff figures in the mosaics of the church of St Demetrios to the fully-modelled figures in some of the Sinai icons. For whatever reason, which we can never know, the artist of this mosaic made his choice and imposed his vision of the lifelike on Photios and his audience.

The church might on occasion attempt to limit the freedom of the individual artist by defining appropriate religious representation. Although such control is not discussed in the course of this sermon, it had been explicitly considered at the Council of Nicaea in 787. The bishops at Nicaea formulated the following position: 'The making of icons is not the invention of painters, but expresses the approved legislation of the Catholic Church . . . . The painter's domain is limited to his art.' In other words the church was to decide what could be represented, and the artist was to put its instructions into practice. How far such a control could be effective is of course another issue.

In the final sections of his speech, Photios comes to an elegant literary conclusion and prepares his audience for the continuation of the service. The service at which the sermon was delivered took place on Easter Saturday, probably at midday. There was a regular ceremonial on this day into which the inauguration would fit. The emperor came in procession to St Sophia, entered the sanctuary of the church and changed the altar cloth; the patriarch censed the church. In addition the emperor went to the treasury and gave a donation to the church in silver. He finally returned to the palace with pomp. This midday ceremonial was probably adapted by Photios to include the unique inauguration of the apse mosaics.

Apart from the necessary didactic function of the sermon (one duty of bishops was to teach and instruct), which influenced the literary genre, Photios had another obligation to bear in mind: prayers for the imperial family. In the church of St Sophia and on occasions when the emperor was present in person, it was no doubt wise to include additional expressions of loyalty and support for the emperor, partly explicitly and partly through the flattery of a specially polished text. The cathedral was not only the seat of the patriarch, it was also the largest church in the empire and was attached to the Great Palace of the Byzantine emperors—it was the site of some of their most important ceremonial appearances to the people. Photios duly offers concluding prayers to God on behalf of the emperors. His words at this point also imply that they are responsible for the apse mosaics, and that any further decoration in the church needs their sponsorship. It is difficult to decide whether this means that the financing of the operation was literally due to the imperial treasury, or whether this statement is just general flattery. Art historians have on the whole assumed that the size of the church made the patriarch dependent on the emperor for such a major work, and that Photios and others had to negotiate for financial contributions from the palace.

In the course of his prayers for the emperors Photios speaks of their position as the gift of God. Earlier on, he had emphasized the legitimacy of their power and piety in comparison with the half-barbarous iconoclasts. His remarks in the sermon are a little ironic in view of the pedigree of the emperors, and the fact that in a matter of a year or two he himself was ousted by one of them from the patriarchal throne. One of the two, Michael III (842–67), the son of the iconoclast emperor Theophilos, was aged two when his father died and first his mother Theodora and then her brother Bardas acted as regent. He gained his position as emperor through a dynastic succession, and when he died at the age of 27 he had spent little time in any active control of affairs. The other emperor was in 867 the adopted son of Michael III: he was Basil I (866–86), the 'Macedonian' who established the dynasty which was dominant until the middle of the eleventh century. Basil was born in Thrace in about 836 and had an Armenian peasant father and (probably) a Slav peasant mother. His first language was Armenian, and he never learned to read or write. In 856 he went to Constantinople as a groom, and his incredible physical strength was by chance observed by Michael III; a homosexual relationship followed. In the spring of 866, when they were about to embark with the fleet on a campaign against Crete, Basil murdered Bardas in front of Michael. The two returned to Constantinople, and on 26 May 866 Basil I was crowned co-emperor in St Sophia by Photios. On 23 September 867 Michael III, said to live in a perpetual alcoholic haze, was murdered by Basil. These were the men whom Photios lauded in his sermon as true Constantinopolitan emperors.

One question, perhaps the key one, raised by the occasion of the sermon is the choice of the particular image in the apse by a society emerging from the period of Iconoclasm. Why focus attention on the Virgin with Christ as a child and on the two accompanying archangels? Photios never sets out an explicit explanation.

There are a number of superficial reasons for the choice. One is, for example, that it was believed to be a restoration of the original scheme, and so it is another case of supposed traditionalism. This, as we have seen, is the implication of the written inscription around the apse. Another simple argument of this kind relies on the view that it was normal practice in the Middle Ages to begin the decoration of a church at the east end, for practical reasons. For example, in this way the sanctuary area was made ready for services first, and the scaffolding could then be moved to the other parts of the building as needed. Applied to St Sophia, this would mean that the timber used in the apse decoration was now waiting for further use in the dome and upper areas of the nave. These parts were indeed eventually decorated. Since the choice of figure for the dome mosaic was that of Christ, one might say that the apse Virgin was just one element of a whole plan for the church which followed a standard scheme. This argument is entirely simple: decoration always starts in the apse and apses always have the Virgin. Since there was nothing 'normal' about introducing decoration to St Sophia at this time, this easy solution is hardly satisfying.

There is a more theological explanation for the choice of a Virgin and Child with which to proclaim the refutation of Iconoclasm. This is explicit in the sermon. Photios says that Christ was born in the flesh, and this is seen and confirmed in pictures. He refers therefore to one of the main iconophile arguments for the legitimacy of icons of Christ—that since Christ himself represents the divinity in human form, there can be no logical objection to the portrayal of God in human form in icons. Such an explanation for the choice of the image is more satisfying than the last, but it does not exhaust all the signs likely to be read by the Byzantine public. To appreciate these requires us to turn away from this particular sermon and consider a much larger question in the second part of this chapter: the importance of the cult of the Virgin in Byzantium.

The sermon celebrated and justified the decoration of the most important public church in the Byzantine world with its first image. This occasion is recorded in a public statement by the man responsible for the organization of the commission, and it is presented as the restoration of the church to its original and proper state, as it had been before the actions of a series of bad emperors. It inaugurates a new period in history, marked also by the return of heretics to orthodoxy and by the conspicuous declaration of the orthodoxy of the emperors through their patronage of art. The argument is expressed that no Christian can entirely understand the world or live a full life unless able to see pictorial representations of saints and church history. Through their particular way of showing truth, icons supply a medium of knowledge different from, and in some ways superior to, words. Icons are therefore defended as essential for intellectual and spiritual life.

This text confirms that the ninth-century perception of the seventh-century use of art coincides with our interpretation of the texts we have already looked at. Photios believed that the practices of this period before Iconoclasm, as he discovered them, constituted the traditional norms of the church. The non-figurative religious art of Iconoclasm appeared therefore as a challenge to the conventions held by a majority of Byzantine society. Photios records some of the reasons why he thought the iconoclast ideas had failed; these constituted innovation and therefore heresy and they took away areas of the experience of the visual from the human mind. Iconoclasm not only took away figurative art from the church, it also crippled human understanding.

What lies behind the choice of an image of the Virgin Mary for the first monumental image in St Sophia after Iconoclasm? To consider this question requires a broader look at the role of the Virgin in Byzantine thinking.

The cult of the Virgin had developed in distinctive ways in Constantinople in the period before Iconoclasm. There were some special reasons for this, among them the fact that the city had become the possessor of a number of supposed relics of the Virgin. The major ones were acquired in the fifth century, and in the later sixth century were the subject of increased attention when they were rehoused in new architectural settings. The robe of the Virgin was in the Vlachernai monastery (the monastery to which the mother of St Stephen the Younger had dedicated her son in the belief that its icon had brought about his conception). The Virgin's girdle was at the church of the Chalcoprateia (near St Sophia, and administered by the clergy of that church). The city also owned her shroud, and the swaddling clothes in which Christ had rested against her breast, and on which could be seen the marks of her milk. The robe and the girdle were displayed in their new settings through the patronage of Justin II (565–78). The imperial interest in these relics was reflected in the increasing ceremonial centred on them and in the veneration they were given. Public interest in the cult of the Virgin intensified still further in the early seventh century, when belief in the powers of relics and icons led to attitudes towards the Virgin in Constantinople similar to those towards St Demetrios at Thessaloniki and towards the *soudarion* at Edessa.

A seventh-century text about the Virgin's robe, which had turned up in the time of Leo I (457–74), describes the conditions in Constantinople in 619 when the capital, like Thessaloniki in the same period, was beseiged by Avar tribes. Since the church of the Vlachernai where the purple robe of the Virgin was kept lay very close to the land walls of the city, the casket containing the relic was taken to St Sophia for security. When it could be safely returned to the monastery, it was carried back in procession among emotional scenes of veneration. When the robe was examined the monks declared that its state of preservation was 'miraculous'. The text records a prayer which asked the Virgin to protect her city and to turn away barbarians, to give lasting peace and freedom from famine, disease, earthquake and other disasters. The climate of thought shown in this text, almost contemporary with the first book of the *Miracles of St Demetrios*, shows many similarities with Thessaloniki; but there, it must be admitted, the local saint takes an even more prominent role in the prayers of the community than does the Virgin at Constantinople.

In the summer of 626 the city faced a more severe siege from the Avars, and this occurred during the absence of the emperor Heraclios in Persia. On 7 August the citizens finally fought off the siege, but only after the icon of the Virgin from the Vlachernai was carried in procession on the walls by the patriarch Sergios, and placed on the gates of the city; and after the Virgin with her sword appeared to encourage the people and a veiled lady was seen by the leader of the Avars. This event sealed the belief that the Virgin was the special supernatural defender of Constantinople. The expansion of the cult of the Virgin can therefore be measured in Constantinople through the growing attention given to her relics and the places in which they were venerated. This evidence can easily be supplemented and broadened with other cases of special devotion and prayer to the Virgin: there is, for example, the record that Heraclios, when he sailed from Carthage to Constantinople to seize the throne from Phocas in 610, carried images of the Virgin on the masts of his ships; and when he became emperor, he carried icons with him on campaign.

Between 726 and 843 Iconoclasm put a brake on the public involvement of the people with the cult of the Virgin by banning access to her icons and even discouraging prayers to her. If the years after 843 were a time of conscious return to the conventions of the earlier period, a conspicuous display of devotion to the Virgin is to be expected and this can indeed be documented. The choice of an image of the Virgin in the apse of St Sophia is only one example of a trend. Photios put an image of the Virgin on his personal patriarchal seals used for letters and documents. Seals of the emperor Michael III also use the image of the Virgin. If we look back to the seals of the late sixth and early seventh centuries, we find examples of the image of the Virgin used in the imperial chancellery. Devotion to the Virgin has become by the time of Photios an essential element in the beliefs of an iconophile; iconoclasts can be attacked for their refusal to venerate the Virgin.

By the end of the ninth century, probably, a mosaic in the southwest vestibule of St Sophia, at an entrance both to the church and to the patriarchal palace (Figures 54–56), showed two emperors— Constantine, on the right, and Justinian, on the left—anachronistically

BELOW LEFT 54 *After Iconoclasm the church of St Sophia was progressively decorated with special images. This lunette mosaic was in the southwest vestibule of the church, over one of the entrances into the inner narthex. This was one of the special ceremonial places of the church; the vestibule lay beside the patriarchal palace and the baptistery, and opened on to the courtyard between the church and the Great Palace. To the right of the entrance door can be seen a porter's lodge and the entry to the patriarchal palace. The composition shows the enthroned Virgin and Child placed between two emperors.*

RIGHT 55 *The emperor on the right side of the Virgin and Child, Constantine the Great, offers the city of Constantinople to them in his hands. Perhaps this refers to the belief generally held by the ninth century that the city lay under the special protection of the Virgin, and so this interpretation of the foundation directly reflects the contemporary view of the powers and associations attributed to her.*

OVERLEAF LEFT 56 *The other emperor in the mosaic of the vestibule, Justinian I, is to the left of the lunette and so at the right hand of the Virgin and Child and in the position of greater honour. He is shown offering them the church of St Sophia. The dedication of the church was to Holy Wisdom, and there were no mosaics of the Virgin in the original sixth-century decoration. The prominence of the Virgin in the mosaics after Iconoclasm makes this particular period notable as one in which it was generally expected that the visual environment would be marked by her images; however there is also the possibility that in this particular case the Virgin is being used as a reference to the feminine gender—and so to the Wisdom of God.*

offering the city and the church of St Sophia to the Virgin and Child. This mosaic conveys through visual means the idea that the city and church had the special protection of the Virgin. Another work of art of the same date as this mosaic shows how deeply involved even the emperor had become in the cult of the Virgin: this is the ceremonial sceptre of an emperor whom the inscription identifies as Leo (Figure 57), probably Leo VI (886–912), the son of Basil I. He showed himself being crowned, not by Christ, but by the Virgin. Although there are later examples of emperors shown crowned by Christ (Figure 58), and there-

fore emphasizing the direct relationship between the heavenly and earthly kingdoms, the representation of the Virgin on this late-ninth-century ivory extended the range of divine associations enjoyed by the emperor.

After Iconoclasm, there are increasing examples of visual expression of special devotion to the Virgin among all levels of society, both in

LEFT *58 This ivory plaque showing the emperor and Christ also conveys the ceremonial of coronation; it probably represents Constantine VII Porphyrogenitos (913–959) around the year 944 when he became sole ruler. In contrast to Figure 57, the emperor has no sceptre or orb and bows his head to Christ. In this case, the effect of the visual image is to emphasize the special relationship of emperor and God.*

RIGHT *59 This illustration and Figure 60 are from a commissioned Bible, one of the small number of grand productions of the tenth century. It was written and embellished for a court official called Leo, who held the titles of Patricios, Praepositos and Sakellarios (the latter a treasury post in the palace). Leo is shown on this page in his official court dress; he has grey hair, but his age is not matched by a beard, no doubt indicating that he was a eunuch. A poem at the beginning of the manuscript states what can be seen in the paintings: that the Bible was offered to Mary and to St Nicholas (the special protector of Leo), and that it was given to a monastery of St Nicholas (location unknown). Several of the miniatures, and the poems written by the donor in the frames around the pictures, extract references to the Virgin from the Old Testament text, and in this picture Leo is shown offering his book to her—in the expectation that she will act as a mediator for him to Christ.*

60 *The second donation picture in the Bible of Leo shows two figures in prayer in front of St Nicholas, both of whom are identified. The 'most pious' abbot of the monastery, Makar, is the figure in a black habit on the left. The bearded figure in court dress on the right is the founder of the monastery, the Protospatharios Constantine, brother of Leo, but now deceased. The images are accompanied by the epigram in the frame: this is a prayer to St Nicholas that the founder of the monastery may as a reward have a quick passage to paradise ('the mansions of life') and that both may be given grace—according strength to one and expiation of sins to the other. The prayers on their behalf are mediated to Christ by St Nicholas, i.e. from a lower level in the hierarchy of saints than shown in Figure 59.*

Constantinople and throughout the empire. Such devotion did not exclude individuals from relying also on the potential help of other saints; for example, in the tenth-century Bible of Leo, the donor shows himself bowing in front of the Virgin (Figure 59), but in another picture his brother is portrayed kneeling at the feet of St Nicholas (Figure 60). It is clear that the Virgin was understood to have greater powers in

Heaven than other saints. Her power was proved for the citizens of Constantinople through the miracles recorded in connection with her relics. In the empire as a whole, outside such miracles, her eminence was enhanced by her position as mother of Christ. Through human eyes this meant that she had the ability to influence her son on behalf of anyone who prayed to her. The rise of the cult of the Virgin reflects many facets of Byzantine society, from the acceptance of the norms of family life to the practices of private devotions. The appearance of a monumental image of the Virgin in the apse of St Sophia in 867 would clearly have stimulated a whole range of overlapping responses in the mind of the Byzantine spectator. Whether the motivation for its choice was theological or otherwise, this new image of the Virgin would have evoked many meanings and taken on many functions.

Why did the cult of the Virgin maintain such a major place in Byzantine life throughout the empire? What led to the promotion of the relics of the Virgin? Why were they not totally subordinate to, for example, the remnants of the True Cross found by Helena on the site of Golgotha, of which Constantinople had a reasonable tally? The cult of the Virgin was not, as we have seen, special to Constantinople. The ciborion of St Demetrios at Thessaloniki included an icon of the Virgin, and services in honour of that saint included a substantial element of worship of Mary. Nor is the growth of the cult of the Virgin special to Byzantine Christianity; the same phenomenon is seen in the West. The promotion of the relics of the Virgin at Constantinople is one of the features of the cult which can more easily be assessed; other aspects are more deeply interwoven in the fabric of society.

Since Photios in the course of Sermon XVII dwells on the role of the Virgin as mother, and the feelings of a mother towards her child, it might seem likely that periods of special veneration of the Virgin Mary coincided with a greater promotion of family life. In fact this would be an oversimplification. We cannot divide Byzantine society into iconophiles who both worshipped the Virgin and encouraged family life, and iconoclasts who abhorred the cult of the Virgin and had little concern for the family. After all, although iconoclasts certainly did ban images of the Mother of God and prayers to her, they also on occasion took positive steps against celibacy. This is, at least, one obvious interpretation of the emperor Constantine V's persecution of the monks which included their defrocking and an insistence that they consort with women and marry. This convinced iconoclast was, it might be suggested, trying to reform a group who had renounced sexual relations in favour of childless virginity; for life in a monastery for both monks and nuns was one of sexual isolation and abstinence.

The church and Byzantine society in general encompassed a wide range of sexual statuses, which do not seem to match closely with attitudes to the Virgin. Within Byzantine religion the 'secular' clergy (outside the monasteries) were divided into parochial priests, who were allowed to have been married before ordination as subdeacon, but who were excluded from the upper hierarchy of the church, and the celibate clergy from whom bishops were chosen. Outside the church the different types of sexual and family behaviour were infinite, ranging from the emperor, who as a monarch was perceived to live in luxury and sexual licence, through the adulterous married woman to those who restricted their sexual relations to the narrowest definition of Christian marriage. However hard we look, we cannot match the worship of the Virgin with any one of these categories; nor can be we be sure that it was her image as Mother (rather than Virgin) which predominated.

The necessary role of the Virgin in the functioning of society becomes clearer if the ways in which she is represented visually are considered with some care. This requires asking how she was regularly seen by the public (aside from her miraculous appearances). Because only fragments of the decoration in churches before the ninth century have survived, it is difficult to visualize the whole environment within which so much time was spent. From this century onwards the material becomes more plentiful and complete. If one looks at the whole environment it is easier to appreciate the way that the cult of the Virgin entered into the calendar of the church and into regular experiences. We can therefore look at the implications of the regular exposure of the people to icons of the Virgin.

Ever since the emperor Justin II in the second half of the sixth century enlarged and redecorated the churches in Constantinople in which the two major relics of the Virgin were kept, the rituals surrounding her cult had developed more and more. The public experience of the Virgin was increasingly prominent on all sorts of occasions. Two festivals in particular were surrounded during the sixth century with enhanced ceremonial. The first was the Annunciation of the birth of Christ to Mary by the archangel Gabriel, commemorated on 25 March. For this day a special hymn was written by Romanos, a Syrian of the first half of the sixth century famous for his poetry in Greek; this *Akathistos* (literally 'unseated') was sung standing up and it became the most popular hymn in Byzantine devotions, despite (or because of) its length. It consists of twenty-four stanzas, each beginning with a different letter, in alphabetical order. The first twelve stanzas are concerned with the Annunciation and the childhood of Christ, and the second twelve with Christ as the saviour of the world and with the Virgin as his mother, the Theotokos. The hymn includes a remarkable number of varied epithets applied to the Virgin, which attribute to her powers and activities which strictly belong to God alone. Every other stanza is followed by a string of salutations ending with the same refrain: 'Hail, Virgin Mother'. The Byzantine audience which regularly heard this hymn became accustomed to the idea that the Virgin was among human beings the closest to God.

The commemoration of the death of Mary became even more prominent in the church year, being fixed (following the example of the church of Jerusalem) on 15 August. This festival gave rise to one of the most carefully designed icons in any decoration. Before looking at these icons, we need to consider the narrative on which they were based. No one could discover the story of the death of the Virgin from the text of the canonical Gospels, where it is not even mentioned. Instead the church relied on an apocryphal narrative attributed to St John the Evangelist, now generally referred to as the *Transitus* (the 'passing') and known in several forms and languages. The earliest version seems to have appeared at the end of the fifth century. In the course of the sixth these accounts circulated and made their impact on all Christian communities. The essential elements in the story are as follows.

The archangel Gabriel appeared to Mary when she was praying at the Sepulchre of Christ in Jerusalem and told her she was about to die. She went to Bethlehem, where she was staying with three virgins, and she prayed to Christ. She asked him to bring John to her and all the other apostles. John immediately arrived in a cloud from the city of Ephesus, and subsequently all the other apostles were similarly transported to her bedside. For protection both the Virgin and her visitors were miraculously transported to her own house in Jerusalem. On the morning of the day of her death, Jesus came to her and received her soul. Some of the apostles embraced her feet hoping to gain blessing from the contact. When the funeral procession was on its way to the tomb in the garden of Gethsemane the Jews attacked it; one of them, called Jephonias, grabbed the bier—but an angel cut off his hands and left them hanging in the air. This miracle of divine protection converted him to belief in Mary as the mother of God and his hands were restored to his arms. The body of Mary was placed in the tomb. After three days, Jesus returned and the angels took up her body to Paradise where it was reunited with her soul.

Not only was the narrative derived from the apocryphal writings circulating in the centuries after biblical times and produced in unknown circumstances without any historical authority, it was full of material which lent itself to theological controversy and differing interpretations. As a result, artists were faced with a difficulty: they had to take care that clear visual depictions were not taken as statements which were contrary to church teaching. It also means that we do not know exactly what individual Byzantines made of the stories. Church debate soon centred on whether the body of Mary could have been taken up to Heaven, and whether her death could therefore be described as a bodily 'Assumption'. This view was taken as the correct one in many discussions in the West, starting with the formulation of St Gregory of Tours (died 594). The Byzantine church was much more uncertain. For example, in an influential statement on the subject by the early seventh-century archbishop John of Thessaloniki, the author of Book 1 of the *Miracles of St Demetrios*, a very cautious view is taken. He records that Thessaloniki was one of the last cities to introduce the festival, and he offers a much shortened account of the story in which all the emphasis was on the universal motherhood of Mary. In contrast to his passionate interest in St Demetrios, John seems lukewarm towards developments in the cult of the Virgin.

But other Byzantine theologians who devoted sermons to the issue advocated the doctrine of the bodily Assumption. In the eighth century, Germanos, the patriarch dismissed by Leo III at the outset of Iconoclasm, produced the most extravagant arguments for her passing into Heaven and thereby becoming the effective intercessor of mankind, and protector of sinners against the wrath of God. Germanos described himself as 'slave' of Mary, as had a pope of Greek origin, John VII (705–7), on a mosaic in his chapel in St Peter's at Rome—in contrast, for example, to the emperor Justinian II who had been called 'slave of Christ' on his coins. After Germanos, the doctrine of bodily Assumption was supported by John of Damascus, by Tarasios (the uncle of Photios), and by Photios himself. A feature of the attitudes of both Tarasios and Photios is an emphasis on the Virgin not only as a tender mother, but also as an awe-inspiring woman in whom the divinity is somehow reflected—as she appears, of course, in the mosaic apse of St Sophia. The view of the church of Rome, when finally defined (in 1950), seems compatible with the view of Photios: 'a dogma revealed by God that the Immaculate Mother of God, Mary ever Virgin, when the course of her earthly life was finished, was taken up body and soul into the glory of Heaven'. This definition avoids the question of whether Mary died, or of when she was taken up to Heaven. The name given to the festival in the Byzantine church was the *Koimesis of the Virgin* (the 'Falling Asleep' of the Virgin, or the 'Dormition'), and most modern writers have kept to this term, rather than translating *Koimesis* as the Assumption, and so have avoided laying stress on possible differences between Byzantine and Catholic dogma.

Apart from the Gospels and Apocrypha, and the versions of their contents disseminated in sermons and other such texts, the citizen of Byzantium became familiar with the events of the Virgin's life (and death) through art. In the course of time, certain of the scenes which illustrated the events of her life became a standard part of the decoration of any church, some of them being frequently connected with a particular part of the architecture. So, for example, churches of the eleventh century and later generally had a Virgin composition in the apse, an Annunciation on the arch around the sanctuary, and the Koimesis on the western wall of the church. This site for the portrayal of the Koimesis, over the main door of the church, made it conspicuous to anyone as they turned to the west or left the nave. The general composition of the scene is very similar in all known examples, though the choice of figures and their position in the scene, as well as more subtle variations and emphases, allowed the artist to evoke different emotions or reactions to the story in the mind of the spectator.

Two well-preserved examples show how the story was translated into visual form, and as they are in churches located quite close to each other and dating from the same century, they can be directly compared. Both churches are on the island of Cyprus, and contain wallpaintings of the twelfth century (Figures 61–64). The earlier of the two is in the small church of the Virgin at Asinou (dated 1105/6), and here the Koimesis is painted on the western wall of the nave above the door (Figure 61). It bears the title 'Koimesis of the Theotokos' (Figure 62),

61 Out of the numerous surviving examples of the Koimesis of the Virgin, the two illustrated in Figures 61–4 are twelfth-century wallpaintings from nearby churches on the island of Cyprus. Comparing these two shows what variations were possible within the set conventions of Byzantine narrative art. This version, the earlier of the two, was painted in the western bay of the church of the Virgin at Asinou. The paintings on the piers and vaults are fourteenth-century, while those of the west wall date from 1105/6.

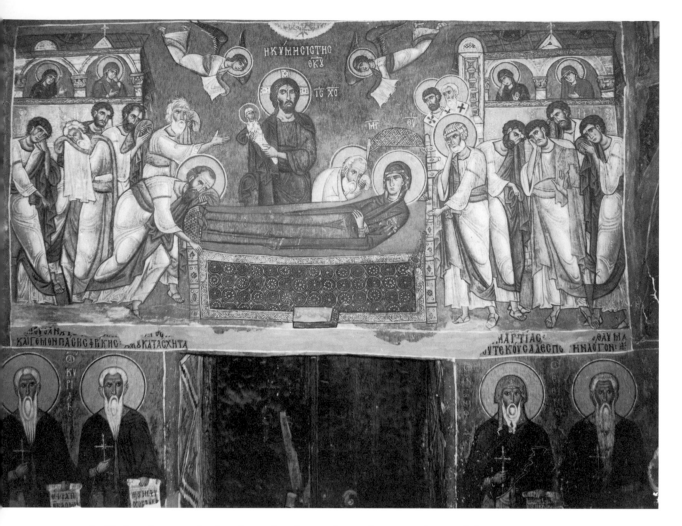

and all the elements in it relate closely to the written versions of the apocrypha. Christ ('Jesus Christos') appears in his human form at the centre of the composition, and takes up the soul of the Virgin wrapped in a funeral shroud (just the same kind of shroud was used for the wrapping of the body of the dead Lazarus in the miracle of his Raising which is portrayed on the wall beside the Koimesis). Christ holds the soul of the Virgin ready for the flying angels to take it to Heaven; they have their arms covered in preparation for receiving a sacred object. The Virgin ('Mother of God') lies on her bed with her arms crossed and her eyes closed (Figure 63).

All the rest of the figures belong to biblical times or the early history of the church. In the foreground of the picture are found the twelve apostles; none are named with an inscription but some conform to set portrait patterns with which they had come to be associated in Byzantine art (Figure 62). St Peter stands to the right of the bed, holding a censer, a sign, as the apocryphal texts point out, that a prayer is being said. Another apostle, white-haired and bearded, kneeling between

62 *The scene of the Koimesis was the largest composition at Asinou, and was prominently placed immediately over the western door of the nave (see Figure 61).*

63 This detail of the wallpainting at Asinou (see Figure 62) shows how the artist portrayed St John the Evangelist mourning the death of the Virgin. He was prominent in the scene, both because of his role in protecting her after the Crucifixion, and because he was the supposed author of the apocryphal text describing her elevation to Heaven.

Christ and the Virgin, is weeping into a handkerchief (Figure 63). He is probably to be identified as St John the Evangelist, as this is his common portrait type in Byzantine representations. His prominent position close to the Virgin is easily explained, as he was thought to be the author of the apocrypha which described the Koimesis, and he takes an important role in the story because of the biblical record that he took on the protection of the Virgin after the Crucifixion. The apostle at the foot of the bed is portrayed with the high forehead and features normal for St Paul (included among the twelve apostles in most Byzantine representations). The apostle standing beside Paul and depicted with dishevelled white hair is probably St Andrew, often shown with this feature in Byzantine art.

The two figures behind St Peter cannot be identified by reference to the apocryphal writings, but they are regularly added in the visual representations of the Koimesis. Their garments identify them as bishops—they wear the *omophorion*, decorated with crosses. Their presence can be explained by reference to theological writings. A text

173

of the late fifth or early sixth century by the mystical theologian Dionysios (the Pseudo-Areopagite), a figure also depicted in the miniatures of the Khludov Psalter (Figure 43), was interpreted by St John of Damascus in the eighth century to mean that four bishops were present at the time of the death of Mary. Three of the four were converts of Paul—Dionysios himself, present because of the belief that he was the first bishop of Athens; Timothy, first bishop of Ephesus; and Hierotheos, also a bishop of Athens. The other bishop of these four was James the brother of Jesus, the first bishop of Jerusalem. Only two are chosen for depiction here: perhaps the older figure with a long white beard is St James, and the other Dionysios. There are also four women inside the buildings (which are depicted symmetrically in the background on each side of the scene), three presumably the virgins with whom Mary was staying at Bethlehem; the fourth, unless added purely for aesthetic symmetry, might be Elizabeth, the mother of St John the Baptist, or Anne, the mother of Mary, both of whom, according to the apocrypha, were seen by the apostles on the third day after the funeral.

The same scene is painted in the later twelfth-century church of the Virgin tou Arakou at Lagoudera (Figure 64), a church in the Troödos mountains of Cyprus above Asinou (dated 1192). This time it is placed unusually on the south wall of the nave. The title is written on either side of the angel in the sky: 'Koimesis of the Most Holy Mother of God'. This is an oddly unbalanced composition compared with the calm and symmetry of the version of Asinou. Despite the regular form of the pointed lunette, Christ is pushed over to one side and is 'upstaged' by the kneeling apostle at the head of the Virgin, presumably St John. Christ holds the wrapped soul of Mary, and just one angel comes down from Heaven to collect it. The position of the Virgin's body is reversed from that in the composition at Asinou. St Peter stands at the head of the bed, holding a long staff—not a censer. On the other side is St Paul, and perhaps St Andrew. There are three quite prominent bishops also squeezed in, but no mourning women. The bishop in the centre is holding a chalice or a censer, and the others hold books.

The ways in which the figures and the background architecture are represented at Lagoudera are substantially different from Asinou. The figures are tall and thin, with sinuous folds and trailing draperies, while the buildings are not flat against the picture plane and are more obviously placed behind the figures to give a greater impression of space. Both scenes are illustrations of the same texts, but through their stylistic treatment create different effects. Death and mourning is portrayed at Asinou as a time of calm and decorum, and the raising of the soul of the Virgin to Heaven is carried out as part of a balanced ceremonial act. At Lagoudera all is agitation and disorder and the participants are cramped around the bier; it is as if Christ rushes in to snatch up the soul of the Virgin.

The comparison shows the ways in which Byzantine artists were able within a traditional art to manipulate the means of expression at their disposal. Some of the features which differentiate the two renderings might be put down to the individual styles of the artists or the influence of the fashions of their periods of production, but their great value for us is to show how Byzantine art could interpret texts. Both paintings condense the whole text of the apocrypha into one single image. Death and mourning are simultaneous with the celebration of the mystery of the Assumption of the Virgin to Heaven. The pictures combine in one place and time representatives of the whole community of saints in Heaven, and show the transfer of the soul from earth to Heaven.

It is not surprising that such a message should be placed so centrally in church decorations: its prominence elevates the apocryphal writings on to the same level of truth as the scriptures. This is just one way by which visual decoration of a church could work to confer authority on a dubious text. Such icons are far more than illustrations; the sermon of Photios documents how the Byzantines themselves could appreciate how pictures worked differently from the texts from which their subject matter was derived. The particular examples considered here date from the twelfth century and come from the region which is the environment of the holy man to be considered in the last chapter; but the general

principles which they illustrate are perennial through the whole period of Byzantium.

One feature, then, of the Byzantine church after Iconoclasm was the inclusion of a representation of the Koimesis in a prominent place, generally over the western door of the nave. This means that if we think of any Byzantine church as a unit of space, then the image of the Koimesis usually faces an image of the Virgin opposite in the main apse. Was this an intentional pattern in church decorations? The suggestion has been made that an opposition between the role of the Virgin at the birth of Christ and that of Christ at the death of the Virgin illuminated two sides of the same truth, the incarnation of Christ. The idea of setting the images opposite to each other in a church is therefore interpreted as something consciously imposed by theologians interested in the rhetorical devices of Antiquity, in this case in the device of antithesis; art, that is, was used to make juxtapositions and oppositions first formulated in the literature of sermons.

This suggestion assumes that learned theologians like Photios consciously organized the icons of a church on the same principles as their writings, or by directly imitating the ideas in texts. Such a narrow understanding of art in terms merely of literary sources is not supported by the consistent evidence which we have observed of the range of evocations which could be conveyed only through art, and of the clear signs that Byzantines themselves were aware of the complex ways in which the visual functioned in their society. From our viewpoint we can see that Byzantine art took on the role of helping Christianity to succeed in doing something which all religions needed to do: to give credibility to paradox. Visual representations of Christian history assisted in making the non-rational beliefs of the religion appear reasonable—the proposition, for example, that there could be life after death was by its depiction given concrete statement and the semblance of reason. The sermon of Photios studied earlier in this chapter exhibits his knowledge of the literary devices of the writers of Antiquity, but the several binary oppositions which he makes are due less to his artificial imitation of oratory than to the paradoxes embodied in the Christian message. To see antitheses between facing images on the walls of churches as simple reflections of Antique rhetoric is to underestimate the value of images in embodying the paradoxes of religion.

The scene of the Koimesis embodies paradoxes within its many elements. It must also have enhanced the role of the Virgin as an intercessor, because of the varying ways in which it could be interpreted. The scene illustrates the end of the life of a human being to whom immediate entrance to a heavenly paradise was granted. As the Virgin was in a mystical sense also described as the 'church' and therefore in a position of motherly grace towards all Christians, the picture offers the hope of life after death for all believers, and the perpetual presence in Heaven of someone to whom appeal could be made through prayer for personal intercession with God. This message was conveyed visually to any person who entered a church and looked at a majestic image of the Virgin in a focal position in the apse and then left the building below another image which guaranteed the presence of the Virgin in Heaven. Byzantines could hope for the help of the Virgin at the time of their own death.

This role of the Virgin as intercessor may be taken a stage further. The image of the Koimesis shows that at the 'rite of passage' of the death of the Virgin, Christ was present; the promise is implicit that the help of a saint may be expected at this rite of passage for any good Christian. It may be that the Virgin Mary herself was seen as a mainstay at other rites of passage and that this stimulated her cult and the conspicuous visual representation in icons of other events of her life: for example, the birth of the Virgin, the birth of Christ, and the marriage of the Virgin were images which showed to Christians that holy persons went through the same experiences as themselves, and could be relied on for help and sympathy by humans passing though the same circumstances.

The sermon given by Photios on the occasion of the inauguration of a new image of the Virgin and Child in the church of St Sophia at Constantinople was composed at a time of radical change in the allowable conventions of a society, and it points to the emergence of beliefs which were to fashion the future profile of the culture. From the middle of the ninth century after the collapse of Iconoclasm, the use of icons in the church and in the home was officially sanctioned; church and emperor agreed on the principles of how their religion should be outwardly seen. The importance of figural religious art was admitted and supported, and the further development of the visual sanctioned. The various aspects of the sermon, and some of the ways in which the cult of the Virgin expanded into various areas of thought, show the particular ambivalence of this period after a century in which traditional Christian art was banned. In order to justify the provocative new image in St Sophia, only commissioned twenty-five years after the end of Iconoclasm, Photios makes great play of its being a restoration and of the fact that the orthodox church must be on its guard against innovation. The statements of writers such as Photios about restoration, their expression of the aesthetic standards of Antiquity and their study of classical authors have so impressed some modern scholarship that the Byzantine revival after Iconoclasm has been characterized as a thorough kind of Renaissance of Antiquity.

In some sense this suggestion of a turning back to an earlier period has validity; but all the examples we have seen concern a return to the conventions or even decorations of the times immediately preceding Iconoclasm rather than to the more distant past. More strikingly, despite Photios' tactical affirmation of traditional conservatism, he is a considerable innovator and his acts encouraged the development of new patterns of religious convention. It was his decision that the church of St Sophia should for the first time be decorated with figurative mosaics, and this established future norms for the environment of churches. When pride of place was given to the representation of the Virgin, the cult received a massive new impetus. When in the late ninth century the emperor Leo VI was shown on his ceremonial sceptre being crowned by the

Virgin (Figure 57), this was evidence both of the public acceptance of new frameworks for the power of the Virgin and, more parochially, of the fact that this emperor was the personal student of Photios himself.

In the period before Iconoclasm, interest in the Virgin often appears to be primarily theological: as the human mother of God, how was she to be fitted into the proper definition of the nature of Christ? After Iconoclasm, as can be detected in the sermon of Photios, the emphasis was changing and less importance was attached to the majestic role of the Virgin as the vessel of the divine, and more to her motherhood and receptiveness to prayer. This shift in her role points to changes in the religious attitudes of Byzantine society and even in the functions of Christianity in day-to-day living. The years after the end of Iconoclasm were those of a stated revival of old conventions, but they show how in the new circumstances of stable empire an environment emerged which would have been scarcely recognizable to earlier generations. The explicit cult of the Virgin and its ubiquitous visualization is one of the most obvious signs of complex developments which affected all levels of society.

5

PARADISE SOUGHT:
THE IMPERIAL
USE OF ART

BYZANTINE emperors were as much locked into the conventions of behaviour as their subjects; they only differed from them in their ability to exploit these conventions. They could form and manipulate public opinion through all the means open to them. This chapter focuses on two emperors whose activities throw light on the effects of specifically imperial patronage of art and how that patronage might determine the perceptions of the emperor by his public. Emperors were in a position to decide and to promote their public image quite as much as any leader in the twentieth century. Their methods betray both the means at their disposal, and how effective these means might be in such a society, where the existence of the emperor was taken for granted but his character was open to redefinition with each new reign. Both the emperors selected for detailed consideration in this chapter undertook extensive building activities which changed the appearance and use of large areas of their capital, Constantinople: the first is Constantine IX Monomachos (1042–55), and the second is John II Comnenos (1118–43). Their patronage will be compared, but some allowances have to be made in pursuing the comparison, for in the case of Monomachos much of the material which he sponsored does survive, but not his own statements of his intentions, whereas in the case of Comnenos, the material is less well preserved, but his own written statement of intentions for his major work of patronage is available for us to study.

These particular emperors are chosen as well-documented cases which clarify the perceived place of the emperor in Byzantine society at two moments in time; both their particular personalities and the historical circumstances of their reigns do show a number of differences, but the nature of their control of the visual means at their disposal has much in common. Unlike the holder of the office of patriarch, such as Photios, the emperor in Byzantium had the freedom to use the resources of the state in any way: his rank and his access to both private wealth and the established imperial treasury meant that he had the power to choose whether to spend money on his private palace environment, and to enjoy the pleasures of royal amusements and possessions, or to use his funds on social welfare and the declaration of a Christian 'conscience'. Because of his own career, Photios understood more than any other patriarch the possibilities offered by both civil and ecclesiastical powers. As patriarch, and particularly as patriarch after a period of failed Iconoclasm, Photios needed somehow to find the money, materials and artists to carry out a redecoration of Byzantine churches according to a definition of 'restoration' which he needed to formulate and promote as the correct church policy. The use of art by Byzantine emperors, whether iconoclast or iconophile, had only the restraints of cost and of public acceptability, for the achievement of imperial power gave the pleasure and the pain of the responsibility for deciding the visual environment in which the emperor would be understood by his subjects.

The emperor was only the pinnacle of a complex power system and his position is only understandable in terms of the other elite groups in Byzantine society. It is necessarily difficult to investigate these groups, for the analysis of power is always a schematization of a complex 'reality' and so differs according to the particular theoretical perspective adopted. The Byzantines saw the workings of their society in one way, but their perceptions were not shared by the medieval West, and differ also from those of modern historians.

When Byzantine writers refer to the working of power in their society they speak of the 'rich' and the 'poor' or the 'powerful' and the 'weak' or other such dichotomies. Such language does not admit of a definition of the 'upper classes'; on the contrary it suggests that there was no obvious constitutional basis for the existence of such a group. What can be discovered from these sources is how at different periods membership of the aristocracy depended to a varying extent on the four main factors of birth, office, wealth and merit. The Western medieval view of Byzantium was distorted because the Crusaders and other visitors thought the absence of an obvious stable noble hierarchy meant there was no social hierarchy at all. They thought that power was entirely derived from wealth, and they did not therefore understand the opportunities for social mobility or the tensions between various groups.

The traditional Byzantine aristocracy can be divided into two groups: the civil nobility attached to the capital and the provincial military nobility with property holdings in the regions. Intermarriage did, of course, sometimes soften the edges of this division, but broadly speaking these two groups represented different avenues to power and different forms of responsibility. The image presented of these aristocratic groups in Byzantine literature is that of a relatively stable and relatively small range of families: in the eleventh and twelfth centuries some eighty-one civil noble families and sixty-four military ones have been identified. However the fact that different families emerged into prominence at different times might suggest greater mobility within the elite than is immediately apparent, and also perhaps the possibility of mobility into the aristocracy from groups outside.

The opportunities for advancement for members of the aristocratic families changed in different periods of Byzantine history, but not always in predictable ways. Under Basil II (976–1025), an emperor perpetually occupied in campaigns around the empire, it might be thought that the military aristocracy would advance more easily into positions of power. This was not apparently the case; perhaps surprisingly, it appears that military families were not favoured over civil families, who still gained the highest posts in the state. This was also the period when (perhaps because of the absence of the emperor from the city) a large number of new families gained prominence, and when military families increasingly took the option of marrying their daughters into the civil aristocracy.

A noticeable shift occurred in 1081, when Alexios I Comnenos (1081–1118), a member of a military family, seized control. What mattered now was to be related to a Comnenos. The Comneni monopolized the military system, and so the aristocracy which was not Comnenian was forced into civil careers. The effective aristocracy therefore became a close political family, much like royal families in Western kingdoms at the time. John II Comnenos (1118–1143), who will be studied later in this chapter, represents the time of the greatest power of this family.

Both the emperors considered in this chapter were born into aristocratic families, the first into a civil family, the second into a military one. One underlying question must therefore be whether these different origins can be related to different images of the emperor in the eyes of the public.

The architecture of the imperial palace served as one form in which the power of the emperor was expressed. Sometimes this could be of extreme importance, if the emperor chose rarely to emerge from his palace and that building came to symbolize, in its architectural forms, the grandeur and remoteness of its rarely-sighted occupant. Recent modern history provides clear examples of this effect, such as Queen Victoria in her later years, or even President Andropov of the Soviet Union who spent his last months inside the Moscow Kremlin, seen by the public only through photographic portraits which were no longer true to his appearance. Among Byzantine emperors, there are cases of the emperor retreating into the palace, though the requirement to attend services in the churches of the city, especially in St Sophia, meant that he was still to be seen on occasion in processions and ceremonial. In the sixth century Justinian in his later years, after the death of his wife Theodora, became something of a recluse inside the palace.

Justin II (565–78), the successor of Justinian, reacted to these years of imperial remoteness and sponsored new public buildings: among others, the new surroundings for the famous relics of the Virgin. Such works conveyed to the public an image of piety and concern, and they also supplied new places for prayer, worship and public rituals. Justin II also built a new palace for the patriarch on the south side of St Sophia. This enhanced the surroundings of the clergy of the church at a time

when the ceremonial of the liturgy also received additional elements.
But Justin II was an emperor who also devoted considerable funds to
his own surroundings. The palace buildings started by Constantine the
Great were already very extensive, and took up much of the acropolis
district of the Roman city, but Justin II was one among several emperors
who added even more amenities. One of his works was a new throne
room inside this 'sacred' palace, his so-called Chrysotriclinos: this
Golden Chamber was a building with a central dome, probably very
similar in appearance to a church (SS Sergios and Bacchos) erected by
Justinian. This new building gave the emperor a domed reception room
inside the palace, a room very richly ornamented in this and in later
periods.

The effect of imperial patronage of this kind was to enhance the
private majesty of the emperor in places where the public could never
enter; only the court, the privileged members of the administration and
of the church, and foreign ambassadors might see this environment.
The Islamic-style kiosks, displaying warbling mechanical birds on the
branches of a golden tree, and other inventions of this kind installed
in the palace by the iconoclastic emperor Theophilos, were only stories
for the Byzantine public. Even the image of the emperor as presented
to them was a filtered one; it derived from his public appearances and
representations; from the sight of the palace from outside and from
stories of its interior. Even when the emperor did show himself in public
he had his special place, like his box in the Hippodrome, or his own
part of the south gallery of St Sophia, or the special enclosure in the
right side of the nave.

Palaces are only one aspect of the construction of the image of the
emperor and this is a question that needs to be looked at more broadly.
The two emperors considered in this chapter come from the eleventh
and twelfth centuries, when the stability and military successes of the
period after Iconoclasm were coming to an end. At the close of the
eleventh century Byzantium found most of Asia Minor passing into
the hands of new Islamic invaders. In the twelfth century pressure from
Crusaders from the West was added to the threat from the Turks and
in 1204 the Crusaders finally managed to occupy Constantinople, if only
for half a century.

Constantine IX Monomachos became emperor as the third husband
of the empress Zoe. She was the daughter of the emperor Constantine
VIII and as a member of the Macedonian dynasty she was accepted as
his successor in 1028, aged fifty and unmarried. An unsuccessful attempt
had been made to marry her to the German emperor Otto III in 1002,
but she arrived in Italy for the wedding only to learn of his death.
Shortly after her succession in 1028 she was married for the first time
to a man who became the emperor Romanos III Argyros; and again
in 1034 to Michael IV. Finally, in 1042, when she was aged 64, she
married Constantine. Although a third marriage was against Orthodox
law (and Constantine too had already been married twice), the patriarch
showed his diplomacy by carrying out the ritual required of him but
avoiding laying his hands on the couple during the coronation in

St Sophia, and only embracing them after the marriage and act of crowning had been performed.

Constantine was emperor at a time when Byzantium had reached its greatest extent since Justinian as a result of the successful campaigns of Basil II (976–1025). The military victories of Basil II must still have dominated public attitudes to the emperor and his duties. Visually Basil had portrayed himself as the victorious Christian general who had received his crown and weapons from Heaven and could rely on the assistance of the saints in conquering his enemies (Figure 65). Constantine, however, made no attempt to emulate that kind of rule. He is portrayed as a man with little interest in the army and military campaigns, who preferred the hedonistic life of the capital. Indeed, although he did not live to see the collapse of Byzantine control over most of Asia Minor after defeat at the hands of the Turkish armies at the battle of Manzikert in 1071, some modern historians have blamed

65 *The frontispiece portrait of Basil II (976–1025) in his specially-commissioned psalter is one of the most effective images in Byzantine art of the emperor as the Christian ruler and soldier. The visual elements are explained in an accompanying poem: the emperor, crowned by Christ and armed by the archangels, is victorious over his enemies and fights with the assistance of saints. The company of military saints on whom he can rely are represented as icon images within the picture.*

him for the failure of the Byzantines on the battlefield on this occasion. Whatever the bias in this image, it is certain that his reign saw changing patterns of provincial administration, an adjustment to the territorial changes and apparent security after the reign of Basil II. The system whereby a military general acted as the governor of a provincial theme changed into one where a civilian judge or a praitor was appointed from Constantinople to act as governor, usually for a period of three years. The new system favoured the civil aristocracy over the military; that is, it favoured the group (of which Constantine Monomachos was himself one representative) which was on the ascendant in the middle of the eleventh century.

The reign of Constantine is traditionally written off by Byzantine historians. They suppose that a look at his portrait in St Sophia (Figure 66), and a reading of the descriptions of his reign by his contemporaries, is enough to dismiss him from serious history. Here is one such opinion:

Seldom are we presented with a more degrading spectacle than the governing triad of an emperor, his vacuous face forever on the grin, toying with his wife's niece, and two miserable old women, gloating over coffers of gold or boiling up messes in a cauldron. Efforts have been made to relieve this picture of some of its darker colours. Pretty books were written—it is said—and pretty poems, and pretty churches and chapels built and decorated. But it will not do. The contemporary testimony to the general folly and vice of Constantine's government is explicit and unanimous.

66 *This is the inscribed mosaic portrait of the emperor Constantine IX Monomachos in the east bay of the south gallery of St Sophia. Only the head is a representation of this emperor: gaps in the tesserae visible above the crown (below the cross) and across the neck are clues to the fact that this head is no more than an insertion in place of an earlier emperor's head on this particular body.*

This kind of history, however stylistically elegant and however well based on a knowledge of 'primary' sources, finds itself with few questions to ask. It assumes that participants in events control them, and that individual Byzantine emperors caused the conditions in which everyone inside their borders lived, and presumably those of some of the people outside. Such an approach often also carries with it a wish to reach moralizing assessments of each person involved in any policy or decision. The aims and methods of this study have been quite different. In exploring and attempting to understand the workings of Byzantine society there has been no occasion to pass moral judgements. Although the image of Constantine as presented in literature and art will now be looked at in detail, it is not appropriate to ask such questions as whether Constantine was a 'good guy' or a 'bad guy'.

The key primary source for the eleventh century in Constantinople is a book by a courtier, Michael Psellos (1018–96 or 97). This *Chronographia* is a racy and anecdotal series of biographies of great men (and their women) by an intellectual who advanced to his greatest period of power in the time of Constantine Monomachos. This history has been described as one of the few books of Byzantine culture that can be read for pleasure as literature, and maybe this assessment has led paradoxically to its neglect as a document for analysis. Not only is it a source for empirical information about the period, but equally it can provide an insight into the stereotypes and commonly held attitudes of Byzantine society. In particular it can show us what general perceptions of the position of the emperor were common in Byzantium—only from this basis can we investigate how new or different imperial images could be promoted.

What did Psellos expect to see in an emperor? He hints that Constantine had various qualifications suiting him for high office, but only one emerges strongly—his birth. His last name, Monomachos, was recognizable to a Byzantine as the name of an old-established aristocratic family, and Psellos says that he was its last male member. But the account of Constantine mainly records objections to his style of ruling, which did not fit in with the ideas of kingship in which Psellos had come to believe. He says bluntly that Constantine had no clear conception of the nature of monarchy and did not realize that this entailed responsibility for the well-being of his subjects and a perpetual watch over the sound administration of the state. Instead of devoting his energies to these concerns, Constantine delegated to others, and imagined that with his new and increased wealth he could retire into a social life of pleasure and luxury.

Psellos describes his own intellectual pedigree as an integration of Plato with Christian philosophy. This no doubt formed his conception of the ideal ruler. It was not an intellectual biography shared by the emperor, who was more pragmatic and perhaps more conventional than Psellos. One story related by Psellos, but no doubt reflecting the kind of court gossip that reached the ears of the public, seems almost to mock at his crude fatalism. Constantine, it is said, was in the habit of sleeping in the palace without a guard outside the door. His simple justification for this disregard for his own safety was that he occupied the throne by the grace of God and therefore already had the perfect guard, and did not need inferior human protection. A similar fatalism is presented in the stories of Constantine's interest in prophecies and auguries about his reign: the emperor enjoyed recalling extraordinary visions and dreams (his own or those of soothsayers). Psellos properly denies that Constantine had any powers of prophecy and gives the official church view—that the outcome of events must be ascribed to the will of God and cannot be discovered from divination.

Through the criticisms which Psellos makes of the behaviour of Constantine Monomachos as an emperor, we discover the court view of the monarch, and certain hints of his public image. Psellos disapproved of Constantine's enjoyment of his position, one conferred on him by God and therefore of great responsibility, and portrays his reign as a time of the abuse of power. Constantine spent the contents of the imperial treasury and handed out state honours indiscriminately. Constantine is characterized as a man who, after suffering years of exile on the island of Lesbos under the previous emperor, believed he deserved the consolation of a hedonistic life of luxury in the palace. Psellos is eloquent in his stories of the twelve years of Constantine's reign: his open parading of a mistress in the palace (she had been his companion during his exile before he became emperor, and was only not married to him because of the canon law prohibition of a third wife—only emperors and empresses could hope to challenge the church on this convention); his later affair with another young girl (a foreign princess and hostage) and general sexual indulgence; his irresponsible wasting of money on whims when building the church of St George at the Mangana, and the building of a swimming pool and pavilion for his own pleasure.

Yet the interpretation of these actions given by Psellos is not the only one, and a different picture can be drawn out of the material. Even Psellos allows that in his public life Constantine was on occasion to be complimented. There was the time when, despite an illness which caused him great pain and discomfort, Constantine insisted that it was his unavoidable duty to attend public processions. So he was carefully lifted on to his horse and kept in position on the saddle by attendants on each side; he even managed to keep on his face an expression of pleasure, despite his suffering, and to change his position on horseback to meet his public (despite some actual physical paralysis). Such an account as this suggests that, contrary to the picture that Psellos tries to convey, this emperor had strong feelings of responsibility and believed it essential to foster his public image as a benevolent monarch.

It is only by a consideration of the artistic patronage of this emperor that sufficient evidence can be found to make sense of his reign in social terms. Only from this evidence is it possible to discover and to appreciate how the public through the whole extent of his empire perceived the emperor. His interest in the arts is of far greater significance than the mere production of an affluent environment.

Constantine's budget for art was enormous. In Constantinople he made extensive improvements in the palace, but his major commission was a monastery which immediately became one of the most famous in the city; this was the monastery of St George of the Mangana (or Arsenal). This was not merely a church and a surrounding residence for monks, but was in all a palace, hospital, monastery and church. It served as Constantine's mausoleum when he died in 1055. If its ruins have been correctly identified in the city today, the church was spacious, and had a dome 33 feet in diameter. All the literary records emphasize how lavish the emperor was in donating decoration and relics to the monastery. His interest can hardly be ascribed, as Psellos believed, to the fact that his mistress lived in this part of the city, and building a monastery was the best excuse for frequent visits to her.

Another of Constantine's deeds was an enormous donation to St Sophia, some time before 1050 when his wife died. This was not, as it happens, the first donation to that church to be given by a husband of Zoe. She and her first husband, Romanos III Argyros, had together given a substantial sum to the church, together with a supplementary annual income paid out of the imperial treasury. This donation was partly used to pay for the gilding of the capitals in the building. This previous donation of Zoe and her first husband had been com-

67 This photograph shows the present condition of the panel in St Sophia in which Constantine Monomachos, his wife the empress Zoe, and Christ were represented (between 1042 and 1050). The panel marked an act of imperial generosity to the church, stated obviously here by the inclusion of the purse of money in the hands of the emperor and the legal document held by the empress; the regal figure of Christ accepts their offering. Through this image the record of a particular act is translated into an affirmation of imperial virtue and status.

68 *The indications are that the portrait head of Zoe on the panel in St Sophia belongs to the same date as the head of Constantine Monomachos shown in Figure 66 (as does the head of Christ), but that there was an earlier version of the panel predating Constantine's accession. This was a similar commemoration of a donation to the church, but the figures involved were Zoe and her first husband on each side of Christ. As the elder daughter of an emperor without male heirs, Zoe was regarded on his death as his successor and so could bestow imperial rank on her wedded husband. By the time of this portrait she was in her late sixties and with her third husband.*

memorated with a mosaic in the south gallery of St Sophia. The new donation of Constantine and Zoe was to enable the clergy to celebrate a daily liturgy—apparently their celebration was previously limited to the great festivals and Saturdays and Sundays. Presumably the money was used for salaries to increase the number of celebrating clergy and for the purchase of any necessary new liturgical accessories.

Constantine no doubt wished to overshadow the earlier sum given by Romanos. Psellos certainly picked up this competitive aspect when, as a court orator giving an official speech of praise to Constantine, he said: 'All previous imperial donations faded as soon as Monomachos made just one donation of his own.' But a visual device also proclaimed that the earlier donation had been overshadowed. The earlier commemorative mosaic in the south gallery which showed emperor and

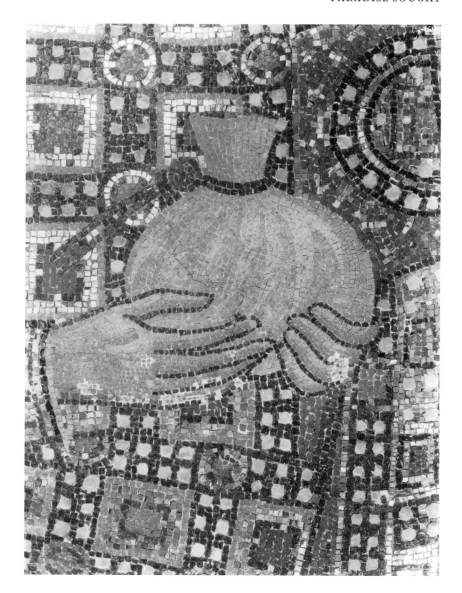

69 The Christian generosity of the imperial couple was conveyed visually on the panel in St Sophia by the most obvious symbol—a full purse.

empress in the presence of Christ (Figures 66–69) was altered. The face and name of Constantine replaced that of Romanos, and the face of Zoe was at the same time remade beside that of her new husband. The changed panel not only recorded in public the imperial couple's magnificent donation to the church, but also annulled the record of the previous donation and of Zoe's previous marriage. But the depiction of the body of Zoe's first husband, and the bag of money in his hand was retained (Figure 69). This consistent element in the mosaic makes imperial generosity to the church on both occasions quite explicit; it highlights the church's dependence on the financial support of the emperor. Compared with the sermon of Photios in 867, we have entered a century when the emperor showed less interest in definitions of faith and more in the outward ceremonial.

189

LEFT 70 *The Nea Moni (New Monastery) on the island of Chios was only one of several communities to which Constantine Monomachos gave donations, but it is one of the few that have survived (despite earthquake damage) to the present day. Direct imperial sponsorship meant in this case that it was built and then decorated with mosaics by commissioned workers from Constantinople. The domed church at the centre of the community was surrounded by the usual necessary outbuildings, for example cells and a refectory; the complex was protected by a high wall. This follows the same pattern as the monasteries of Sinai and Mar Saba and was the standard layout—with variations depending on the site—throughout the Byzantine period. This sketch by Barskij shows the appearance of the monastery in 1732.*

The public face of the Christian emperor as philanthropist was even more firmly emphasized in Constantine's many other grants of aid outside the capital. There was virtually no part of the empire or the neighbouring states which did not see evidence of his universal patronage. He gave funds to the church of the Holy Sepulchre in Jerusalem for a major rebuilding which had been made necessary as a result of the arson of the Islamic ruler, Caliph al-Hakim, in 1009 (the dome of this period is visible in Figure 4); he gave money to the city of Euchaita in Asia Minor (near Amaseia in the Pontus) and to the cult centre of the military saint Theodore the General which it housed, commemorating this generosity with an image of himself; and he gave money to the monastery of Nea Moni on the island of Chios so that he became in its legends the official founder, despite the fact that it was apparently founded in the reign of Zoe and her sister Theodora (April to June 1042), just before he came to the throne. He was regarded as its greatest benefactor, and indeed the buildings and mosaics belonging to his patronage still survive in the monastery, which itself is still in use, but now as a convent (Figure 70).

Another aspect of his patronage is found in a manuscript which contains a representation of Constantine together with Zoe and Theodora; this is a book of the *45 Sermons of St John Chrysostomos* (now in the library in the monastery of St Catherine on Sinai; see Figure 71). Written in the border of the page is a special prayer addressed to the Saviour, asking that 'the one Pantocrator of the Trinity may protect the shining trinity of earthly sovereigns'. The desire to be connected with this book, containing some of the sermons most commended for their theology

RIGHT 71 *Constantine Monomachos ascended to the throne through his marriage with Zoe; but she was not the only surviving member of the Macedonian dynasty—she had a younger sister, Theodora, who also lived in the palace. This manuscript miniature implies, in an interpretation unique to this reign, that Byzantium had now acquired three crowned rulers of equal status. The idea is communicated visually, but is also stated verbally.*

by the church, and the reference to the reigning dynasty as a trinity, is evidence of Constantine's desire to protect and legitimate his own rule by reference to theology—both in written and in visual form.

Constantine used art in his contacts and diplomacy with rulers outside the empire. He was in touch with the Hungarian court, as is shown by the set of enamel plaques which seem to have been part of a crown sent to Hungary from Constantinople on which Constantine, Zoe and her sister Theodora are represented as well as dancing maidens with haloes (Figure 72). It is hard to tell if the figures convey the idea of imperial power and luxury, or communicate some more religious message; perhaps King David among the women of Israel who danced in front of him. It is likely that Constantine extended patronage to the Russian court as well; he seems to have been involved in the decoration of the church of St Sophia at Kiev with mosaics and wall paintings. No doubt such generosity consolidated his friendship with the Russian court after a period of hostilities.

Constantine also looked towards the West. He sent money to the mother house of the Benedictine order, Monte Cassino in South Italy. He donated a regular annual subsidy of gold to the monastery, starting in the year 1054. Ironically this was the year when the patriarch of Constantinople, Michael Cerularios, provoked a violent and lasting schism

72 The artistic patronage of Constantine Monomachos ranged geographically over the whole area of the Byzantine world, and over the various available media. This enamel crown, probably sent to Hungary during his reign, was made up of a series of enamelled plaques. It represents the Byzantine ruling family, but the impression is of entertainment and revelry, more like descriptions of the Islamic court than those of Byzantium. Such visual ambivalence was open to the Byzantine artist and here the reference might be in part biblical (for example to the reign of King David and its celebration).

between the Orthodox church and the Catholic church; the emperor appears more sensitive than this patriarch who was attempting to assert the independence of the church from the emperor.

The sum total of the artistic patronage of the reign of Constantine was enormous, and must have been of great importance in making the emperor and his wife known throughout the Mediterranean world. How would public perceptions have been affected by these visual representations? Most obviously a public image of the 'piety' of the emperor was being built up. In St Sophia, in a new large monastery in Constantinople, in the Holy Sepulchre, in a new monastery on an Aegean island, in cult centres in Asia Minor and in new foundations in the Russian lands and in Italy, a majority of the Mediterranean community were able to see the visual proof of the philanthropy and the piety of the imperial family; and, where inscriptions accompanied the visual images, there too the role of the emperor as devout Christian was emphasized. This public perception went beyond appreciation of the emperor's Christian devotion, and gratitude for imperial munificence. Icons were witnesses of the imperial support for the church, but at the same time made the point that the church needed imperial sponsorship for major enterprises. Because the emperor's portrait could be set up where he wished in a church, the imperial image was thereby surrounded with all the associations of a holy place; his image could be put where ordinary people could not go, and it put him in a relationship both physically and symbolically closer to God than the ordinary citizen. This both confirmed his special status on earth and made a promise of his future station in Heaven after death. The use of coins in earlier periods for demonstrating the relationship between God and the emperor has already been mentioned. By the eleventh century such a statement was not only standard on the coin issues, but was also made on a monumental scale in the churches of the Mediterranean world.

The piety of the ruler which is emphasized by all these donations, and by any accompanying inscriptions, is no empty slogan within the patterns of belief of the time. The purpose of the Mangana church was to give a place of repose for the body of Constantine after his death, and the reward which he was promised by religion for imperial piety and virtue was instant entry to Heaven after death, and remission from punishment for human sins. The range of his patronage over all sorts of establishments—from the central church of the empire and the holiest site of Christendom, the Holy Sepulchre in Jerusalem, to remote monasteries within the Orthodox community and outside it in a Western monastery—makes it appear that the emperor was trying to guarantee his future salvation at all costs. Although piety was a duty of the good Christian ruler, it had clear practical benefits.

Constantine Monomachos comes through the biography of Psellos as a man with an understanding of the need to put on a good public face; he conformed to the expectations of society by his assiduous attendance at public ceremonies. The visual image of the emperor is also that of a Christian emperor dedicated to duty. Of course, in his anecdotes Psellos reads the emperor's actions in terms of personal commitment, almost to the extent of superstition, but the underlying patterns can be found through a consideration of the forms that his patronage took.

One enigma in the interpretation of the reign is the role of the empress Zoe. She is prominent in the stories of Psellos, and appears on the icons with Constantine—in the mosaic icons of St Sophia she stands beside her new consort, hardly looking like a woman of 64 years or more (Figure 68). Psellos describes her as even more committed to religion than Constantine: 'there was no moment when the name of God was not on her lips'. A case might be made that Zoe personally was responsible for the reproduction in several media (from coins to mosaics) of a particular image of Christ called 'Antiphonetes' (literally 'Responder'), for she owned her own small image of this type. It answered her questions by changing its colour, and she thought it could be used to divine the future. When it turned pale, she expected disaster; when it took on a fiery red colour, she believed this to be a good omen. Zoe not only clasped the icon in her arms at times of distress and spoke to it, she also built a church of Christ Antiphonetes in which she was buried. Yet despite the record of such stories about Zoe, we cannot determine a particular role for her or for women in general in the way that visual images were constructed. Once Zoe was married to an emperor, her importance in conferring legitimacy could be forgotten. Whatever the court knew about the life of the empress in the palace was of little relevance in the promotion of the public image of the emperor. It was through visual means that an instant and conventional portrait of the emperor could be conveyed to the public; the stories that later filtered through from the palace were insubstantial compared with the firm and traditional statements of the art.

★ ★ ★ ★

John II Comnenos (Figure 73) was emperor a century later than Constantine Monomachos, and his career and personality have been treated by modern historians as of quite a different order from those of Constantine. He came, it is true, from a different family background: from the military aristocracy and from a family established by his father Alexios I Comnenos as a new ruling dynasty. He spent much of his reign on active campaign. His empire was diminished in size from that of the previous century through the loss of much of Asia Minor, but he was able to consolidate the European territories that were left, despite the threats of the Crusaders. The verdict of moralizing historians on John II Comnenos both in his own time and later is universally favourable; they see him as a person of commendable virtue and seriousness. A writer of the second half of the twelfth century, Nicetas Choniates, wrote in these terms:

He was a man who governed the empire excellently and who lived a pious life. In morals he was not lax and licentious. He was generous in his donations and contributions, as his distributions to the citizens show, and as do the beautiful and great churches which he founded.

73   This portrait of John II
Comnenos (detail from
Figure 75) was in the gallery
of St Sophia as a pendant to
the panel of Constantine
Monomachos and Zoe
(Figure 67). See caption to
Figure 75.

By John's reign, many circumstances of the empire had changed: apart
from the presence of Turks in Asia Minor (since 1071) and the Crusaders
(since 1096 when Westerners on the First Crusade reached Constantinople), changes had occurred in the internal workings of empire.
Monastic institutions had grown in wealth as they, rather than the established church, received endowments; inside the monasteries new
ceremonial and rites were in the course of development, which led,
among other things, to the additional use of icons around the sanctuary.
In the secular sphere, access to power had increasingly come to lie in
the gift of the Comnenian family; nepotism was a feature of the time.

Yet approaching John through his artistic patronage reveals surprising similarities with Constantine Monomachos, as the following comparison of their methods and aims will show.

Two visual examples of the way that John II Comnenos was presented
to a Byzantine audience offer the chance of direct comparisons with

Constantine. One is in an illuminated manuscript of the Four Gospels which has a dedication miniature which portrays the emperor and his eldest son and heir, Alexios, who was co-emperor (Figure 74). The emperor and co-emperor are shown with full titles and in full regalia

74 This imperial image, from a manuscript of the Four Gospels, communicates a number of perceptions of the reign of John II Comnenos: the Christian loyalty of the emperor, the legitimacy of his crowned son and heir, and the declaration of Mercy and Justice as the signs of this reign.

RIGHT 75 The mosaic panel of John II Comnenos and his family in St Sophia is most obviously claiming generosity on a scale equal to that of the earlier reign of Constantine Monomachos, whose donations were presumably by now legendary (compare Figure 67). Some elements of the panel, such as the choice of the Virgin and Child, instead of that of the enthroned Christ, would have been conspicuous to the Byzantine viewer; their interpretation had to be made from a reading of the visual signs, as there was no explanatory inscription.

OVERLEAF 76 Various parts of the original buildings of the Pantocrator monastery in Constantinople have survived, and its three churches have been partially restored; but the buildings are still in use as a mosque, and have not yet been fully investigated archaeologically. The monastery stands in an undeveloped part of the city of Istanbul.

with Christ, the source of their power, crowning them. The qualities with which John wished to be associated are conveyed through two personifications, the crowned women who lean towards Christ. These represent the virtues Mercy and Justice. This is an image of the just ruler; such is the claim of the emperor.

The second image is a mosaic panel in the gallery of St Sophia (Figures 73, 75) which from its position must be seen as a pendant to the Constantine and Zoe panel (Figure 67). It too records a donation of the emperor to the church, although the precise occasion has not been discovered. Since the panel represents John with the empress Eirene, who died in 1134, and their son Alexios who was crowned co-emperor in 1122, the representation belongs between those two dates.

The two panels of Constantine and John are similar in many respects: both show an emperor holding a purse of money and so pointing to his generosity, and his wife holding the signed and sealed legal document which confirmed the donation. Byzantine spectators, seeing the mosaics side by side in the church, would have recognized a similarity of purpose and of the methods used to achieve it. But there are differences between them. In the later panel there is an additional figure to the right; by including their son in the group the Comnenians were able to declare that, unlike Constantine Monomachos, they had a dynastic successor to the throne (though in the event Alexios died before his father). Another difference lies in the depicted recipient of the donation: in the earlier panel the donation is made directly to Christ, whereas in the

later the figures of the Virgin and Child are the recipients. The difference would obviously have been noted by the Byzantine spectator, but it cannot be certain how much they would have made of the change. It is at least tempting to suggest that it marked the idea that the Virgin had taken on an even greater role in the legitimation of the imperial power.

One surviving monument in Constantinople and the document which records the circumstances of its foundation provide the best means of penetrating to the patronage of John II Comnenos, and gaining a context for comparing it with that of Constantine Monomachos. The monument is the monastery of Christ Pantocrator (Figures 76, 77) and the document is its charter of foundation or *Typikon*. John built this new and very extensive foundation, together with his wife, and it was the major project of the reign.

Even in its modern condition, partly restored and archaeologically investigated, and partly clumsily adapted for use as a mosque, the monastery of the Pantocrator on the top of a hill over the Golden Horn

77 *The Pantocrator monastery was the largest new monastery built in Constantinople in the twelfth century. This record of the state of the foundation in the nineteenth century points to the contrast between the massive brick masonry and domes of the churches and the surrounding wooden houses of the ordinary people, which must have been a common feature of the medieval urban environment; such an opposition may have suggested the security of the church in contrast with the ephemeral nature of private housing.*

78 Of the three adjacent churches of the Pantocrator monastery, the one designated as the main site for the regular monastic ritual was the south church; its dedication was to Christ Pantocrator, the Ruler of All, and it was the most lavishly embellished. Today the most conspicuous surviving decoration in the building is its intricate marble pavement. Its icons and mosaics have now disappeared, and the original columns have been replaced during its use as a mosque. Some of the currently visible fittings are also Turkish, for instance the mimbar built on the right of the apse.

remains impressive. Three large churches, side by side, and some of the outbuildings of the monastery of John, are still to be seen; and there are the vestiges of their original luxurious decoration of mosaics, wall-paintings, marble floors (Figure 78), sculptured fittings (Figure 79), and even stained glass. The founder was able to lavish on the work all the imperial resources of the first half of the twelfth century. It was, therefore, the direct equivalent of the Mangana monastery of Constantine Monomachos. Like the Mangana, the Pantocrator monastery had an impressive church nucleus, an imperial mausoleum (for the new dynasty) and an attached hospital. It therefore provides an ideal focus for a historical comparison of imperial thinking and planning.

It is our knowledge of the original *Typikon* (or 'Charter') which makes it possible to consider the exact nature of the Pantocrator monastery. This *Typikon* is couched in legal and technical language, not always easy to understand, but the choice of contents is an indication of the preoccupations of the emperor. The original document itself survived until 1936, when it was burnt in a fire in the Greek monastery

79 *The Turkish fittings in the Pantocrator monastery are in great part constructed out of re-used sections of the Byzantine sanctuary sculpture; for example, the twelfth-century marble columns of the original sanctuary screen can be identified. The panels with stylized plants used in the mimbar were themselves already being re-used in the Byzantine period, for they are sixth-century pieces, originally in the nearby church of St Polyeuctos which had collapsed by the twelfth century and which was then ransacked for building materials. Several pieces of the sculpture of St Polyeuctos were taken by the Crusaders to Venice in the thirteenth century; the Venetians occupied the monastery of the Pantocrator between 1204 and 1261, and various pieces now in the Treasury of San Marco probably derive from the Pantocrator.*

of the Megaspileon; it had been found there in 1902 but was never fully transcribed. Fortunately, three copies of it were made in the eighteenth century and a modern edition has been constructed from these. A monastic *Typikon* was a legal document intended to ensure the stability of the foundation named in it and the continued acceptance of the wishes of the founder. Like all legal documents it incorporates a structure and a number of clauses adapted from its predecessors. Since this *Typikon* contains rules and instructions for the arrangement of the monastery, down to the most detailed consideration of hygiene and the activities of the community throughout day and night on every day of the year, it provides an insight into the social and religious background of the patronage of art and architecture in Byzantium.

The *Typikon* was signed by John Comnenos in October 1136 as 'Pious Emperor in Christ the God, born in the purple and Ruler of the Romans'. The dedication of Pantocrator for the monastery and its main church means that its divine patron was Christ, worshipped as 'Ruler of All'; a second church was dedicated to the Virgin Mary, and a third, the mausoleum, to the Archangel Michael, traditionally thought to be the angel present at death.

The opening sentences of the text had been lost from the original parchment manuscript even before the copies were made and the text now begins abruptly with the opening statement by the founder. This introduction is a thanksgiving to God for keeping John safe during life. In it he records his deliverance from conspiracies and from his enemies. He gives the names of the foreign adversaries over whom he has been victorious, but, as was conventional in court literary language, they appear in the vocabulary of classical antiquity: Persians, Scythians, Dalmatians, Dacians and Paeonians. They probably represent the Islamic armies of Asia Minor, the Petchenegs, Serbs, Hungarians and Bulgarians. John says that in gratitude for favours received from God, he has, together with his (now deceased) wife, constructed a church dedicated to the all-powerful Wisdom of God with representations of Christ in front of the church and in the sanctuary. The ways of God and providence are mysterious, but he makes his offering of a community of 'Nazirites' who will pray on his behalf for the forgiveness of his sins. These monks will be supported by a full complement of priests and the staff needed to man the church for services. Furthermore he has endowed a second church dedicated to the Virgin. As an additional way of gaining forgiveness of his sins, through the witness of 'ambassadors' of his philanthropy, he has made arrangements for the care of the old, the infirm and the poor in the monastery, and also for a hospital for lepers and the wounded, and for food and clothing for those in need. To ensure the success of the monastery and its establishment, he has drawn up rules and regulations; from these we find that the community is to contain eighty monks, fifty clerics, a hospital of fifty beds, a hostel for twenty-four invalids and a special ward for lepers.

The regulations are detailed and precise, and some must be standard for the time. They reveal clearly the mentality of the Byzantines and the fruits of the application of the bureaucratic mind to the institutions of religion.

The organization of the daily monastic office is set down first, then the details of how incense is to be used in the church and the prayers to be chanted during the censing. Priests and monks are told where they should stand in the church, these places being decided according to rank. Their conduct during services is also carefully prescribed. Other instructions about ceremonial are given, including the placing of lamps and candles. The instructions about lighting are divided into two sections in order to separate the arrangements made for normal services from those for special festivals (when there were also special donations to be dispensed).

Such detail in the description of arrangements has the advantage that it also gives us information about the now lost decoration. The church of the Pantocrator was the south church of the complex and was originally decorated with mosaics and portable icons (Figures 78, 79). The visitor to the church in its present condition needs an effort of imagination to recreate its original appearance at the moment of its completion in 1136. Time and its conversion into a Turkish mosque have robbed the church of its original columns and much of its decoration; all that can now be seen is the intricate marble floor and some of its sculpture. Originally it also had figured stained-glass windows (a few fragments were found during conservation work), and possibly even enamel icons on its sanctuary screen—according to fifteenth-century Byzantine clergy, this was the source of enamels in the Pala d'Oro on the high altar of the church of San Marco in Venice. Text and archaeology put together show us that the visual environment of this twelfth-century imperial commission had all the luxury and artistic multiplicity which one connects with an Italian church of the High Renaissance.

Few sections are more extraordinary to the modern reader of the *Typikon* than its thorough instructions on the daily handling of the bread to be distributed during the liturgy. The instructions concern not only the weight and quality of the bread but how it is to be divided. The reason for the complicated instructions is that in the Orthodox rite at the time a part of the eucharist bread was used for consecration, and the rest was blessed and distributed to the congregation. Already in the ninth century it was customary for the priest at the eucharist to pierce the bread with a liturgical spear to symbolize the passion of Christ. By the time of the foundation of the Pantocrator in the twelfth century the procedure was altogether more complicated, as was also the symbolic interpretation that went with it. To understand the terms in the *Typikon*, the practice of the twelfth century needs to be appreciated. The celebrant priest would first remove a small portion from the main loaf and this piece alone, called the lamb, was consecrated. He also had a number of other loaves with which to commemorate the Virgin, the saints, the living and the dead, for whose memorial small particles were cut out from each loaf and placed on the paten alongside the 'lamb'. The number of allowable additional loaves was fixed at five in the fourteenth century. The *Typikon* lays down that the daily allowance of flour should be used to bake bread as follows: two large loaves for the commemoration of Christ and the Virgin and five additional loaves, one for the saint commemorated on that day and the four others to commemorate the memory of the founder's father, grandmother, mother and wife. For every Saturday the instructions involved the use of far more loaves, since twenty-four people were to be commemorated. On a few Saturdays this list is increased still further with the addition of eight more names. A final but major instruction concerns further commemorations to be added to the daily eucharist after the deaths of the founder and his children: bread must thereafter be offered daily on behalf of himself and his four sons and three daughters. The text lays down such commemorations as part of the eucharistic celebration, and to be included in the prayers of the liturgy; it also adds a number of details about the arrangements of the tombs.

This section of the *Typikon* was of essential importance to the founder: it aimed to ensure the continuation of prayers on his behalf after his death, when his body would lie in the sarcophagus placed in the church next to that of the Pantocrator, and his soul would be judged. He wanted the benefit of a symbolic place during the liturgy next to the body of Christ.

The *Typikon* is not only concerned about the organization of all the services; the monks who maintained the church had to be disciplined in all aspects of their life. They must after all be suitable to serve both the heavenly and the earthly king.

A series of rules was laid down to ensure that the monks ate communally in the refectory. Again the instructions are detailed and comprehensive, beginning with the particular psalms to be chanted as, in order of rank, they entered for their two daily meals. The etiquette to be followed at these meals is meticulously specified. The various prayers and the grace are laid down and the monks are told, for example, when to be silent (during the reading of a lesson) and when to eat (after the abbot begins).

A long section is devoted to the arrangements for food on different days and at the different seasons of the church year. The focus is on what, when and how much; on which days, for example, they would be served fish, and on which days cheese and eggs. The allowable diet during fasts was, of course, given very special attention, but predictably Lent received even more. On weekdays during Lent only one meal a day was allowed, and the portions of bread and wine had to be smaller than usual.

All other aspects of life are covered, including baths—normally two a month, but absolutely none during the whole of Lent. However, even during Lent, one eventuality is allowed for: a monk may take a bath if illness makes this essential. A prohibition normal for monasteries is also applied in the Pantocrator: no women may enter it, however distinguished, virtuous or aristocratic. If it is necessary for a woman to attend the service of burial of one of her family, she must not enter the monastery through the gate, but she is to be allowed into the church of the Virgin Eleousa (the north church of the three in the complex; see Figure 80). Probably the side doors of this church had direct access to the street, and this arrangement would certainly keep women out of the view of the monks.

The number of monks was specified as not less than eighty: fifty should be entirely concerned with carrying out the divine office in the church while the others, clearly of second rank, carried out all the domestic duties of the house (which included such chores as washing the other monks in their baths). The 'church' monks must show all the serious qualities expected of the monastic life. They must live entirely as a community, even to the extent of making their confession to the abbot in public. No member of the laity could live in the monastery, and no monk could spend the night outside it. The enclosed community of monks is to be its own paradise. In this monastery the monks were supplied with clothes (in others it was common to allow the purchase of clothes as needed). Annually at Easter each monk was to be given a cotton mantle (the cotton had to weigh four pounds) and two pairs of shoes. Every two years he got a new black habit and a shirt. But no one received his new outfit without showing his old clothes to the abbot for inspection.

The question of the selection of a new abbot brought out the full legal ingenuity of the founder and any advisers he had for the drafting of the *Typikon*. A method for eliminating argument was contrived and

a special procedure invented (for, as the document notes, the selection
of a new abbot was a notorious source of trouble in monastic communities). The incumbent abbot was required to write down a secret list
of three candidates. When he died the list was to be read out at a meeting,
and if one of the candidates was unanimously acceptable to those

80 The north church of the Pantocrator monastery was dedicated to the Virgin Mary as the 'Eleousa'. In its present state it has lost the original high windows of the apse, its sanctuary screen, its original columns, and, perhaps most conspicuously of all, its figural decoration in mosaic. Its stark whitewashed interior is a legacy of its use as a Turkish mosque; nothing could be further from the way in which a Byzantine monastery was embellished in the period after the failure of Iconoclasm.

present, he was declared elected. If there was no such agreement, the name of each candidate was to be written down on a separate sheet and these sheets were to be placed on the altar by one of the monks who could not read. After three days of prayer, a different monk, another one who was illiterate, was to choose one of the names and display it for all to see. This name would be reckoned to be the candidate chosen by God. As if all this forethought were not enough, the *Typikon* allows for another contingency. If an obvious candidate in the community is not on the previous abbot's list, a special appeal could be made through the court to the emperor (*if* the majority of monks agreed).

In the ceremony of recognition of the new abbot, in which he was given his staff of office, the icon of the Pantocrator took a central part; it was seen to be the agency through which Christ granted the position of abbot, and the abbot is reminded that he will give account of his conduct to Christ Pantocrator on the day of Judgement.

The abbot, because of his responsibilities (which included overall charge of the monasteries affiliated to the Pantocrator and listed in the document), was to be given special treatment. The monks are told they will have no reason to feel any jealousy since they have joint responsibility for his election. He is to be given more varied food and larger helpings, and he is also to have his own superior wine.

The *Typikon*, predictably, gives as much detail for all the other parts of the monastery, turning next to the other two churches on the site. Both of these have survived, though in a condition far from their original splendour. The church of the Virgin is the north church of the complex, in which now only the original sculptured cornices can be seen and a very small patch of ornamental mosaic (Figure 80). As in the south church of Christ Pantocrator, the original marble columns have been removed and have been replaced in this case with stone piers of the Turkish period. Between the two large churches is the oratory of St Michael, still in use as a mosque in recent years and not archaeologically investigated (Figure 81). This small domed church is called in the text the '*Heroön*'—in classical Greek the word originally designated the tomb of a hero, and its use here is unusual and evocative. This was the place in the monastery designated for the grand marble sarcophagi of John II Comnenos, his family, and his Comnenian successors.

The church of the Virgin (Figure 80) was the only part of the monastery into which women were allowed entrance. The prescriptions for its use begin with the question of its lighting. In Byzantium the lighting of a church and its icons was not only a practical consideration, since a number of monastic services took place at night, but also an important symbolic part of prayer. As we have seen already in the seventh century, candles were important as ex-votos in the ciborion of St Demetrios; by the twelfth century, candles and lamps seem to have been prominent in any church. The *Typikon* runs through the recommended lighting in the church of the Virgin. These instructions again reveal something about the various kinds of icons in the original church, which fell into two categories: some were designated for

81 *The central of the three churches of the Pantocrator monastery was dedicated to the archangel Michael (the Angel of Death); it was the mausoleum of the Comnenian imperial dynasty (the Heroön), where their bodies were put to rest in large marble sarcophagi. This illustration shows the impressive ribbed dome over the nave.*

veneration, and needed candles specially arranged in front of them, while others were to be used in processions. The *Typikon* also mentions monumental images on the walls of the three churches in the complex.

Unlike the Pantocrator church which was serviced by the 'church' monks, the Eleousa was manned by fifty separate clerics (including eight priests, ten deacons, sixteen singers, and even eight young orphans to carry the candles during processions). The clerics were allocated into two groups and expected to work in shifts, a week at a time. Oddly perhaps, an arrangement was made for four women also to look after the church (they must be of suitable age and conduct). One of the specified services was a weekly litany on behalf of the founder for the forgiveness and remission of his sins followed by a distribution of money to those who attended it. The salaries of the clergy were defined and included supplementary payments for participation in the memorial services of the Comnenian dynasty. Special arrangements for the festivals of the Virgin were set out.

The *Typikon* devotes equal attention to the arrangements for lighting and ritual in the Heroön (Figure 81), which lay in between the two main churches. Here the Psalms and the rest of the offices were to be said by the monks of the Pantocrator—unlike the church of the Virgin, the Heroön was architecturally linked to the Pantocrator church through a wide archway. The clergy of the Virgin church, however, also had duties in the Heroön. The three churches were accessible to each other through a common narthex along the west. The monastery was responsible for the lighting of the Heroön, and allowance for this was made in the allocation of oil and wax to the community. The liturgy was to be celebrated here three times a week.

The important days in every year for the Heroön were to be the commemorations of the empress Eirene (who died in 1134), of John (when he died) and of their son Alexios (assuming he would be buried here too). All the necessary financial arrangements were made to ensure that the services would take place and that the congregation had an inducement to attend.

The annual commemorations of imperial deaths were to be marked by one special arrangement in the church. This involved the use of an icon, and can be treated as a test case of the essential role now taken by the visual in Byzantium. The *Typikon* sets out carefully the required ceremonial on these anniversaries. The icon of the Virgin from the Hodigitria monastery is to be brought in procession to the Pantocrator. This is the famous icon, which tradition was to identify as the work of St Luke, listed in the *Letter to Theophilos*. It was a large icon and it must have been very heavy. It was to be brought over on the day before the service of commemoration and to arrive to the accompaniment of prayers for the dead and thirty repetitions of 'Kyrie Eleison'. The icon was to be set up for the night in the church of St Michael near the tombs so that it was present during an all-night service attended by both the monks and the clergy; it remained in position for the liturgy on the anniversary itself. The fact that John Comnenos insisted on the physical presence of this icon of the Virgin during the memorial liturgy and prayers on behalf of him and his family is one of the best proofs that can be quoted of the dominant and necessary presence of the visual for the working of Byzantine society.

The *Typikon* now comes to the various philanthropic works to be associated with the monastery. All the other establishments constructed for these would be located within the walls of the precinct, which must have covered a large area of the hill in this part of the city. The enormous extent of the city of Constantinople within its fifth-century walls enabled emperors to take over considerable open areas of land without necessarily dispossessing large numbers of people—or so, in the lack of any recorded complaints, we may imagine.

The organization envisaged for the hospital predictably left nothing to chance. It was to have fifty beds, and quotas were laid down for the types of patient to occupy them. Women patients were included in the allocations. Arrangements for bed coverings and clothing for the patients are fully considered. Numbers of staff are also laid down, and it is expected that doctors and their assistants will work in alternate months. Services in the church of the Virgin attended by patients and doctors are to be held according to the instructions of the *Typikon*. Instructions are likewise given for food, baths and equipment, and attention is given to the salaries of the staff. A cemetery was also carefully organized.

The usual precision was applied to the endowment of the Old People's Home. Only men were eligible to come here, and a quota of twenty-four was envisaged, with six servants to look after them. The abbot, or anyone else, was specially forbidden to give a place to anyone strong and healthy who could quite easily maintain himself. Here the *Typikon* anticipated a possible source of corruption in the community. The annual allowance of food for each man was written down—their diet was to consist of bread, dried vegetables, cheese, oil and wine. One of the monks was chosen to be in charge of the home; the requirement was that he should be the most pious of their number. On Holy Thursday, to commemorate the Washing of the Feet of the Apostles by Christ, the abbot had the annual duty of ceremonially washing the feet both of the old people from the home and of the patients from the hospital. After the ceremony they were given money. A similar practice of giving such 'Maundy' money has survived in royal ceremonial in Britain, although here the full ceremonial with the Washing of Feet has been abbreviated, and the nature of the charity is different.

The *Typikon* made special provision for the care of lepers. For the Byzantines, this disease, and not epilepsy, was the 'holy disease', and so called for attention from the founder if he wished to ensure the widest recognition for his philanthropy.

So much of the *Typikon* is concerned with money that it is not surprising to find a long section listing the properties on which the monastery's prosperity would depend. The length of the list is testimony to the size of the Comnenian family's holdings in land; since it was the endowment of just this one monastery it can only have been a fraction of the complete wealth of the dynasty. In addition to these assigned lands, the monastery might also have benefited financially from the special legal status that the emperor was able to confer on it: it was to be free and independent from outside authorities, both ecclesiastical and secular.

The closing prayers of the founder show his expectation that the beneficiaries of his endowment will in return pray for him, and that he will be rewarded in heaven for his generosity.

★ ★ ★ ★

The importance of the Pantocrator monastery, which any modern visitor might guess from its size and the extent of its site (Figure 77), is entirely confirmed from the *Typikon*. The care taken by its founder to give it financial stability was successful in achieving its survival throughout the rest of the period of the Byzantine empire, while after the Turkish capture of the city in 1453, the structural soundness of the monuments ensured their continued use to the present day. Even after the death of John II Comnenos, the foundation was the subject of continued attention from the family. For example, although John had tried in vain to obtain the body of St Demetrios from the church in Thessaloniki, his son and successor, Manuel I Comnenos (1143–80), persevered in the request and did obtain from the church a piece of the ciborion and a covering of precious metal from one of the icons. These were brought to the Pantocrator in time for the festival of St Demetrios in October 1149, and received enthusiastic veneration from the public of Constantinople.

On the death of Manuel and his burial in an ornate black marble sarcophagus in the Heroön, another famous relic was brought to the monastery and set up near his tomb. This was the red stone on which it was believed the body of Christ was laid to rest when he was taken down from the Cross. Manuel had brought it from Ephesus in 1169/70 and is said to have carried it on his own shoulders from the harbour of Constantinople to the church of the Pharos in the Great Palace. This stone was probably installed under the archway between the Pantocrator church and the Heroön where there are now three pairs of dowel holes in the marble floor. There can be no doubt that in the twelfth century this foundation must have appeared as a monument in the city to the wealth, concern and religious devotion of the Comnenian emperor.

The reigns of Constantine Monomachos and John Comnenos are particularly valuable for the historian since here, as rarely, it is possible to set written texts beside artistic material. Both emperors devoted enormous attention to philanthropy and the visual display of it. Both impressed the public with their image of Christian devotion and piety. But their success raises the question of how far they conformed to an image of the Christian ruler and how far they created the image. The court idea of the ideal ruler can be extracted from assumptions made in written eulogies of various emperors and in the prefaces which introduced imperial decrees. The essential element of the view of the elite was that it must be recognized that God chooses the emperor, and that through this special relationship the emperor loves and imitates God. At the same time, the emperor, like God, feels responsible for his subjects and their well-being. On their side, his subjects must trust the emperor to ensure that justice is done in the state, and they expect from him generosity and philanthropy. These views formulated by the elite would have been in the mind of a responsive emperor, and in some form must have been communicated to society at large. The question for us is what part the visual played in such communication.

The image of a Byzantine emperor held by the ruling classes, who could observe or discover the actual behaviour of the emperor in the palace, would have differed from that of the public, whose opportunity for observation was more limited and whose sources of information were indirect and no doubt biased. The closest contact ordinary subjects had with the emperor was through his participation in processions and church services, or through their observation of the overt signs of his power, such as his artistic commissions and the representations of him which accompanied them. The public appearances of Constantine Monomachos, to which he attached so much importance, and the quantity and nature of his spending on public works, seem to have operated successfully to promote a favourable public image. In the same way John II Comnenos, despite his absences on military campaigns, was able to impose his 'presence' on the city through his patronage at St Sophia and the Pantocrator. His military successes might be expected to lead to popularity in any case, but it was as a pious and generous emperor that he was primarily seen.

Both Constantine and John used their imperial wealth to finance massive commissions, among which the two most directly comparable works are the commemorative mosaics in St Sophia and the monastic complexes of the Mangana and the Pantocrator. In the case of Constantine the text of Psellos obviously helps us to approach his expressed ideas; in the case of John the *Typikon* gives us a statement of intentions in the frame of reference of the founder himself, and we can deduce his own understanding of imperial philanthropy. His patronage of a monastery and a hospital is seen to offer returns, above all increasing his chances of gaining the forgiveness of sins. This was a particular concern because of the Byzantine beliefs about the procedures after death.

No pious emperor could doubt that he would go to the Christian Heaven; but his passage there could be delayed if he was required to spend time paying the penalty for his sins in the various 'customs houses' through which each soul had to pass, accounting in each for a particular kind of sin. Although the Byzantine church did not have a specific definition of 'Purgatory', everyone believed that the passage of the soul to Heaven could be long delayed by punishments for sins committed in life. The Virgin, of course, was the proof that it was possible for a human to go directly to Heaven and the imitation of her virginity by holy men and women could offer to them the hope of immediate acceptance into Heaven after death. In Byzantium, the most special of all cases was the emperor. If his position was decided by God, still he could not live the life of a holy man, but had to conform to certain conventions. Emperors were expected, for example, to include among their responsibilities to their subjects the continuation of the empire and the transmission of power to a successor, which of course normally meant marriage and the production of offspring. How could an emperor live a good Christian life with all the restraints of his position? How was he to accelerate his own passage to Heaven after his temporal life? The way in which these two emperors resolved this issue can be seen from the evidence we have considered. They saw that the patronage of institutions which involved massive projects of architecture and decoration was a solution. These benefited large numbers of people, satisfied their own feelings of piety, and could promote public enthusiasm for the reign. In return for their spending on a monastery and mausoleum, they not only gained the promise of perpetual repose for their bodies after death in a planned and maintained setting, they also deserved the favour of God for their soul. Patronage of art led quite directly to the 'purchase of paradise'.

This pursuit of personal patronage brought with it further advantages, some of which have already been described. An emperor could through his special position so endow and legally protect a monastery that its chances of future survival were much enhanced. His investment was the best insurance for the safety of his physical remains after death and the maintaining of prayers of intercession for his soul. It had another practical advantage (and there is a hint of the recognition of this in one section of the *Typikon*): a monastery offered a place of retirement for the emperor in old age or in the event of other contingencies; the inclusion of hospital facilities in the Pantocrator and the Mangana was not entirely altruism. All of these advantages came accompanied by a public recognition of philanthropy and generosity.

The hidden benefit of this kind of imperial patronage lay in the way that it solved a major dilemma of the philanthropist. It is one thing to accept the duty to use some of a personal fortune for the benefit of humanity; it is another to persuade humanity of the wisdom of choosing the particular beneficiaries. For the Byzantine, endowment of a monastery was the perfect solution, because it enabled the donor to delegate the decision about who should benefit to another authority. It eliminated the need to make a possibly invidious choice of individual beneficiaries, and it cushioned the emperor from criticism when the choices had been made. Someone else chose the patients at the hospital, and someone else handed out the rations of food and clothing in the community. The patron of the monastery avoided face-to-face contact over the details of his donations. At the same time such patronage must have enhanced the status of the emperor, especially when impressive visual portraits of him were set up to record his donations. Both the contents of these portraits and their position in a church would convey to the spectators the special relationship of the emperor with the divine.

Such patronage also enhanced the status of art in Byzantium. Since Iconoclasm, icons had again become an expected part of a Christian environment, and their role continued to expand. The evidence of the reigns of Constantine Monomachos and John Comnenos shows how prominent icons were in churches and how new uses were still being developed for them. Both emperors sought to demonstrate through art how their reigns conformed to a commendable notion of the Christian monarch. Particularly in the Pantocrator monastery, there is evidence of the use of icons within the prayers for the living and dead members of the imperial family. Moreover, unlike ordinary people, emperors were able to summon into their own presence when alive, and into their tombs after death, one of the most sacred cult objects of the Virgin, the icon of the Hodigitria. Since icons were an increasing part of the consciousness of the Byzantines, there was an obvious consequence. Art was the essential point of contact between all levels and all members of society. It was a symbolic language open to all, displayed in churches frequented by all. It does not follow that the universality of art through the empire meant that everyone interpreted it in the same way. But the consistent language of visual signs was strikingly different from the spoken and written Greek of the Byzantine empire, which followed different conventions of grammar and vocabulary at various levels of society. The associations and evocations of art were exploited by Constantine Monomachos and John Comnenos. Photios had told the emperors in St Sophia in 867 that art was more direct than writing in influencing belief and behaviour; these eleventh- and twelfth-century emperors put art to the test.

6

PARADISE GAINED:
THE PRIVATE USE
OF ART

THE palaces and vast monasteries of Constantinople and the
atmosphere of sophistication and urbanity in the capital city
are far removed from rural Cyprus, to which we now move
to look at the life and thinking of a twelfth-century holy
man, St Neophytos of Paphos (Figure 82). The caves in which he lived
for over fifty years have in large part survived in the form in which
he and his fellow monks adapted them for their monastic use. But
although the personality of Neophytos may at first sight seem bizarre,
and his aspirations and way of life far removed from those of any Byzantine emperor, yet his religious attitudes and his use of art in communicat-
ing these are more closely allied to those of contemporary
Constantinople than at first appears. St Neophytos and his monastery
provide us with the best focus for the use of the visual in Byzantium,
and bring together the various strands so far traced in this book.

Although Neophytos was in the same religious tradition as St
Theodore of Sykeon and shared his belief in the value of asceticism,
the comparison of these two men, both recognized in their lifetimes
as saints, reveals changes between the seventh and the twelfth century
in the role and attitudes of the holy man. By the time of Neophytos
art has taken on a prominent role in the monastery; partly, no doubt,
as a result of the encouragement given to the visual as a medium of
communication through the triumph of the iconophiles. Neophytos
himself makes thoroughgoing use of the visual arts. Although there are
many similarities in the spiritual aims of these holy men, the ways in
which these were realized and expressed were very different. Whereas
Theodore had a wide role to play in late sixth- and seventh-century
society, offering help and support to many people in the face of all kinds
of adversity during a time of decline and fear, it appears that Neophytos,
living in a century of relative prosperity and hope, at least until its closing stages, held a marginal place in society and was more respected from
a distance than approached as a person who had something to contribute
to the community at large.

82 Neophytos of Paphos was depicted on the wall of his cell in the Enkleistra kneeling at the feet of Christ and raising his hands in prayer—the text of his prayer is written beside him. This portrait was painted in 1183 when he was in his fiftieth year.

The nature of the relationship of each man to the society in which he lived—the participation of Theodore in a public life, and the total retreat of Neophytos—is an illustration of the changes which had taken place in Byzantine society, due in part to developments over the intervening centuries within the organization of Byzantine life, and in part to pressures from the other Mediterranean powers and societies with which the Byzantine empire had to coexist. Life has become less obviously social, more apparently private. The case of Neophytos marks the career of the holy man as a professional with a status within a highly organized church sphere. Neophytos might be said to have had little to offer the public at large, yet he can receive the admiration of the church establishment and the virtual veneration of his fellow-monks for his isolation from society. Only in the visual is there an obvious common language between the saint and the rest of society; but in his use of art, Neophytos is found to push the conventions to extremes.

Once again the argument of this chapter is structured around the career of an individual actor and the art surrounding him. This has the advantage that it permits a renewed focus on a distinctive type of figure in Byzantium—the holy man; and it allows us, through this figure, to understand some of the wider elements of continuity and change that characterized the history of Byzantium. While the strength of the imperial power system remained constant over the centuries, the world of the individual changed between Late Antiquity, when Constantinople was founded as the capital of a massive empire, and the Middle Ages when Byzantium became just one of several struggling powers in the Mediterranean area.

However, the attempt to view Byzantium through the person of individual actors in the period has its difficulties as well. Too much emphasis on this approach can lead us to see the individual as an isolated figure *confronted* by a monolithic power structure, rather than as a *part* of a community. One recent analysis of Byzantine society has characterized it as a world of 'individualism without freedom'; people are seen as confined within the family unit and lacking any real membership of a larger co-operating community. Such a view of each Byzantine as a Kafkaesque individual intimidated by the single remote authority of a semi-divine emperor is uncomfortably close to a twentieth-century literary stereotype. It underestimates the cohesive power of the church, and the opportunities for communal life in monasteries like that of the Pantocrator. It does not consider the ways a communal identity could be promoted through the common veneration of icons, nor does it assess the effects of the ubiquitous presence of such images as the caring Mother of God, which might be understood to be watching over society as well as being available for the reception of prayers.

The application of any concept of 'individualism' to Byzantium raises a number of theoretical problems. What is it to speak of an individual in Byzantium? Did people think of themselves as individuals? How far is one applying a modern way of thinking based on such notions as 'personal identity' and 'human rights'? Byzantium was certainly far different in this respect from our own world of post-Romantic, post-

Reformation Christianity which privileges the individual and the creativity of personal genius. In broad terms, Byzantines grew up learning the traditions of the past in such a way that they found their identity not in themselves but in the common mind of the group. Yet even so, while keeping in mind the dangers of anachronism, we can usefully study the lives of single actors in Byzantium as *representatives* of their society. We can also be sensitive to changes in Byzantine views of the 'individual' or 'self'; even though they were probably always different from our own, they were not necessarily static. Indeed, as we shall see, the twelfth century shows various signs of changing attitudes.

The evidence for the study of Neophytos is found in his own writings, some of which give details of his life, and in the visual decoration of the caves in which he lived, and these two sources can be directly compared. The writings are all theological or monastic (some sixteen volumes according to his own boast), and the art all consists in the decoration of his monastery. With the help of both these media, we can come more closely to an understanding of the ways by which, in this society, text and image could be used to communicate messages which are in one sense complementary, but which evoked different responses. The relation between text and image, and the appreciation of the different values of each, can be better explored in the case of St Neophytos than in the other material so far considered.

The outline of the life of this holy man shows his part in the twelfth-century society of Cyprus. During the earlier part of his career Cyprus was a province of decided strategic importance to Byzantium as a base of operations during the upheavals in the eastern Mediterranean caused by the establishment of Crusader Kingdoms. By the time of the death of Neophytos in the early thirteenth century the island was no longer the subject of Byzantine investment and support and was itself one of the declining Crusader dominions.

Neophytos was someone whose obituary could be given in one sentence: 'He was a peasant, shrewd but of limited education, born in 1134, who confined himself to a couple of small caves for most of his life and died in one of them in 1215 or soon after.' Yet such a bald summary leaves much unsaid: why should anyone have spent over fifty-five years of his life in a cave, and how could he attract a small group of monks to devote themselves to him? Nor does it recognize that, despite an outwardly uneventful life, the environment which Neophytos developed around himself tells more about the ways of thinking in Byzantium than do the actions of many of those at the centre of the political arena of the time.

The facts of his life are to be found in the *Typikon* of the monastery which Neophytos himself founded. He was born in 1134 on Cyprus, at Lefkara, an inland village in the hills between Larnaca and Limassol. His parents were probably farmers and had seven other children. His mother became a nun in later life and one of his brothers, called John, became a monk and later abbot at the monastery of St Chrysostomos at Koutsovendi in the mountains on the north of the island; this was a foundation of the year 1090, still in part surviving today. Neophytos ran away from home in 1152, seven months after his betrothal, and arrived at the monastery of St Chrysostomos. His parents found him and brought him back home, but two months later he was allowed to return to the monastery and he received the tonsure.

For the next five years Neophytos lived in this monastery, at first being allowed only to farm the vineyard—some such job was regularly considered appropriate for a second-class member of the community who was illiterate. After learning to read and write, and memorizing the psalter, he became assistant sacristan for two years.

Neophytos had decided that he wanted to live as a solitary hermit, rather than as a member of a regular controlled community; in 1158–9 he moved to the Holy Land and spent six months travelling there searching for some hermit who would receive him as a disciple. His travels took him to many of the holy places visited by Theodore of Sykeon centuries before him, including the Holy Sepulchre in Jerusalem (now remodelled both by Constantine Monomachos in the eleventh century and more recently by the Crusaders) and also the monastery of the Virgin at Choziba near Jericho where Theodore had been granted the 'angelic' habit of a monk. Neophytos found no suitable or willing hermit, and returned to the monastery of Chrysostomos; he was, however, refused permission by the abbot to set up his own private retreat on the adjacent mountain slope, so he left again to try another option. He went to the harbour of Paphos to find a boat which would take him to Mount Latmos, near Miletus, an area of western Asia Minor famous as a retreat for monks and hermits. While he was trying to find a boat from the castle of Paphos for the passage to Asia Minor, Neophytos was arrested by the guards and robbed of his savings (two gold nomismata). He wandered off into the hinterland of Paphos.

Some three miles inland he found the cliff and caves in which he spent the rest of his life (Figures 83, 84); this was on 24 June 1159. He

83 *The Russian pilgrim Barskij, who sketched Nea Moni on Chios in 1732 (see Figure 70), also visited the monastery of Neophytos and stayed there for three days. In his sketch of 1735 the Enkleistra lies in the ravine to the left. He visited the caves and saw the wallpaintings of the nave: his response was that they 'induce contrition in every devout worshipper'.*

converted a natural cave into his home, with walls of rubble masonry and plaster; over a period of about a year he created a cell, a tomb and a chapel. On 14 September 1160 he dedicated the altar in the chapel on the festival day of the commemoration of the finding of the Holy Cross by St Helena. He decided to call the caves the Hermitage of the Holy Cross; this was a happy choice as five years later he acquired a fragment of the Holy Cross from somewhere on Cyprus. The special Greek name he used for the hermitage was *Enkleistra* (because he was 'locked in').

The next change of circumstances was in 1170 when Neophytos was ordained priest and accepted a resident disciple. He was apparently persuaded to accept these changes by the bishop of Paphos, a man named Basil Kinnamos, who provided a subsidy to meet the extra expenses involved. The elevation of Neophytos to the priesthood meant that he himself could celebrate the eucharist, and did not need to rely on the services of an outside churchman. The expansion and the decoration of the Enkleistra now followed; cells were constructed all along the cliff. The first *Typikon* for the community (perhaps dating from 1177, but now only known through references to it in the later document which superseded it) laid down a 'very small' number of monks.

In 1182/3 the Enkleistra, partially decorated before, was now given a complete embellishment of wallpaintings. What survives of this period of decoration is in the cell of Neophytos, in his tomb, and in the sanctu-

84 The monastery of Neophytos in its present state is centred on a large domed church surrounded by the cells and other monastic buildings; the rock-cut Enkleistra can be seen in the distance in the ravine to the left. The building of the new monastery dates from the early sixteenth century; at the time the Enkleistra too was restored and parts repainted—an inscription in the nave records that this renovation took place in 1503 and that it was due to the initiative of the 'second founder' of the monastery, a monk with the name of Neophytos.

220

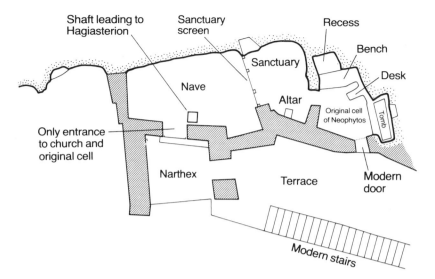

Plan of the Enkleistra.

Shaft leading to Hagiasterion

Sanctuary screen

Recess

Bench

Sanctuary

Desk

Nave

Altar

Original cell of Neophytos

Tomb

Only entrance to church and original cell

Narthex

Terrace

Modern door

Modern stairs

ary around the altar (see plan). To the west of the sanctuary there is now a larger nave, described in an inscription as the church of the Holy Cross. This inscription (belonging to 1503 when the Enkleistra was restored) claims that this part was cut out and painted through the initiative of Neophytos in 1195/6. The painting in the nave is certainly later than the work of 1183, and might belong to 1196/7; it is not possible to be certain on the dating because of a number of discrepancies between the archaeological indications and the statements made by Neophytos.

Neophytos and his community gained a new embellished environment of great artistic quality in 1183, but the conditions of political life on Cyprus changed for the worse in 1184. Neophytos himself (probably in 1197) wrote a book about these difficulties which is known as the *Misfortunes of Cyprus*. In 1184 Isaac Ducas Comnenos, a great-nephew of the emperor Manuel I Comnenos (1143–80), arrived on the island with forged documents and declared himself emperor of Cyprus and independent of Constantinople. Seven years of fighting and resistance followed, with many leaving the island and many thrown into prison. In 1191, by his maltreatment of some shipwrecked Crusaders, Isaac gave a pretext to King Richard Lionheart of England to conquer Cyprus. He in turn sold it in 1192 to the Knights Templar; and they presented it to the French knight Guy de Lusignan. For the rest of the life of Neophytos Cyprus was ruled by the Lusignan kings (who from 1197 were also the kings of Jerusalem), and the island never returned to the political control of the Byzantines.

Neophytos made a conspicuous change in his arrangements in the Enkleistra during the year 1196/7; by 24 January of that year Neophytos had dug out a new cell with his own hands—the New Zion. This cell was higher up the cliff above the church and allowed him to live in greater privacy in the community. The new cell and its adjoining chambers were connected by a shaft to the nave of the Holy Cross. Probably the decoration of this church belongs to the same programme of work as the cell, but it is also possible that the paintings were done in the ten years or so after 1197. Whatever the timing, the organization of the paintings in the church does seem to have been planned by Neophytos himself, and was certainly carried out, as we shall see, with reference to the position of his new cell on the cliff. The refectory cave was decorated at the same time as the church, and in the same period a pair of processional icons was acquired by the community: one of Christ Philanthropos and one of the Virgin Eleousa.

The legal arrangements of the community were set out in a revised *Typikon* dated May 1214. It allowed up to fifteen or even eighteen monks in the community, to be supported by property already acquired by the monastery. In the *Typikon* Neophytos laid down detailed instructions for his burial, and he appointed to succeed him as abbot of the community his nephew Esaias, who was already a priest and monk. Shortly after writing this *Typikon* Neophytos died. His death was said to have taken place on 12 April, presumably (he was now over eighty) in 1215 or very soon after.

Neophytos spent altogether over fifty-five years in the Enkleistra. In all these years he kept up a regime of prayer, all-night services in the church, study and writing, and he never ate cooked food. His devotion to his ideal of the Christian life is undoubted, although his cultural horizons may seem limited. He collected a library of books for himself and his fellow monks to consult; at least thirty manuscripts which once belonged to the Enkleistra have survived in various modern library collections; in all the community probably owned at most about fifty books, including service books. What survives is of routine content, such as the writings of Church Fathers and Lives of Saints, and there is not one secular book.

From his own writings Neophytos has been characterized as pompous and conceited. More important for our purposes than any assessment of his character is a comparison with Theodore of Sykeon. Both were holy men, both achieved wide renown. The fame of Theodore relied on his biographer; that of Neophytos came from his own writing and from the visual images of his holiness which he himself had planned. Two texts written by Neophytos allow us to establish something of the processes by which he projected a verbal image of his holiness, and it is useful to look at these before considering the visual expressions on the walls of his monastery. The first represents the contribution of the saint to a topical theological issue of his period, and it shows that a provincial monk knew of and could participate in such a controversy, while the second text is the *Typikon* of the Enkleistra.

The theological problem, about which Neophytos wrote a pamphlet, roused sufficient feeling to divide the Byzantine world at the end of the twelfth century. It concerned the precise nature of the bread and wine used in communion: did the bread change its character in the course of the eucharist and in some way reflect the progress of the body of Christ itself from the human to the divine? Did it start like a human body, subject to moral laws and corruptible? Did it then, when eaten at the communion and lying inside the stomach, become incorruptible and eternal and no longer subject to mortal laws?

The debate in this form is known to have been initiated in Constantinople by a monk named Michael Glykas. He had been sentenced to be blinded in 1159 for various heretical views, but lived, still active in theological controversy, until after 1185. Various of his writings are known: a history and a learned commentary on the Bible. His contention was that the bread and wine of the eucharist when consecrated by the priest and received by the communicant was mortal and corruptible, like Christ's body at the time of the Last Supper; only after consumption did the elements gain incorruptible immortality and join with the soul of the recipient, as Christ's body became immortal in the tomb.

The doctrine of Glykas found acceptance with two patriarchs of Constantinople at the end of the twelfth century and the beginning of the thirteenth. One of these patriarchs is known to have discussed the question with the bishop of Paphos, Bacchos, when he was in Constantinople trying to sort out the ecclesiastical status of Cyprus under the Crusaders. Bacchos declared the doctrine to be innovation and therefore anathema; the orthodox view, he insisted, must be that the body of Christ was always incorruptible. The patriarch, however, argued in support of the view of Glykas, and the controversy continued in Constantinople. The next patriarch asked the emperor to call a synod to discuss this issue, and this met in the imperial palace in 1199/1200. The thesis of incorruptibility received the majority of votes, but the minority which supported the formulation of Glykas was sufficiently large that the question was regarded as still open. The imperial solution to this impasse was to decree silence on both sides. The fall of Constantinople to the Crusaders in 1204 was a more effective termination to the argument.

Neophytos joined in this debate, presumably learning about it from the bishop of Paphos, whose side he took. He wrote a short essay on the issue, probably soon after 1200. He was not entirely clear what the views were on each side, but concluded that the flesh of Christ was incorruptible before and after the communion, and so the view of Glykas must be opposed. But the content of the proofs he brings forward hardly supports his own case. His method of theology was to rely ultimately not on logic, but on the benefits of direct revelation from the Holy Spirit which he is prepared to claim for himself.

From the beginning of the text Neophytos imposes himself; he speaks of his 'rustic' status, but mitigates it by the immediate claim that the Holy Spirit is speaking through him. The same claim of his privileged relation with the divine is repeated at the end of the text. The debate according to him is whether the flesh of Christ was corruptible or incorruptible. His answer depends on a collection of anecdotes, which may be taken as indicative of the kind of conversation at the Enkleistra. One concerns a priest monk in the second half of the twelfth century at a village near Lefkara on Cyprus who was celebrating the eucharist, but went out of the church before finishing and forgot to come back. When he returned to the church on the next morning and took the cover off the chalice, it was full of blood and flesh. Out of surprise and shame, he tried to get rid of the contents by burning them; but instead of being reduced to ashes in the flames, the lump of bloody flesh still remained.

In alarm the man tried to dispose of the flesh by hiding it, but the archbishop and the governor of Cyprus heard the story and transferred the relic into a silver casket.

Another story was told to Neophytos by a second priest monk. He customarily gave the bread of the eucharist to his son as well as to the congregation, but one day the child became ill after eating the holy mysteries and vomited them with disgust, complaining that he had been given meat. A monk who had travelled in the Holy Land told Neophytos how he was at the monastery of St Euthymios at Jerusalem and present at the liturgy. When the priest was about to cut the bread, one of the youngest monks of the community rushed up to him and grabbed his hand to stop him. When the abbot questioned the youth, he replied that he believed that the priest was about to kill a child, and so ran up and held his hand to stop a murder.

According to Neophytos, these stories prove that the bread and wine are not corruptible even before they have entered the mouth of the communicant. To our eyes, the stories hardly seem to prove the point. The first two might be said to be evidence that the body of Christ in the eucharist was literally incorruptible before and after communion, but the Jerusalem story implies that the body of Christ could have been killed and was therefore mortal.

The revealing aspect of the pamphlet (leaving aside the questions of logic) is the kind of argument that Neophytos happily puts forward. These or similar anecdotes can be shown from other texts to have circulated widely, and it is clear from the writing of Neophytos that in his mind they took the chief role in deciding about abstruse theological controversies. They do not seem to differ much in intellectual standing from the compilation of miraculous icons in the *Letter of the Eastern Patriarchs to Theophilos*, which was taken as a proof of the divine demonstration of the legitimacy of figural icons in the church. The nature of religious debate does not here seem substantially different between the ninth and the twelfth centuries, or between elites and non-elites.

This text also tells us that a provincial monk in the countryside of Cyprus under Crusader rule believed his opinions in current theology deserved expression and notice. From a modern point of view, Neophytos might seem merely an eccentric, but in the context of the twelfth century, we can see that religious debate involved the whole region of Byzantium. Issues of theology were not only discussed at the centre; they were reworked and reformulated by isolated hermits in the outlying provinces. Even when the Byzantine empire was losing political control at its margins, the Byzantine world was bound together by its common concern for common religious problems.

Our second text from the pen of Neophytos is the *Typikon* of the monastery (including Neophytos' *Will*) written in 1214. Such monastic charters, as we have seen in the case of the Pantocrator *Typikon*, bring out the bureaucratic and managerial side of Byzantine life, but they can also illuminate the physical arrangements of the community concerned. In this case it is helpful to consider the *Typikon* before looking at the caves themselves.

The *Typikon* is known to us in one clean copy written by a priest, Basil, who was a notary and teacher on the staff of the bishop of Paphos. The text was written in May, 1214, and is now in the manuscript collection of Edinburgh University. It has some pages missing, but its pristine state does suggest that, like most of the other writings of Neophytos, the book lay unread after his death in the library of the community. It was drafted by an old man of eighty facing death who sees his life from the point of view of someone already accepted as a saint.

The *Typikon* spells out all the rules for the community, which partly derive from the community's earlier *Typikon* of 1177. Some rules enacted are traditional in documents of this type, but others appear distinctive to the monastery of Neophytos. Consideration of some of these prescriptions will help to show the character of the establishment and the preoccupations of Neophytos in ordering his monastery.

Neophytos' first concern was with the size and exclusiveness of the monastery. The very small number of monks allowed by the earlier *Typikon* of 1177 is said to have been criticized by powerful men in society who suggested an increase to twenty or twenty-five. Neophytos refused to increase the community to this size, as he thought such numbers would lead to all sorts of troubles, but he agreed to a community of fifteen or even up to eighteen. Out of these, the two most suitable were to be delegated to serve as *oikonomos* (manager) and *docheiarios* (quartermaster). Within his community, Neophytos banned the establishment of a school for lay children: it would, he said, be indecent and wrong. Women and even all female animals were likewise banned. These prohibitions clearly reveal the exclusiveness of the community. Neophytos justifies the idea of a small male community as the ideal of Christian religion and attempts to ensure its practical achievement.

He was also concerned with the character of the personnel within the monastery. All monks were to live a spiritual life and not to forget the inscription which he had put up in the narthex of the church: this prohibited anyone who had fallen into sin to remain in the monastery. One particular section of advice covers how a monk is to prepare for death through the spiritual life and good works and the glorification of God. At the head of these monks was to be an abbot, a position to be held after his death by his nephew, already a monk in the monastery.

The monks were to live under a strict regime. Neophytos was concerned to justify the rule of poverty and appealed to New Testament precedent and its moral value. Although pragmatic to the extent of realizing that in the present circumstances of the Crusader occupation of the island the monastery could not rely on charity as in the past, he stresses that the possessions of the monastery (some arable land, a vineyard and some cattle) were but a necessary evil; the monks must beware losing their souls in pursuit of wealth. Church services were closely regulated: the liturgy was to be celebrated on Saturdays, Sundays, festivals and holy days and in each liturgy an offering of bread was to be made for Neophytos as well as for Christ (a much simpler procedure than that set out on behalf of the emperor and his dynasty and court in the Pantocrator *Typikon*). Neophytos also gave attention to the day-to-day conduct of the monks: each monk was to remain in the monastery, live an ascetic life and refrain from sexual contact with the other monks. Any monk who fell into bodily sin was to be confined as appropriate.

The *Typikon* itself was to form part of the ritual of the church. It was to be read out three times a year in the presence of every single monk—on the feast of the Nativity of the Virgin (8 September), on Christmas Day, and on the feast of the Annunciation (25 March). The emphasis on festivals of the Virgin Mary in the church year is a further confirmation of the importance of the Virgin in the ordering of life in Byzantine society, seen already (in Chapter 4) in the context of the ninth century, but still increasing and perhaps accelerating at this time.

The description of the Enkleistra in the *Typikon* gives information on the functions of all the caves which survive today and their fittings. The cliff along which the community lived was approached by a bridge or arched terrace by the stream. There was a gate outside the Enkleistra, which in 1214 had no seats or roof; there had been an earlier more comfortable gateway, where the monks would sit in shelter, but Neophytos had this taken down in the belief that it was used not as a place of rest, but as a rendezvous for all sorts of corruption. Inside the enclosure was a bakery, kitchen, cells and stores. There was also the terrace, rock-cut refectory, narthex and church of the community. In addition to all these there were the very special arrangements made for Neophytos himself, which we shall examine in detail presently. The caves used by Neophytos exclusively belong to the two periods of his life in the Enkleistra; the period of the original cell and the first sanctuary, which have their decoration from 1183, and the upper cells developed after 1196, which were higher up the cliff over the church. The *Typikon* describes these caves as the upper treasury, the *Hagiasterion* (the Holy Room in which Neophytos attended services), the new Enkleistra or New Zion for him alone, and another cell, dedicated to St John the Baptist.

Neophytos recorded the wish that at some future date the community should construct a proper church nearby to be dedicated to the Holy Trinity. What he says about the financing of this new church is revealing; he told the community not to arrange the raising of the money themselves, as that might put them under unfortunate obligations. They must wait for it to be donated by an emperor or a member of the ruling class. The sentiment shows not only the level of support which Neophytos thought practicable for such a community, but also the expectation of how and for what purposes money might be invested in a provincial rural group.

Neophytos formally left all the sacred possessions of his Enkleistra to the community. These are specified as holy icons, sacred vessels, the relic of the Cross and other relics and bones of martyrs (thirty in all). After he had been summoned to God, then the brothers were not to mourn him excessively, but should follow the usual prayers and services and bury his relics in the tomb in the Enkleistra which he had already prepared. He gave very precise instructions for his burial in his original cell, the first Enkleistra, where he lived before moving up the cliff to the New Zion above the church. He wished to be wrapped in the burial clothes which he had woven for himself some years before and to be put in a coffin made of pine, cedar and cypress wood (the same materials as the True Cross). The monks were to build a wall there and fill in the door, and on this new wall they should paint an icon, under the inspiration of God. The purpose of this work was to hide the place of his burial from strangers so that his body would be undisturbed until the day of the last trumpet.

As for his original cell, which he rather pompously called the *Protokathedros Enkleistra*, and which, he reminded the monks, was painted with holy icons, this had gained the status of a sanctuary. To prove its (miraculous) status, he reported that one or two people had tried to sit down in it, but were unable to do so. It was not, he believed, an ordinary cell and its special powers would continue.

The *Typikon* of Neophytos demonstrates the world of a twelfth-century ascetic community, just one of literally hundreds of monastic communities which by this period marked the whole landscape of Byzantium, both in the cities and in the countryside. The document reveals a number of idiosyncrasies associated with Neophytos himself, but many of his assumptions about the monastic life would have been standard at the time. One can see that he is encouraging people to enter into a marginal role in society, and that he denies any place for sexuality in the spiritual way of life. However, his asceticism does not rule out the spending of money, preferably by rich outsiders, on the decoration of the monastery. He expects such a holy area as his own cell to be ornamented with icons, and the various parts of the monastery are demarcated and given meaning through their ornament.

The aim of this chapter is to compare the ways in which art was used in the Enkleistra with the ways in which the thoughts of Neophytos were expressed in his writings. The principal question which lies behind the analysis is whether the visual decoration of the environment worked differently from written or spoken texts. This question has been examined already from other evidence in this book, but here in this set of painted caves the quantity of the material and our knowledge of the functions of the various rooms allow a fuller answer.

The modern visitor to the monastery of Neophytos will find a flourishing community under his name (Figure 84). Most of the buildings on the present site are, however, later than the time of the saint. The Enkleistra continued in existence after the death of Neophytos, but probably along the lines of a more conventional monastic community without following his stricter regime. The tomb of the saint proved (properly) to have miraculous powers, and the monastery was maintained through a regular annual income. The paintings of the rock-cut church were restored in 1503 (when some panels were repainted) at the expense of a monk called Neophytos who styled himself the 'new founder' (he died in 1512). Probably it was at this time that the new church which had been recommended by Neophytos was built (though not where he suggested) and dedicated to the Virgin. In 1585 the possessions of the monastery were confiscated, but after some years of decline the efforts of one of the abbots saved the community from destruction, and permitted its restoration. The manuscripts were sold to agents of the French government in the seventeenth century, and when it was visited by the Russian pilgrim Barskij in 1735 it had a very small and rustic community (Figure 83). At that time Neophytos' remains were still in his tomb, but the relics were later (in 1756) transferred to the main church of the Virgin. The monastery was later restored, but, like monasteries in Greece, suffered Turkish damage after the Greek Revolu-

85 In this cell, which he designed and cut out for himself, Neophytos lived from 1160 to 1197. He provided for himself a bench for sitting and sleeping, a desk and a number of storage niches. In the decoration of 1183, a Deisis (including the portrait of Neophytos in Figure 82) was painted to the right, the Crucifixion to the left, and on the wall to the left of that a set of standing saints. Medallions containing portraits of saints were on the vault above.

tion of 1821 when the church was identified as a place of refuge for dissidents.

The caves in the cliff, where the community began, continued as the centre of the monastery until the sixteenth century, and had needed a substantial restoration in 1503. The cleaning of the paintings in 1963 restored the environment of Neophytos as it was in the Middle Ages, with the exception of the wallpaintings that have been lost over the years and the addition of the repainted material of 1503. We shall be concerned here with the original cell of Neophytos and the sanctuary next to it, both decorated in 1183, and the church of the Holy Cross, decorated in 1196/7 or soon after. Other caves, such as the Refectory and the New Zion, have too few of their paintings left to be of use for our argument.

The cell of Neophytos received its current wallpaintings in 1183, when he was in his fiftieth year (Figure 85). It is its form and fittings at this date which we need to visualize.

When the cave received these paintings, there was a masonry partition between the cell and the sanctuary of the church. This was an addition made by Neophytos after his initial occupation of the cell in 1160 and it gave him the advantage of privacy from the place where the services of the church took place. A couple of much later alterations visible on the plan (see p. 221) have rather changed the aspect of the room. There is now a low wall in front of the tomb, which makes the recess more cramped; this can only have been put there after 1756 when the relics of Neophytos were taken away. There is a door now in the eastern wall of the cave, leading directly on to the terrace, which must have been knocked through in recent times in order to allow women visitors access to the cell and the tomb directly from the terrace. Without it, women would only have been able to reach the cell through the sanctuary, something expressly forbidden in all Orthodox churches. In 1183, without this exterior door, the cell must have been darker and more enclosed.

This cell in which Neophytos lived for thirty-seven years (from 1160 to 1197) is very small: it has a ledge which could double up as bed and seat, a masonry table, an alcove for his books, and a few other small recesses in the wall. Neophytos carved out the corner opposite the bed as a tomb chamber.

The painter of the *Protokathedros Enkleistra* recorded his name, Theodore Apseudes, on the wall, and inscribed the date, 1183. For a painter to take care to record his name in church decorations in this way seems to be a development of the twelfth century, paralleled perhaps by the care which Neophytos took in the *Typikon* to mention the exact dates of the events of his own life. Perhaps, as was suggested in the introduction to this chapter, this development is part of a changing view of the position of the individual in Byzantine society and a feature of a growing tendency to 'self-projection' in those outside the top ranks of society.

At the time of the decoration in 1183 Neophytos was resident in the cave and effectively isolated from the practicalities of the outside world. The suggestion of new decoration, its organization and its financing was most likely to have been the responsibility of some other person. The obvious candidate for the sponsorship of this work is the bishop of Paphos, Basil Kinnamos, who was in office from 1166 until the early 1190s. It was he who ordained Neophytos as priest in 1170 after four years of urging, and persuaded him to accept a disciple and a supporting grant of money. From that time the Enkleistra was developed and began to evolve from a hermitage to a regular monastery.

It was frequent practice for a bishop to be responsible for the organization of artistic commissions, helped by his contacts with other bishops and with influential people in the capital. Basil Kinnamos was probably related to the aristocratic family Kinnamos, prominent in Constantinople at the period; he could have communicated with his relations there in order to find a suitable artist to work in the Enkleistra. It has been suggested that the work of Theodore Apseudes shows a knowledge of contemporary stylistic fashions in the capital, and that he therefore travelled from Constantinople to work in the Enkleistra. This is quite possible. It does not however seem significant to decide where this artist was trained; there was so much work in the regions of the empire at the time that many artists must have been forever travelling around, meeting and influencing each other on the job, and training assistants and pupils on their commissions. So far no work has been attributed to this artist before this commission, and so nothing can be said of his age and experience in 1183.

The features of the decoration are so often to be connected with the writing of Neophytos that one may assume that the chief influence on the choice of subject was the saint himself, possibly in consultation with the bishop. The artist might therefore be conceived as working (in accordance with the recommendation of the Council of Nicaea) as the agent of the church; in practice the degree to which each of those involved influenced the decoration cannot be determined, and may not have been straightforward even at the time of production.

From the paintings of 1183 Neophytos gained a permanent company of saints and Christian narrative scenes in his cell, in the presence of which he could follow his ideal of human life. They were a source of spiritual support and offered the promise of salvation. These icons and the inscriptions with them supplied the outward signs of the religious beliefs and thoughts in the Enkleistra. Every part of the walls of the cave around Neophytos was covered with paintings which together form a connected visual statement.

Above him in the dome-shaped vault was a group of portraits painted in gilded medallions. These are a set of Old Testament prophets, holding texts from their writings. Only two of the texts are now legible. They both speak of God seated on his throne and may refer to the representation of Christ enthroned on the wall of the cell. However, since they are just above the place where Neophytos himself sat, they may also suggest a parallel between the position of the holy man and the figure of God. The saints painted in the other part of the ceiling have now disappeared except for a fragment of St Damian; the choice of a medical saint may have in part depended on the fact that this was the living room of Neophytos—St Theodore of Sykeon had icons of the medical saints in his room. There was a further text written over a part of the ceiling, and although this is now in fragments, enough remains to show that it was autobiographical, mentioning the monastery of St Chrysostomos and probably the events at Paphos before the saint came inland and found the Enkleistra site. It seems that Neophytos wanted a record of the story of his life inscribed in his room in 1183. This is another pointer to the emphatic personal bias of the visual decoration.

The icons around the walls were of single saints or of scenes. Five individual figures were represented, of which the three identifiable figures are military saints: Theodore the General, Demetrios and Procopios, all repainted versions of an earlier decoration in Neophytos' cell. Christian warriors are so frequent in church decorations in Byzantium that it is difficult to assume any special associations with these figures for anyone in Cyprus in the Crusader period. The most obvious reference of the cycle is the assistance given to men by the saints.

The Crucifixion on the partition wall belongs to 1183, but was not the first painting on the wall (an earlier and simpler icon of the Crucifixion lies underneath it, and shows through at points where the present paint surface is damaged) (Figure 86). The second version now visible

86 From where Neophytos sat in his cell, the Crucifixion lay to his right. Below this painting was the only way out of the cell, leading directly to the altar and sanctuary of the Enkleistra.

is a powerful and effective image: the sagging body of Christ, the misery of St John and the Virgin Mary and the women beside her, and the large, brutal figure of the centurion Longinus, were, in comparison with traditional schemes, treated with more emphasis and sweeping movement. In addition the figures are set in a carefully constructed architectural space. Such a 'style' enhances the emotional reactions of the spectator, for it increases the narrative content of the scene over its dogmatic statement of a Christian truth. From the viewpoint of Neophytos

87 To his left Neophytos looked onto the Deisis. This was the most powerful visual image in the cell, with dominant figures of Christ enthroned with the Virgin and St John the Baptist; below them, at his own eye level, was the representation of Neophytos at prayer.

this icon of the Crucifixion was the central scene of the wall between him and the altar on which the liturgy of the sacrifice of Christ took place. Although the inclusion of a Crucifixion is to be expected in the decoration of a monk's cell, this particular position for the scene may have been chosen so that it carried a perpetual image of the symbolic rites which occurred behind it.

The most conspicuous image in the cell is on the wall facing the Crucifixion (Figure 87). This too was a traditional composition which was treated in a special way in this decoration, and it also replaced an earlier (smaller) panel of the same subject painted before 1183. This icon uses both pictorial and written elements for its effect. The composition was one of great popularity in Byzantine art, and is known today as the *Deisis*—the 'prayer'. In it Christ was normally represented between two figures, the Virgin Mary and St John the Baptist, the two saints traditionally regarded as most effective at interceding with God in Heaven. In the version produced for Neophytos in his cell, Christ sits on an ornate throne, dressed in swirling garments. He holds a closed book and lifts up his right hand in a gesture of blessing. The Virgin and the Baptist stand on each side of Christ with their hands outstretched in prayer. Their prayer is on behalf of Neophytos who is included in the scene, although he is on earth, not in Heaven. He is kneeling below Christ, wearing his monastic habit (Figures 82, 87).

This portrait of the monk is on the wall just beside the place where he spent his days in prayer, worship, study, writing and sleeping. His portrait is accompanied by a text addressed to Christ and recording his perpetual prayer:

Christ, through the prayers of your Mother and your Baptist
who stand reverently by your holy throne
be merciful now and for evermore
to him who lies as a suppliant at your feet.

In this case the visual and verbal meanings of the *Deisis* are very similar. However, there is a difference between the two: whereas the text is a prayer which could often be repeated in his meditations by the saint, the picture conveys both the prayer and an answer to it. To the outsider the prayer written on the wall could apply to anyone; it is the portrait of Neophytos which tells the spectator that this is not a general prayer, but a very personal and special request. Furthermore the gesture of Christ in the picture conveys to everyone that Christ has answered the prayer of this particular suppliant. The text only makes a request; words are too explicit to risk a verbal answer. This is only one image among several in the Enkleistra which demonstrate how the visual can operate in different ways from the verbal and sometimes make more daring religious statements.

The painted area around his tomb seems as carefully considered as the rest, surprisingly perhaps since it was partly obscured from view during the lifetime of the saint, and was to be entirely hidden after his death. Three separate figural icons are now preserved within the tomb chamber (Figures 88, 89). These are the Crucifixion, the Anastasis and

88 The tomb chamber in the cell was provided with a set of wallpaintings as part of the decoration of 1183. Above the place designated for the coffin of Neophytos, the chosen scenes were a Crucifixion, the Anastasis, and a devotional image of the Virgin and Child with saints.

an image of the Virgin and Child with two saints. Each icon has a specific reference to death and no doubt acted as encouragement to the saint, as during life he awaited death. The choice of a Crucifixion again meant that the scene on the partition wall was repeated within a very small space. This time it is depicted over the place for the coffin, and so has no direct reference to the liturgy of the sanctuary, but rather to the mystery of life after death. In choosing the representation of the Crucifixion here, Neophytos no doubt intended to suggest a parallel between his own death and that of Christ.

The other scene above the tomb is the Anastasis, a standard scene in which were represented the descent of Christ to Hell after the Crucifixion, and his Resurrection on the third day (Figure 89). The version here has many parallels in Byzantine art. Christ has broken down the gates of Hell, and rises to Heaven taking with him various of the dead from their tombs: he takes Adam by the arm, while lined up to follow are Eve and David and Solomon. The other figure present is St John the Baptist; he, as usual in this scene, holds a scroll with the words: 'See the one of whom I have said he comes to free you from the bonds of hell'. The funerary purpose of the picture is plain enough, and no attempt has been made to make any special point here in the details of the scene—unless, that is, Adam at the moment of his resurrection has some portrait resemblance to Neophytos.

The third image in the tomb chamber is in the small niche and as a result is smaller than the other two. It shows the Virgin enthroned with the Child, St John Chrysostomos and St Basil. These two saints were fourth-century bishops, and probably the most famous of the church Fathers. Their frequent portrayal in Byzantine churches is partly to be connected with their authorship of the two standard versions of the Byzantine liturgy. For this reason they were usually painted in the sanctuary of a church where the liturgy was celebrated. Since this niche was not at the time of decoration part of the sanctuary of the church, their choice might instead refer to one of the prescriptions of Neophytos in the *Typikon*—that there should be a regular commemoration after his death in the liturgy celebrated in the church. But other functions for the images can be detected. For example they make links with other paintings on the wall: John Chrysostomos points towards the Crucifixion and holds a scroll with the text: 'A strange sight is Christ crucified', while Basil has the text: 'Whatever it is that you see with amazement, say what it is.' Both texts emphasize the power of sight in understanding Christian mysteries, as did Photios in his sermon on the apse Virgin of St Sophia.

89 Part of the Anastasis painted above the place designed for Neophytos' coffin—from where he expected to be raised at the end of the world—includes the 'historical' event of Christ upon his own resurrection on Easter Sunday raising Adam and Eve from their tombs.

Another possible connotation may be a reference to the biography of Neophytos; he may have wanted to commemorate John Chrysostomos as the patron of the monastery which first accepted him as a member. The element of biographical reference in the paintings was originally made more explicit, for, as already mentioned, there was an inscription incorporated in the decoration (on the ceiling beside the icon of St Damian); this text is now scarcely legible. It mentioned the monastery of Chrysostomos; but it is no longer possible to compare the written message of the cell with that of the images.

The central images of the niche are the Virgin and Child. Mary is shown affectionately leaning towards her son, but the focus of the representation is less the visual portrayal than the text on a scroll which she holds up in this almost secret part of the cell. It begins with the words: 'Grant, my son, remission to him who lies here.' It is a prayer, spoken by the Virgin on behalf of Neophytos, which transmits his hope that he will, by the merit of his pure way of life on earth, have earned himself a place in Heaven without facing terrible punishments directly after death. The text ends with the answer of Christ: 'I grant it, moved as I am by your prayers.' The text and images make clear to us what the expectations of a Byzantine holy man were; he hoped for his soul's instant acceptance after death in the company of the saints of Heaven. Later, at the end of the world, his body would be raised to Heaven also. In this secret part of the cell writing becomes for once as explicit as the picture of the Deisis.

The sanctuary next to the cell was also painted in 1183 by the artist Theodore Apseudes (Figure 90). This small cave contained the altar,

90 The wallpaintings in the sanctuary of the Enkleistra also belong to the decoration of 1183. The main function of this rock-cut chamber was to house the altar and to give space for the celebration of the liturgy. To enhance the architectural appearance, the rock was roughly shaped in the form of a cupola church. The image chosen for this vault was the Ascension; the artist, Theodore Apseudes, designed this in the available surfaces around the east window and fitted in other images below.

and there was probably a narthex outside it on the west side—although this now no longer survives, since at some point the nave of the main church was built over the area. The sanctuary was lit by two small windows in its eastern wall; it held the altar, and was the place where the eucharist was celebrated. Niches in the walls held the necessary vessels for the bread and wine of the communion. All of the cave was painted, but one of the present images, that of Christ Pantocrator on the vault, is a later work of 1503, when the caves were restored.

The sanctuary provided a setting for the celebration of the eucharist and for other monastic services which needed an altar. It was also the place which gave the only access to the cell of Neophytos, which lay beside and beyond it. At first the relic of the Holy Cross may have been kept here, though later it was certainly kept in the nave to the west. The decoration of the sanctuary relates to its various functions: figures of saintly bishops mark out its connection with the liturgy; scenes from the life of Christ, as found in all Byzantine churches, give even this tiny cave the status of a church; representations of saintly monks and of Neophytos himself identify it more particularly as the centre of worship of this monastic community. This is a combination of the standard and the unusual. Bishops and Christ would be familiar icons in any Byzantine centre of worship, but the great prominence of the monks and even more so of Neophytos gives the whole an idiosyncratic feel.

The scenes and figures around the apse are chosen for their connections with the rites of the altar, and so reflect a choice made in many other Byzantine churches. In the lower register of the eastern wall is a set of standing saints which would be directly beside the place of the celebrant priest (Figures 90, 91). The central figure is the Virgin Mary, and with her are four bishops: St John Chrysostomos, St Basil, St Epiphanios and St Nicholas. The first two of these, as has already been mentioned, were normally represented in the sanctuary of a church as the authors of the liturgy. The inclusion of Epiphanios reflects local patriotism; he was a fourth-century monk who became bishop of Salamis in Cyprus, and wrote defences of Orthodox belief and refutations of all known heresy. Most twelfth-century churches in Cyprus included a representation of this local hero in the sanctuary. The other figure, St Nicholas, bishop of Myra, was a common Byzantine choice in church decoration, although his precise connection with this part of the church is unclear.

The function of such saints in the sanctuary decoration is usually reinforced by the contents of inscriptions which they hold on scrolls. These figures as usual hold scrolls, and, though the texts do not follow the usual pattern of being the first words of a number of different prayers used in the liturgy, they do as usual refer to the service. What has been done here is to write out only one prayer: the first words are held by Chrysostomos (who probably wrote the prayer) and the other saints hold a continuation of the same prayer (with a few gaps). The prayer in question is the so-called prayer of the prothesis, spoken during the cutting of the bread of the eucharist. Perhaps we are to read the choice

of these saints accompanied by this prayer to mean that they were specially to be commemorated during the service.

In the tiny space of the sanctuary were four representations from the life of Christ: on the vault the Ascension (Figure 90); to the left of the altar (around the door which led to the cell of Neophytos) the Annunciation of the Virgin (Figure 92); Christ as a young man (Christ Emmanuel) above the door (Figure 92); and just inside the entrance an enthroned Pantocrator ('Ruler of All')—assuming that the surviving later painting is a replacement of a similar image of 1183. These images span the whole of the earthly life of Christ, from the first to the last event of his earthly existence, and in the Pantocrator they take the viewer to the eternal heavenly rule of Christ. The focus of the community's worship and the structure of the liturgical year was centred on the life and continuing rule of Christ. Here all that was represented in four images.

Around the walls of the sanctuary stand the figures of saintly monks, all holding texts which impress on the members of the Enkleistra the rules of the successful monastic life. Their function is didactic. The saints

91 The space around the altar in the sanctuary of the Enkleistra was used to house images of the Virgin and church Fathers; the wall at this level also had to contain the serving niches needed for the liturgical vessels. To the right of the altar (to the west) is the archway leading to the nave of the church.

238

92 To the left of the altar is the doorway which was the only way into Neophytos' cell in the twelfth century. The paintings of 1183 around this doorway show an image of Christ in his youth (Christ Emmanuel) above the door, with the Virgin and archangel Gabriel on either side depicting the Annunciation. These are among the standard choices of icons for the sanctuary area of a church at this period.

chosen are successful monks in the history of the church—SS Ephraim the Syrian, Kyriakos the anchorite, Gerasimos, Theodore, Pachomios, Hilarion and Euthymios. They hold messages like 'The beginning of a monk's ruin is laughter and talk' or 'He who has fear of God in his heart has no need of many books, for fear of God is sufficient for him' or 'This is the royal road that the Fathers have laid down—to eat once a day.' The life of Christ provided the structure of the monastic routine. For the struggling ascetic members of the community, the life of these monks provided a practical model and the image of a saintly status which was in theory attainable by all.

One special panel of a monk, placed on the cave vault opposite the altar, represents Neophytos himself (Figure 93). It is placed physically near the place of the liturgy and visually is a pendant to the scene of the Ascension of Christ. The parallelism with the ascent of Christ to Heaven is clearly intentional. The composition is one unique in Byzantine art. It portrays visually something which the writings of Neophytos allude to less directly: that Neophytos takes as his model Christ himself and will on death immediately go to Heaven. In the centre of the panel

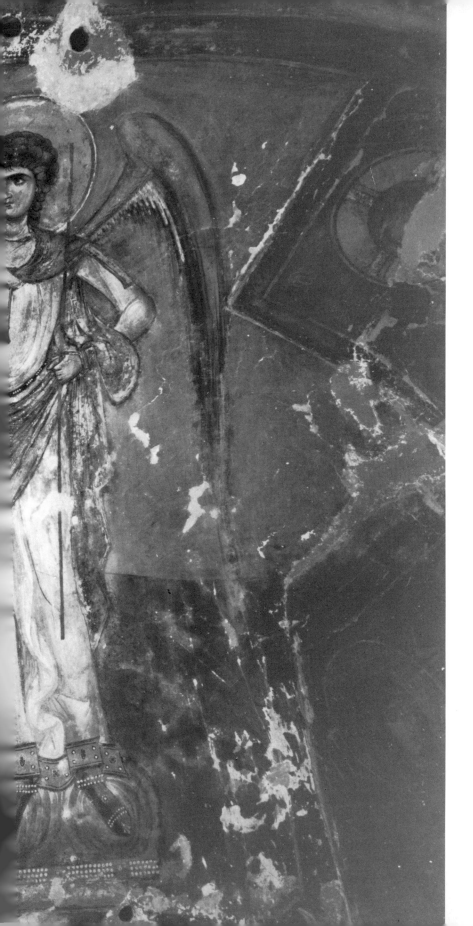

93 The unparalleled image
among the sanctuary paintings
of 1183 is the panel which fills
the wall opposite the altar. In
this scene Neophytos is
represented being, apparently,
raised to Heaven by the
archangels Michael and
Gabriel. The image is
accompanied by a text—a
prayer in the first person that
Neophytos the monk may join
the company of angels.

is a monumental figure of Neophytos, identified by name; he is in a light-coloured monastic habit and has his arms crossed across his chest—in the same position as the arms of the Virgin in the Koimesis on her death-bed at the moment when her soul is received into Heaven by Christ. On each side of Neophytos are the archangels Michael and Gabriel, holding his shoulders and conveying him upwards, towards Heaven. Two lines of verse are written across the top of the picture. They contain a prayer written in the first person and so on behalf of Neophytos, which asks: 'May I join the community of these two angels by virtue of my "angelic" habit.' Once again there is a disjunction between the verbal and the visual. The words ask for entry into Heaven; the icon 'says' the unsayable in confirming the presence of benevolent angels at Neophytos' death, clearly fulfilling his wish to go directly to Heaven. Once the verbal prayer is translated into a visual form, a different kind of statement results. A wish has become fact.

Some of the paintings at the entry to the sanctuary also seem to belong to the decoration of 1183, though the precise appearance of the area at that date is unclear, since we do not know exactly when the nave was enlarged to its present shape. The most important of these for the understanding of the uses of art is a painting of St Stephen the Younger on the wall to the left of the entrance (Figure 94). St Stephen has already appeared in the context of Iconoclasm in Chapter 3. We now see how this saint was visualized centuries after Iconoclasm has ended, and his

94 The other figures in the sanctuary paintings of 1183 are monastic saints. More saintly monks and hermits appear in the nave of the church outside the sanctuary, but most of the painting of this area belongs to the phase of decoration undertaken at a later period in the lifetime of Neophytos (in 1197 or later). One of this series, St Stephen the Younger, is just outside the sanctuary and the paintings might belong to the work of 1183. The eighth-century saint, notable for his opposition to Iconoclasm, is shown holding an icon of the Virgin.

95 *The wallpaintings of the nave include a figure which can be identified as that of Neophytos; this is the third portrait of him in the Enkleistra, and shows him in his old age. Neophytos is to the right of the entrance door of the church and is in the lower register of paintings. Above and to the right of this door are the last two scenes of the cycle which runs around the vaults of the nave and which starts on the wall facing the entrance door: the scenes are the Anastasis (the second in the Enkleistra; see Figures 88, 89) and the* Noli me tangere, *in which the risen Christ towers above the two tiny figures of Mary Magdalene and another woman.*

prominence shows that there is no sign of the Iconoclasm debate dropping out of the consciousness of Byzantines in the late twelfth century. He holds a framed icon of the Virgin and Child (complete with a ring for attaching to a wall). On seeing this picture any spectator would appreciate that he was offered a precedent for the importance of icons in the life of a monk. As well as an icon Stephen has a scroll with an inscription: 'If a person does not reverence our Lord Jesus Christ and his pure Mother shown on an icon, let him be anathema.' This is a standard text for representations of this saint, but the message seems especially appropriate for the Enkleistra on an occasion when an ascetic community had received a contribution for its embellishment. It justifies the attention given to the visual in the caves.

The painting of the nave looks very different in style from the work of Theodore Apseudes in the sanctuary and cell in 1183. It was painted around an opening in the ceiling which communicated with the new cell which Neophytos occupied from 1197. The painting cannot therefore be earlier than 1196/7, and belongs to a separate phase of decoration during Neophytos' old age. A date around 1197 is accepted here, and is supported by the inclusion of a portrait of a monk on the south side of the entrance door which closely resembles the two earlier portraits of Neophytos (Figure 95). He clearly could not resist including his own portrait in this part of the Enkleistra too.

The scheme of decoration of the church of the Holy Cross is one

to be found in many other Byzantine churches—standing figures of saints along the walls, and a cycle of New Testament scenes around the vaults. The effect of the register of standing saints was to make it appear to the members of the community of the Enkleistra that they were in the company of saints from the earlier history of the church as they stood through the offices and liturgy of the church week and year. In this way was created a society of the dead and the living, all to be united, according to their belief, in the afterlife. The upper curving vaults of the church represented one part of the story of Christ. The scenes followed the now conventional system of marking the vaults with a set of pictures which give a permanent and direct visualization of the annually recurring festivals of the church year, but despite the traditional framework, special evocations were produced through the particular choices of scenes and figures.

The figures along the walls have been chosen to show the great models of asceticism and holiness from the past (Figures 94, 96) and twelve examples survive (including St Stephen the Younger who is an integral part of the series): Antony, Arsenios, Euthymios, Amoun, Andronikos, Daniel, Theodosios, John Climacos, Onouphrios, Makarios, Paisios and Stephen. Each one holds a scroll with a moralizing slogan suitable for monks to read, as did the sanctuary saints (where

96 The register of monastic saints in the nave is a stereotyped set of figures, each holding a scroll with a text to encourage asceticism. The paintings can scarcely be described as works of much subtlety or quality. Such monotony of style probably reflects the specific difficulty of obtaining highly-skilled artists in Cyprus at the end of the twelfth century when the island had passed out of the political control of Byzantium; such work should not be used as a basis for any general characterization of the stylistic nature of Byzantine art.

Euthymios had already appeared, but with a different text). Some of these quotations seem allusive to us; that of St John Climacos, for example, which is taken from his book *The Ladder to Paradise* (a series of precepts for monks, which also stimulated striking pictorial images, Figure 100), reads: 'It is better for me to grieve my parents and not my Lord; for he has both created and saved us.' Others are unmistakably direct, like that held by St Amoun of Nitria, a fourth-century Egyptian hermit, which declares: 'Brethren and Fathers, refrain from immoderate eating and untimely drinking; frequent the church and pray constantly.' Neither texts nor images are independent of each other. On their own the images do not convey the message, but project the texts and provide them with moral authority. The texts do not by themselves add up to a systematic guide for life, but in the hands of the saints evoke the whole pattern of a holy life. Texts and images together gave the spectators a tradition to emulate.

The rendering of the individual saints is stereotyped; they are little more than a number of variations of standard portrait types—the artist of this section of the Enkleistra lacked the ease of expression and the talent of Theodore Apseudes. Perhaps the political situation under Crusader rule limited the possibilities for finding artistic talent. Funding arrangements for the realization of the paintings were clearly not too stringent, however, as the haloes of many of the figures are expensively gilded.

Since the church was dedicated to the Holy Cross, and possessed a relic of its wood, it is only natural to find representations of St Constantine the Great and his mother St Helena, who hold a representation of the True Cross between them, in memory of the fact that it was discovered by Helena (Figures 97, 98). In a recess beside their representations was a cross-shaped fitting in the wall where the relic must have been kept. This area of the church shows how the possessions and dedication of a church were an integral part of the planning of its architecture and decoration. The fact that the Crucifixion is shown on the wall directly above the relic is obviously a carefully planned focus of the whole narrative cycle. Although the reason for the inclusion of Constantine and Helena may have been the possession of the relic, the presence of the imperial couple in turn reminded the spectator of his place in the Christian empire. In the *Typikon* Neophytos commends his community to the care of the Byzantine emperor, although after 1191 the island was never again within the boundaries of Byzantine political control. The ideology of Byzantium outlasted its power.

The narrative scenes shown in the upper parts of the church are limited to events from the Passion of Christ. The dedication of the church to the Holy Cross, itself validated through the possession of the relic, in turn became a key factor in the choice of the scheme when the church was painted. The decoration has been worked out so that the scene of the Carrying of the Cross and the Crucifixion were located above the place where the relic was displayed.

The narrative starts at the west end of the church beside the entrance door and is to be read from left to right around the walls. The first

OVERLEAF LEFT *97 At the east end of the nave, on the right side, is a bay with a number of fittings. It is reasonable to interpret these and the choice of wallpaintings as evidence that the relic of the True Cross which Neophytos had acquired was kept here, fitted into the wall. The relic in its slot was between representations of angels and set below the scene of the Crucifixion (the third in the Enkleistra). On the wall to the right of the bay was the site chosen for the depiction of Constantine the Great and his mother Helena (see Figure 98).*

OVERLEAF RIGHT *98 The painting of Constantine the Great and his mother Helena shows the conventional representation of them holding the True Cross between them; such an image can be found in many Byzantine churches, but few of these could claim to own a part of the relic itself. Above this panel is the scene of Christ being taken down from the Cross; the Virgin holds his hand to her cheek, St John the Evangelist kneels at his feet, and Joseph of Arimathea lifts the body. The visual signs of mourning for the dead Christ are understated in this version.*

scenes are now repainted as part of the work of restoration of 1503, but it is clear that the content of the scenes has not been changed. The cycle consisted of: the Last Supper, the Washing of Feet, the Agony in the Garden, the Betrayal by Judas, the Judgement of Pilate, the Road to Calvary and the Crucifixion, the Descent from the Cross, the Lamentation over the body of Christ, the Anastasis, and *Noli me tangere*. Finally, in the highest part of the vault, where the rock was roughly shaped in the form of a dome, there is the Ascension of Christ, witnessed by four Old Testament prophets (Moses, David, Isaiah and Jeremiah), holding texts referring to the power and the sufferings of God (Figure 99). In all, the pictorial programme supplied a symbolic re-creation of the death and resurrection of Christ, commemorated annually in the Easter service and in the regular liturgy.

The effect of the cycle is to emphasize the sufferings of a good Christian life, mitigated only by the promise of a life after death. The heavy and linear treatment of the figures and compositions shows up again the limitations of the artist's technique, although the message itself is clear.

The most remarkable use of art to make suggestions which could not easily be stated in words was in the Ascension of Christ in the 'dome'

99 The nave of the church, like the sanctuary, was architecturally designed with a dome, although the cutting of the rock was quite crude in execution. It was then decorated, as was the sanctuary vault, with a representation of the Ascension. The special visual effect of the design here came from the shaft at its centre which led to a special chamber occupied by Neophytos in the years after 1197. To those in the nave it appeared that the figure of Christ (now fragmentary) was rising into Heaven in the company of Neophytos.

of the church (Figure 99). This use of the visual was only possible as a result of the new arrangements made for Neophytos in 1197, which allowed the visual impact of the church to be created not just through painting but through the spectacle of Neophytos himself as well.

In the *Typikon* Neophytos described the development in 1196/7 of a number of chambers on the upper level of the cliff, in fact directly over the church of the Holy Cross (see plan p. 221). One of them was the *Hagiosterion*, a tiny room into which Neophytos went to participate in the eucharist and in the chanting of holy hymns. The chamber above this was intended as his new living place, and it was to this cell that he gave the name of the New Zion or New Enkleistra. In order that he might be a participant in the services in the church, an opening was made in the ceiling of the church so that there was a shaft which led up into the *Hagiosterion*. The monks at worship in the church of the Holy Cross could therefore look upwards and see Neophytos literally high up above them. Furthermore the shaft through which they saw him was itself an integral part of the painted decoration of the church. They saw him framed within the composition of the Ascension, with the upper part of the figure of Christ projecting on to the side of the shaft. The Ascension scene contained the usual elements (as in the representation of the same scene in the sanctuary in 1183; see Figure 90): Christ at the apex is taken up into Heaven by a group of flying angels while the Virgin, two angels in white and the apostles look on. The position of the *Hagiosterion* above the painting must have enhanced the heavenly status of the holy man in his lifetime. In a sense he becomes here one of the icons of the church.

The name given to the new cell, the New Zion, also stressed the extraordinary status of Neophytos. Apart from its most obvious meaning, the associations of such a name are with the 'upper room' of the Last Supper—the place of the first eucharist—and also with the upper room to which the apostles went after the Ascension. The effect of the visual connections between the scene of the Ascension and the title of the new cell of Neophytos is to suggest his own succession from the apostles.

This series of paintings is one of the most striking instances of the expression of radical new claims, justified and no doubt also stimulated by icons and decorative schemes. Neophytos appeared literally above the humble monks of his community—no longer just their earthly head, but himself inserted into the company of saints that decorated the walls of the monastery. In the community of a self-educated rural hermit on the margins of the Byzantine Empire, we find visual images vividly calling 'normal' human status into question. What was Neophytos to the monks of his community? At one level, of course, he was their abbot and author of their monastic rule—a powerful human being. But as they looked at the decoration around them and at Neophytos on high, many must have seen in him a saint like those depicted in their place of worship who had once been on earth but now resided in Heaven, proof of the rewards of a virtuous life. Some must have found in the visual images of Neophytos a formulation of a question inexpress-

ible and impermissible in verbal terms: was Neophytos a new apostle or even perhaps a new Christ?

★   ★   ★   ★

This book began with an evocation of the conventional view held of Byzantium. Its consistent theme has been the understanding of the place of art within this society at various moments of time. The argument has been that art was not only accepted within the culture as an essential help for the achievement of the Christian life, but was part of the perceptions of all Byzantines in ways they could hardly fully appreciate themselves.

If art is to be seen as a key part of the world of Byzantium, then one overriding question for us today is whether the conventional view of Byzantine art is as much an oversimplified stereotype as the view of Byzantine society. It is easy to find characterizations of Byzantine art as 'unchanging', 'stiff', 'flat', 'abstract', all adjectives that attempt to place it as a form of art at the other end of the spectrum from the illusionistic art of the Antique World or the Italian Renaissance. Such characterizations are not simply unaware of the variety of Byzantine art; it is perhaps of greater significance that they offer no hint of the uses and functions of this art in society. This book has shown some of the areas of Byzantium where answers can only be found when art is taken into account. The ambition to reach a formal definition of Byzantine art is a misplaced one.

RETROSPECT

THE ARGUMENT in this book has ranged over six centuries, all around the eastern Mediterranean, and across the whole spectrum of Byzantine society. While focusing on the function of the visual arts in Byzantium, it has not been a work of 'traditional art history' in the sense of an exclusive concern with dating works of art and attributing them to individual artists, with practical considerations of their production and with analysis of their iconography. Icons have not been considered as autonomous objects which need only to be dated and put in sequence in order to be understood. Instead works of art and literature have been treated as evidence of attitudes and beliefs and, conversely, as instigators of these. This approach has additionally shown up the differences between literature and art in the expression and formation of beliefs and ideas.

The argument has not been of a traditional 'sociological' type, developed by the posing of questions formulated, for example, on the basis of statistical information on family life, demography and social patterns. Yet, in a more general sense, it has been constantly concerned with Byzantine society, with the relationship of art to social practices, and with the functions of visual images in a wide cross-section of the different societies and groups of the empire. In this way a fuller understanding has been gained of the standard historical characterization of Byzantine society as traditional and conservative.

During the whole period covered by the book, Byzantium remained—despite significant changes in the size of its empire and in the ways that its provinces were managed—a society under the rigid control of its ruler. The emperor inherited or usurped his title and claimed a unique position in the political organization as the representative on earth of a divine order in Heaven—a divine order which itself mirrored the scheme on earth. This ideology was not only made explicit in the texts of the period but was also conveyed to society through visual images, most obviously through the structured artistic schemes in the churches which everyone visited. For any subject to question the Byzantine imperial system was therefore tantamount to heresy; yet he might claim that individual emperors (though not the imperial system) had fallen into heresy, and no longer truly represented the Christian order. The Iconoclasm of the emperors of the eighth and ninth centuries was seen as heresy by a sufficient number of Byzantines to form a challenge to the imperial position; and when Iconoclasm was finally abandoned, the new ruling group could claim for itself true orthodoxy. But what was seen as tradition and orthodoxy was by no means constant; paradoxically, an appeal to tradition could be used as an argument for the justification of innovations by the iconoclast emperors.

Byzantium is also a society in which no easy distinction can be made between the political and the religious, or between the lay rulers and the church. This is one of the factors that makes it difficult to compare Byzantium and Western Europe. The Byzantine amalgam is difficult for the modern observer, at least intuitively, to understand. Also, modern preconceptions of words like society, church and state mean that the terms of literary texts are likely to be misleading because of their apparent familiarity. To add visual images to the witness of texts can therefore significantly enlarge the terms of reference. Even more important, it is easier to enter into such an admittedly alien past culture through images simply because of their unfamiliarity. Byzantine art acts as an expression of the amalgam between church and state; images help to show not only the permanence of the amalgam over the centuries, but also the changes in its character demonstrated by the way in which the uses and perceptions of art altered.

★　★　★　★

The first chapter focused on a rural society in Asia Minor in the late sixth and early seventh centuries and on the career of Theodore of Sykeon. His well-documented *Life* allowed issues to be seen as they affected a limited group, and illustrated some of the effects of the workings of the power structures of the imperial system from the point of view of those outside the capital. It was a time when Asia Minor faced the unmistakable signs of change and of challenges to the established traditions of life. One aspect of the period was the threat posed by armies moving through the region—first the Byzantine soldiery on their way to the east, and then the invading Persian armies (soon to be followed by the Arabs). The population which faced this increasing threat of war had already been demoralized and decimated by successive epidemics of the plague. Yet the society of rural Asia Minor looked at here was not a group on its own, isolated from the rest of the empire. It was not possible to speak of a rigid distinction between conventions in town and countryside in Byzantium, and contacts were continually made between people from various parts of the empire and in different walks of life. Yet for all this apparent homogeneity, certain groups and individuals were clearly and recognizably differentiated in Byzantine society; the distinctions were visually displayed by dress and other attributes so that the hierarchies of power and rank could be seen as well as felt. For example, Theodore's successful career depended upon his conversion to a religious way of life which all members of society approved and on his consequent promotion through an ordered church hierarchy. Both the promotion of his Christian virtues and the progress of his career were assisted and reflected by the visual works of art connected with him.

Another angle on Byzantine society in this same period of invasion and crisis was derived from the evidence of the city of Thessaloniki. Unlike the region of northern Asia Minor, a relatively secure and central part of the empire, Thessaloniki represented a frontier; it lay between empire and barbarians, between Christians and pagans, and between the Mediterranean and mainland Europe. In the case of this Byzantine city, day-to-day living was assisted not through the inspiration of one living individual, but through the more complicated processes of the promotion by the church and the ruling class of a local hero of the past. Confidence both in the powers and even in the existence of St Demetrios was built up substantially through visual aids. His legends were recounted verbally and at length, but for a confirmation of his supposed appearance the citizens had fuller and more direct evidence in the icons in his church. These long-established icons also helped to suggest that he had a symbolic presence in the city, and made the stories of his appearances more credible. It was such pictures which lay behind dreams in which his presence was claimed—at least after they had been interpreted when the sleeper woke up—and behind visions where his obviously benign presence needed no further explanations or proof for those who 'saw' and recognized him. The role of bishops and governors in sponsoring visual representations of St Demetrios had the combined effect of building up confidence and trust in a Christian saint and the concomitant associations, and also, through their claims of personal access to him, of establishing the authority of the ruling classes, which were themselves under imperial control.

Only by finally turning to the evidence of Constantinople could the amazing power of the Byzantine emperor be fully observed. The clearest example of his absolute powers was the phenomenon of Iconoclasm, which was imposed in part as a response to challenges to imperial power posed by the increasing reliance of his subjects on other elements in society, such as the church and the monasteries and especially the icons. The spread of icons seems to have offered individuals a special and new channel to the world beyond, which devalued the powers of the emperor as a special representative of God on earth, and icons were also visible proof of the size and power of the church as displayed through the growing community of saints.

The imperial ban on icons in the eighth and ninth centuries has no simple explanation, nor was it purely a church dispute; it was the imposition of a new way of life which impinged on everyone. It can be interpreted as a demonstration of the powers of the emperor and his expectations of loyalty, an especially striking demand if Iconoclasm was, as seems possible, only attractive to a minority of his subjects. By observing the arguments and attitudes of those who openly opposed the emperor and his policies on the nature of allowable visual representations during Iconoclasm, the preoccupations of Byzantine society itself, particularly in Constantinople, emerged in sharper profile. A premium was put by everybody on the continuation of established authority and traditions; the difficulty was to agree on what was established, especially when the traditions incorporated rival elements. From the viewpoint of the present day, we know that much of the Christian community has shifted its values to such an extent that the iconoclast case, as an attack on idolatry and superstition, has come to represent a traditional virtue of the church in Western Europe.

In the ninth century, the failure of Iconoclasm was seen as the triumph of the traditional over innovation. This triumph meant in social terms the predominance of a certain kind of religious thinking, defined in Byzantium as 'orthodoxy'. It did not mean the triumph of the church in terms of political power; for the emperors, by themselves subscribing to orthodoxy, maintained their previous controls over the church hierarchy. However, the emergence of the church as the victor after Iconoclasm set the cultural mould for the rest of the period. The emphasis given by the clergy, for example, to the cult of the Virgin and the patronage by the wealthy of architecture and decoration which publicly communicated her character and special powers, inspired a dependence on her through the stages of human life.

The public organization of Christianity remained in the framework of a service of state; but the conspicuous expansion of monasticism meant that these virtually self-contained communities, to whom special immunities from taxes or outside control might be granted, took over new functions. It was convenient for the emperor to delegate his charitable obligations and the details of the distribution of his donations to monasteries. This delegation was of course expressed in its time in terms of the piety and virtue of the ideal Christian emperor, but it amounted to more than this. From the surviving associated patronage of the arts, what emerges is how public perceptions of the values of the Byzantine system were reinforced and maintained through imperial investments in religious art.

One of the most characteristic developments of this society was the institutional system of the monastery and the spread of such communities inside cities and in the countryside. A foretaste of the possible effects of the encouragement of the holy man in society is given by the case of Theodore of Sykeon, described in Chapter 1. But despite his fanatical and extreme asceticism he was not able to abdicate from social responsibilities, and did in fact fulfil important functions in the wider community as well as offering help and security to his fellow monks. The particular history of Byzantium led to a society which in the twelfth century could support the hermitage of Neophytos of Paphos. Indeed the structures of society were such that this community could survive not only the evolution of the island into a new state of Cyprus outside the Byzantine empire, but all other vicissitudes to the present day.

The life led by Neophytos enclosed in his cell—little different from burial alive in his tomb—and the dogmatic specialization of his literary interests must represent an extreme of Byzantium to a modern observer. But Neophytos was hardly typical of Byzantine society, even though Byzantine society accepted him as an ideal type of Christian. The visual environment which was gradually constructed around him on the walls of his dwelling is by almost any standards extraordinary, and beyond the conventions of his own time. Throughout this book the case has been put that visual material is to be seen as an integral component of the thinking of society. But the environment of Neophytos discloses a use of art which goes vividly beyond the normal readings of the visual. The special function of art is to do more than to express ideas in a way different from written or spoken statements; it is used in the presence of Neophytos to say the unsayable, and even to predict his future in Heaven.

The cases chosen for illustration in this book help to unravel the integral place of visual communication in society. They are examples which demonstrate that art is not to be underestimated as mere decoration, but should be recognized as an influential expression of ideas and a means for constructing a visual environment within which the nature of individual and social ideals can be displayed. Once constructed, this visual environment does not simply remain as a record of the intentions of its creators; its images can take on new meanings and change or extend the perceptions of its audiences. For the historian, the challenge of the visual aspect of any culture lies in understanding its grammar and discovering ways of reading its signs. In the art of Byzantium, there are many more possibilities yet to be explored. It is clear enough that icons did not have as their primary function the artificial representation of 'reality', and so cannot be viewed, as much European art has traditionally been, in terms of progress towards more and more effective illusion. How then is 'development' in Byzantine art to be understood? How are we to interpret changes and shifts in the traditional conventions of Byzantine representation? Is indeed the familiar notion of 'innovation' the right concept to stress? Or does that merely distort our recognition of the positive role of tradition in Byzantine society? Many issues are raised by visual images, images that are inevitably ambiguous. All viewers, whether Byzantines themselves, later Christians or modern scholars, ask their own particular questions of what they see and impose their own interpretations on it. This study is one such interpretation.

BYZANTINE EMPERORS

Overlapping dates show periods of joint reigns.

324–337	Constantine I the Great
337–361	Constantios II
361–363	Julian
363–364	Jovian
364–378	Valens
379–395	Theodosios I the Great
395–408	Arcadios
408–450	Theodosios II
450–457	Marcian
457–474	Leo I
474	Leo II
474–475	Zeno
475–476	Basiliscos
476–491	Zeno (again)
491–518	Anastasios I
518–527	Justin I
527–565	Justinian I the Great
565–578	Justin II
578–582	Tiberios I Constantine
582–602	Maurice
602–610	Phocas
610–641	Heraclios
641	Constantine III and Heraclonas
641	Heraclonas
641–668	Constans II
668–685	Constantine IV
685–695	Justinian II (first reign)
695–698	Leontios
698–705	Tiberios II
705–711	Justinian II (second reign)
711–713	Philippicos
713–715	Anastasios II

715–717	Theodosios III
717–741	Leo III
741–775	Constantine V
775–780	Leo IV
780–797	Constantine VI
797–802	Irene
802–811	Nicephoros I
811	Stauracios
811–813	Michael I Rangabe
813–820	Leo V
820–829	Michael II
829–842	Theophilos
842–867	Michael III
866–886	Basil I
886–912	Leo VI
912–913	Alexander
913–959	Constantine VII Porphyrogenitos
920–944	Romanos I Lecapenos
959–963	Romanos II
963–969	Nicephoros II Phocas
969–976	John I Tzimisces
976–1025	Basil II
1025–1028	Constantine VIII
1028–1034	Romanos III Argyros
1034–1041	Michael IV
1041–1042	Michael V
1042	Zoe and Theodora
1042–1055	Constantine IX Monomachos
1055–1056	Theodora (again)
1056–1057	Michael VI
1057–1059	Isaac I Comnenos
1059–1067	Constantine X Ducas
1068–1071	Romanos IV Diogenes

1071–1078	Michael VII Ducas
1078–1081	Nicephoros III Botaneiates
1081–1118	Alexios I Comnenos
1118–1143	John II Comnenos
1143–1180	Manuel I Comnenos
1180–1183	Alexios II Comnenos
1183–1185	Andronicos I Comnenos
1185–1195	Isaac II Angelos
1195–1203	Alexios III Angelos
1203–1204	Isaac II (again) and Alexios IV Angelos
1204	Alexios V Murtzuphlos
1204–1222	Theodore I Lascaris
1222–1254	John III Ducas Vatatzes
1254–1258	Theodore II Lascaris
1258–1261	John IV Lascaris
1259–1282	Michael VIII Palaiologos
1282–1328	Andronicos II Palaiologos
1328–1341	Andronicos III Palaiologos
1341–1391	John V Palaiologos
1347–1354	John VI Cantacuzenos
1376–1379	Andronicos IV Palaiologos
1390	John VII Palaiologos
1391–1425	Manuel II Palaiologos
1425–1448	John VIII Palaiologos
1448–1453	Constantine XI Palaiologos

GLOSSARY

Agora A public place, market place, or civic assembly area, usually in the centre of a city (the Latin Forum).

Ambo A raised platform set in the nave of a church from which the scriptures could be read during the liturgy; it was also used for the recitation of litanies and other public parts of services, and sometimes for the display of relics, such as the Holy Cross. By the time of Photios it had become the place from which sermons (originally delivered from the apse) were spoken; hence pulpit is one correct translation.

Anastasis Literally 'Resurrection': in art the Resurrection of Christ portrays the breaking of the gates of Hell, and the rescue of Adam and Eve and Old Testament kings. John the Baptist is witness of the Ascent of Christ from Hell to Heaven

Chlamys A short cloak, distinctively fastened by a brooch on the right shoulder.

Ciborion Normally either a vessel which contained the bread of the eucharist or the canopy (or baldacchino) resting on four columns which was placed over the altar. Uniquely the ciborion (originally of silver, but later of marble) in the church of St Demetrios at Thessaloniki was a special structure on the north side of the central nave which contained an effigy of the saint and acted as an architectural focus for prayer to the saint.

Eparch A Greek translation of the Latin title *praefectus*. In the *Miracles of St Demetrios* the word is met in several meanings: sometimes it refers to the post of Praefectus Praetorio Illyrici (the military commander of the region as it was organized in the Late Roman period), and sometimes to the same post after it had apparently evolved into the governorship of Thessaloniki; the word in the plural refers more generally to imperial officials.

Ex-voto An offering made in fulfilment of a vow.

Hippodrome Major cities in the Roman empire, including Constantinople and Thessaloniki, were supplied with arenas for regular chariot-race meetings and other entertainments. The hippodrome of Thessaloniki seems to have been abandoned in the fifth century, but in Constantinople, where there were several, the main hippodrome beside the Great Palace of the emperor continued in use throughout the period covered in this book.

Iconostasis A high screen in churches of the Late Byzantine period which divided the sanctuary from the congregation and which concealed the altar, except when the central doors (the 'royal doors') of the structure were opened for ritual effect. Literally 'a stand for icons', the screen came to be systematically decorated with ranks of icons: see also *templon*.

Koimesis The 'Falling Asleep' of the Virgin; the theology of the death of the Virgin was complicated and it was developed over the period. Some Byzantine interpretations of the apocryphal texts are very close to the Roman Catholic doctrine of the Assumption.

Liturgy As equivalent for the Greek *leitourgia*, the Byzantine ecclesiastical term for the eucharist or mass.

Loros The long gold-embroidered and jewelled scarf (or stole) worn on Easter Sunday by the emperor and by the twelve highest court officials—on that day signifying visually Christ and the twelve apostles.

Mandylion See *soudarion*.

Mihrab See below *mimbar*.

Mimbar (*also* minbar, mimber) The pulpit in a mosque, approached up steps; from here the leader (the Imam) of the congregation preached a sermon on Fridays. The mimbar was located next to the *mihrab*, a niche which showed the congregation the direction of the shrine of the Ka'ba in Mecca, towards which they faced for prayers, and which was the most highly decorated area of any mosque. The mimbar itself was likewise a conspicuous feature of the interior.

Narthex The western vestibule of a Byzantine church, immediately inside the entrance door (or doors); it was sometimes separated from the nave and aisles by doors or by columns, as in the case of St Demetrios at Thessaloniki. It had various functions including supplying a place for candidates for baptism or for penitents (not allowed to attend the liturgy).

Nomisma (plural *nomismata*) The Greek name for the standard gold coin of the period (the Latin *solidus*). For most of the period from the eighth to the eleventh centuries, it was of 24 carats, and 72 nomismata weighed one pound. In this period, other coins were silver (the *miliareson*), and bronze (*follis*). The gold coins were consistently debased during the eleventh century; finally in the twelfth century a new set of denominations was introduced and the old nomisma of pure gold replaced by a *hyperpyron* (super-refined) nomisma.

Omophorion A long strip (originally wool, then silk or velvet) worn round the shoulder during the liturgy by Byzantine bishops and falling loose towards the ground (corresponding to the *pallium* in the Catholic church).

Proskynesis The act of prostration in front of the emperor, or in church in the presence of the divine. It involved falling to the knees, touching the ground with the forehead, and stretching out the arms in supplication and adoration.

Revetment Any kind of facing. The vertical areas of Byzantine church walls were usually either faced with marble slabs or else rendered with plaster and painted to resemble marble revetment. Other parts of a church, such as tombs, could be revetted with carved marble ornamentation or precious metals. Icons were sometimes revetted—usually with gold or silver covers over parts of the panel.

Soudarion/mandylion Both nouns refer to a cloth, the famous relic of the city of Edessa in the province of Syria (now Urfa in Turkey). The legend concerning this cloth comes in several versions. The oldest versions concern Abgar V (king of Edessa from 4 BC to AD 50) who wrote to Christ and asked him to come and cure his illness. In return he received a letter promising a visit from St Thomas after the Ascension who would heal him and preach the Gospel. This letter written in Syriac is recorded in Edessa in the fourth century as a source of miracles. By the sixth century, an addition had been made to the legend: that Christ had also sent his portrait, miraculously imprinted on a cloth. This cloth was brought to Constantinople in the tenth century, and joined the collection of famous relics in the imperial palace.

Tablion (Latin *tabula*) This word appears in several senses in Byzantine Greek; in this book tablion always refers to an ornamental square of silk (usually of purple or golden thread) sewn on to the chlamys and acting as a badge of office.

Templon The barrier between the congregation and the sanctuary of a Byzantine church. It was a colonnade (frequently of marble) which closed off the area of the altar from the congregation, but, at least in its original form, it was open and did not hide the sanctuary from the laity. In time, icons and curtains were added to the structure, and it finally developed into the opaque iconostasis (see above).

Theme The regional divisions into which the provinces were organized from the seventh century.

Transept The extension of the nave of the church with bays to north and south, usually slightly to the west of the sanctuary. The effect is to increase the ground space around the altar area, and formally to give the ground plan of the church the shape of a cross.

BIBLIOGRAPHY

General Bibliography

BROWN, P., *Society and the Holy in Late Antiquity* (London, 1982).

GUILLOU, A., *La civilisation byzantine* (Paris, 1974).

HODGES, R. and WHITEHOUSE, D., *Mohammed, Charlemagne and the Origins of Europe* (London, 1983).

HOPKINS, K., *Death and Renewal. Sociological Studies in Roman History. Volume 2* (Cambridge, 1983). On pp. 33–6 is to be found the clearest statement of the nature of the political system of Rome in the Late Republic. This allows one to formulate the necessary questions which need to be answered if the political organization of Byzantium is to be understood.

JENKINS, R., *Byzantium. The Imperial Centuries AD 610–1071* (London, 1966).

KAZHDAN, A. and CONSTABLE, G., *People and Power in Byzantium. An Introduction to Modern Byzantine Studies* (Washington, DC, 1982).

MANGO, C., *The Art of the Byzantine Empire 312–1453* (Englewood Cliffs, New Jersey, 1972).

MANGO, C., *Byzantium. The Empire of New Rome* (London, 1980).

OSTROGORSKY, G. (*trans.* J. Hussey), *History of the Byzantine State* (Oxford, 1968).

WEITZMANN, K., *The Icon* (London, 1978).

1 The Visible Saint: St Theodore of Sykeon

ALLEN, P., 'The "Justinianic" Plague', *Byzantion*, 49 (1979), 5–20.

BAKER, DEREK, 'Theodore of Sykeon and the Historians', *Studies in Church History 13, The Orthodox Churches and the West* (1976), 83–96.

BROWNING, ROBERT, 'The "Low Level" Saint's Life in the Early Byzantine World', in *The Byzantine Saint* (1981), 117–27.

DAWES, ELIZABETH and BAYNES, NORMAN H., *Three Byzantine Saints* (London and Oxford, 1948).

FESTUGIÈRE, A-J. (*ed.*), *Vie de Théodore de Sykéon* (Brussels, 1970); two volumes, the first of text, and the second of translation into French and commentary (*Subsidia Hagiographica*, no. 48).

HORDERN, PEREGRINE, 'Saints and Doctors in the Early Byzantine Empire: the case of Theodore of Sykeon', *Studies in Church History 19, The Church and Healing* (1982), 1–13.

KITZINGER, ERNST, 'The Cult of Images in the Age before Iconoclasm', *Dumbarton Oaks Papers*, 8 (1954), 83–150. Reprinted in *The Art of Byzantium and the Medieval West: Selected Studies by Ernst Kitzinger*, edited by W. E. Kleinbauer (Indiana University Press, 1976).

[106, note 84: The translation of *staurodochos* as referring to an icon in a receptacle for a relic of the holy cross makes the impossible assumption that such a village church in Sykeon could have a relic of the cross at that time, an assumption that can be ruled out. Note 85 incorrectly refers to chapter 13 as containing a cure; but it was only a 'cure' for a bad memory.]

MAKRIDES, RUTH, 'Saints and Sainthood in the Early Palaiologan Period', in *The Byzantine Saint*, edited by S. Hackel, *Studies Supplementary to Sobornost* 5 (1981), 67–87, *esp.* 83*ff* on canonization.

ROSENQVIST, J. O., *Studien zur Syntax und Bemerkungen zum Text der Vita Theodori Syceotae* (Uppsala, 1981).

SEVCENKO, I., 'L'Agiografia bizantina del IV al IX sec.', *La civiltà bizantina dal IV al IX seculo: aspetti e problemi. Corsi di Studi*, I (1976); (Bari, 1977).

WICKHAM, C., 'The Other Transition: from the Ancient World to Feudalism', *Past and Present*, 103 (1984), 3–36.

2 The Saint Imagined: St Demetrios of Thessaloniki

BROWN, P., *The Cult of Saints. Its Rise and Function in Latin Christianity* (Chicago and London, 1981).

CORMACK, ROBIN, 'The Mosaic Decoration of S. Demetrios, Thessaloniki: a re-examination in the light of the drawings of W. S. George', *Annual of the British School at Athens*, 64 (1969), 17–52. The dating of the mosaics belonging before the fire of *c*.620 suggested in this paper now needs revision.

CROKE, B., 'Hormisdas and the Late Roman Walls of Thessalonika', *Greek, Roman and Byzantine Studies* 19 (1978), 251–8.

DAHL, E., 'Dilexi Decorem Domus Dei. Building to the Glory of God in the Middle Ages', *Acta ad archaeologiam et artium historiam pertinentia*, 2nd series, 1 (1982), 157–90.

EVANS, J. A. S., 'The Walls of Thessalonica', *Byzantion* 47 (1977), 361–2.

GRABAR, A., 'Notes sur les mosaiques de Saint-Démétrios à Salonique', *Byzantion* 48 (1978), 64–77.

LEMERLE, PAUL, *Les plus anciens recueils des miracles de saint Demetrius*, I Texte, II Commentaire (Paris, 1979–1981). This fundamental recent edition comes to new conclusions about several of the dates of events recorded in the text, and this means that all previous statements have to be reconsidered.

PALLAS, D. I., 'Le ciborium hexagonal de Saint-Démétrios de Thessalonique', *Zograf* 10 (1979), 44–58.

VICKERS, M., 'Sirmium or Thessaloniki? A Critical Examination of the St. Demetrius Legend', *Byzantinische Zeitschrift* 67 (1974), 337–50.

WALTER, C., 'St. Demetrius: The Myroblytos of Thessalonika', in *Studies in Byzantine Iconography* (London, 1977), 157–78: reprinted from *Eastern Churches Review* (1973).

WARD, B., *Miracles and the Medieval Mind* (Philadelphia, 1982).

3 Iconoclasm: the Imposition of Change

ANTONOPOULOS, E., 'Miséricorde, olivier: agents et attributs', *Byzantion* 51 (1981), 345–81.

BROWN, P., 'A Dark Age Crisis: aspects of the Iconoclastic Controversy' in *Society and the Holy in Late Antiquity*, reprinted articles (London, 1982), 251–301.

BRYER, A. and HERRIN, J. (ed.), *Iconoclasm* (University of Birmingham, 1977): especially D. Freedberg, 'The Structure of Byzantine and European Iconoclasm', pp. 165–77.

CAMERON, AVERIL, *Continuity and Change in Sixth-Century Byzantium* (London, 1981): reprinted papers: *esp.* no. XVIII 'Images of Authority: Elites and Icons in Late Sixth-Century Byzantium'.

CRONE, PATRICIA, 'Islam, Judeo-Christianity, and Byzantine Iconoclasm', *Jerusalem Studies in Arabic and Islam* 2 (1980), 59–95.

DE'MAFFEI, F., *Icona, Pittore e Arte al Concilio Niceno II* (Rome, 1974).

DOBSCHUETZ, E. VON, *Christusbilder. Untersuchen zur Christlichen Legenden* (Leipzig, 1899).

DODD, ERICA CRUIKSHANK, *Byzantine Silver Treasures*, Monograph der Abegg-Stiftung Bern 9 (Bern, 1973).

DODD, ERICA CRUIKSHANK, 'The Image of the Word', *Berytus* 18 (1969), 35–79.

DUCHESNE, L., 'L'iconographie byzantine dans un document grec du IXe siècle', *Roma e l'Oriente* 5 (1912–13), 222–39, 273–85, and 349–66. This is a re-publication of the text edited from Patmos ms. 48 (ninth-century) and Patmos ms. 179 (twelfth-century) by Sakkelion in 1864.

In this book a date is accepted for this text close to 843 on the basis of the following considerations:

Was this *Letter* written and sent to the emperor Theophilos in April 836 by three patriarchs as its title claims? There are various arguments in favour of the authenticity of the letter: the three oriental patriarchs can be independently documented; some sort of meeting certainly did take place in Jerusalem at Easter 836; and one of the manuscripts of the text is ninth-century, apparently almost contemporary with the date of the meeting. The arguments against the existence of this letter in this form in 836 are more decisive. It is inherently improbable that a document with this theological content and containing an icon of the Virgin and Child was prepared for despatch to Theophilos. Further anomalies are the vast size of the council, supposed to take place in the city of Jerusalem under Islamic occupation, the intemperate remarks against the Arab empire, and the amazing praise for the piety and goodness of the iconoclast emperor Theophilos.

The easiest solution is to accept that something was written in 836, but to take the *Letter* as we have it as a reworked version not much later in date. This kind of invented document is not entirely isolated in the first half of the ninth century, and indeed the book in which it is found seems to have included another composition of similar type: *The Condemnation and Anathematisation of the heretical and false Patriarchs Theodotos, Antonios and John* (these are the patriarchs of Constantinople who span the second period of Iconoclasm until 843). The best studied of this sort of invented document from this period are the two *Letters of Pope Gregory II to the emperor Leo III*. Only the second of these letters appears to be authentic and then only in part; the first, with its long discussion about images, is a careful Byzantine creation (needed to supplement the second in order to support the iconophile case). The author has been supposed to be a monk, living outside Constantinople, and writing some time between the late eighth century and the middle of the ninth century. Our text seems to be the creation of a similar kind of writer.

Our version of *Letter of the Three Patriarchs* has a nucleus of images in its list, nine in number, from the regions under the control of the oriental patriarchs, but these are supplemented with images and detailed anti-iconoclastic stories from Constantinople; this suggests the capital as the place where it was compiled, after 836. The compilation could belong to the intense period of activity in preparation for the iconophile council of 11 March 843, for there was over a year between the death of Theophilos on 20 January 842 and the ending of Iconoclasm; or alternatively to the subsequent years after the end of Iconoclasm in 843, when it would have acted both as an encouragement to the victorious iconophiles and as a polemic against recalcitrant opponents who might still have anticipated a return to Iconoclasm (Iconoclasm or named supporters of it were condemned at church councils held in 861, 867 and 869). Perhaps there was a significant manufacture of such documents, possibly under the direction of one of the first two patriarchs to take office after 843 (Methodios and Ignatios) who had both been monks under Iconoclasm. A final decision on the date should also take into account the dating of the Khludov Psalter and related illuminated manuscripts, as these would seem to belong to exactly the same kind of circle.

GOUILLARD, J., *La vie religieuse à Byzance* (London, 1981); reprinted papers.

GRABAR, A., *L'iconoclasme byzantin. Dossier archéologique* (Paris, 1957).

GRIERSON, P., *Byzantine Coins* (University of California, 1982).

GUTMANN, J. (ed.), *The Image and the Word. Confrontations in Judaism, Christianity, and Islam* (Missoula, Montana, 1977).

HALDON, J., 'Some Remarks on the Background to the Iconoclastic Controversy', *Byzantinoslavica* 38 (1977), 161–84.

HALDON, J. F. and KENNEDY, H., 'The Arab-Byzantine Frontier in the Eighth and Ninth Centuries: Military Organisation and Society in the Borderlands', *Zbornik Radova Vizantoloshkog Instituta* 19 (1980), 79–116.

HENRY, P., 'What was the Iconoclastic Controversy About?', *Church History* 45 (1976), 16–31.

HERRIN, JUDITH, 'Women and the Faith in Icons in Early Christianity', in *Culture, Ideology and Politics* edited by R. Samuel and G. Stedman Jones (London, 1983), 56–83.

LADNER, G. B., *Images and Ideas in the Middle Ages. Selected Studies in History and Art* I (Rome, 1983).

MANGO, C., *The Brazen House* (Copenhagen, 1959).

MARKUS, R. A., 'The Cult of Icons in Sixth-Century Gaul', reprinted in *From Augustine to Gregory the Great* (*Variorum Reprints*, London 1983); his translations and deductions are not acceptable.

MEGAW, A. H. S. and HAWKINS, E. J. W., *The Church of the Panagia Kanakaria at Lythrankomi in Cyprus. Its Mosaics and Frescoes* (Washington, DC, 1977); *esp.* Appendix: 'A Wonderworking Mosaic in Cyprus', pp. 161–70. One error here might be misleading: it is not correct that the first publication of the *Thesaurus* of Damascenos was in 1676. The British Library has a printed edition from Venice of 1561 (presumably the first edition). Therefore the supposition of Megaw that *The New Heaven* of Ivan Galiatovsky, published in 1665, depends on a manuscript copy of Damascenos is an unnecessary complication.

MIGNE, J. P., *Patrologia Graeca*, vol. 95, 343–86.

ROUAN, MARIE-FRANCE, 'Une lecture "iconoclaste" de la vie d'Étienne le jeune', *Travaux et Mémoires* 8 (1981), 415–36. A new edition of the text is in preparation by this writer with Marie Dupré La Tour; until that appears the text may be consulted in Migne, *P.G.* 100.

STEIN, D., *Der Beginn des byzantinischen Bilderstreites und seine Entwicklung bis in die 40er Jahre des 8 Jahrhunderts* (Munich, 1980).

VASILIEV, A., 'The Life of St Theodora of Edessa', *Byzantion* 16 (1942–3), 165–225, *esp.* 216–25.

4 After Iconoclasm: the Illusion of Tradition

CAMERON, AVERIL, *Continuity and Change in Sixth-Century Byzantium* (London, 1981); *esp.* XVI 'The Theotokos in Sixth-Century Constantinople'; and XVII 'The Virgin's Robe: an episode in the history of early seventh-century Constantinople'.

CORMACK, R., 'Interpreting the Mosaics of S. Sophia at Istanbul', *Art History* 4 (1981), 131–49.

GRAEF, HILDA, *Mary: a History of Doctrine and Devotion*, vol. 1, *From the Beginnings to the Eve of the Reformation* (London and New York, 1963); vol. 2, *From the Reformation to the Present Day* (London and New York, 1965).

LAOURDAS, B., *Photiou Omiliai* (Thessaloniki, 1959).

LEMERLE, P., *Le premier humanisme byzantin* (Paris, 1971).

MAGUIRE, H., *Art and Eloquence in Byzantium* (Princeton, 1981).

MANGO, C., *The Homilies of Photius Patriarch of Constantinople* (Harvard University Press, 1958).

MANGO, C., 'When was Michael III Born?', *Dumbarton Oaks Papers* 21 (1967), 253–8.

MANGO, C. and HAWKINS, E. J. W., 'The Apse Mosaics of St Sophia at Istanbul. Report on Work carried out in 1964', *Dumbarton Oaks Papers* 19 (1965), 113–49.

OIKONOMIDES, N., *Les listes de préséance byzantines des IXe et Xe siècles* (Paris, 1972).

RUSSO, E., 'L'affresco di Turtura nel cimitero di Commodilla, l'icona di S. Maria in Trastevere e le più antiche feste della Madonna a Roma', *Bulletino dell'istituto italiano per il medio evo e Archivio Muratorio* 88 (1979), 35–85; and 89 (1980–1), 71–150.

SPATHARAKIS, I., *The Portrait in Byzantine Illuminated Manuscripts* (Leiden, 1976).

SPECK, P., *Die Kaiserliche Universität von Konstantinopel* (Munich, 1974).

WENGER, A., *L'Assomption de la T.S. Vierge dans la tradition byzantine du VIe au Xe siècle* (Paris, 1955).

WILSON, N., *Scholars of Byzantium* (London, 1983).

5 Paradise Sought: the Imperial Use of Art

BOURAS, C., *Nea Moni on Chios. History and Architecture* (Athens, 1982).

CONSTANTELOS, D. J., *Byzantine Philanthropy and Social Welfare* (New Brunswick, 1968).

GAUTIER, P., 'Le typicon du Christ sauveur Pantocrator', *Revue des Études Byzantines* 32 (1974), 1–145.

JENKINS, R. J. H., *Byzantium. The Imperial Centuries. AD 610–1071* (London, 1966). The quotation about Constantine IX Monomachos comes from page 345.

JONES, C., WAINWRIGHT, G. and YARNOLD, E. (eds.), *The Study of Liturgy* (London, 1978).

KAZHDAN, A. P., *The Structure of the Ruling Class at Byzantium in the eleventh and twelfth centuries* (in Russian) (Moscow, 1974). A useful summary of the book is given by I. Sorlin in *Travaux et Mémoires* 6 (1976), 367–98.

KAZHDAN, A. in association with FRANKLIN, S., *Studies on Byzantine Literature of the Eleventh and Twelfth Centuries* (Cambridge, 1984).

LAIOU, A. E., 'The Role of Women in Byzantine Society', *Jahrbuch der Österreichischen Byzantinistik* 31/1 (1981), 233–60.

MAGDALINO, P. and NELSON, R., 'The Emperor in Byzantine Art of the Twelfth Century', *Byzantinische Forschungen* 8 (1982), 123–83.

MANAPHES, K. A., *Monastiriaka Typika-Diathikai* (Athens, 1970).

MANGO, C., 'Notes on Byzantine Monuments', *Dumbarton Oaks Papers* 23–24 (1969–70), 369–75, *esp.* 372ff.

MATHEWS, T. F., *The Byzantine Churches of Istanbul, A Photographic Survey* (Pennsylvania State University, 1976).

MEGAW, A. H. S., 'Notes on Recent Work of the Byzantine Institute in Istanbul', *Dumbarton Oaks Papers* 17 (1963), 333–71, *esp.* 335–64 concerned with Zeyrek Camii. This is the essential archaeological treatment of the Pantocrator monastery; some of its considerations were distorted by the incorrect belief that Eirene founded the Pantocrator church before her death, here thought to be in 1124 (instead of the correct date of 13 August 1134). Also in need of reconsideration is the date of the templon screen of the south church: excavation in the city has now revealed that the sculpture used in this was sixth-century *spolia* taken from the ruined church of St Polyeuctos; the date when this sanctuary screen was set up could be after the departure of the occupying Venetians from the church in 1261 rather than in the twelfth century. (On the screen see A. W. Epstein, 'The Middle Byzantine Sanctuary Barrier: Templon Screen or Iconostasis?', *Journal of the British Archaeological Association* 134 (1981), 1–28.

RENAUD, E. (*ed.*), *M. Psellus, Chronographie* (two vols.) (Paris, 1926–8): Assoc. G. Budé.

ROSENTHAL, J. L., *The Purchase of Paradise. Gift Giving and the Aristocracy 1307–1485* (London, 1972).

SEWTER, E. R. A. (trans.), *The Chronographia of Michael Psellos* (London, 1953).

Travaux et Mémoires 6 (1976), *Recherches sur le XIe siècle.* LEMERLE, P., *Cinq études sur le XIe siècle* (Paris, 1977).

WHITTEMORE, T., *The Mosaics of Haghia Sophia at Istanbul. Third Preliminary Report. The Imperial Portraits of the South Gallery* (Oxford, 1942).

6 Paradise Gained: the Private Use of Art

BELTING, H., *Das Bild und sein Publikum im Mittelalter. Form und Funktion früher Bildtafeln der Passion* (Berlin, 1981); see also the English version of pp. 142–98 of this book:

BELTING, H., 'An Image and its Function in the Liturgy: the Man of Sorrows in Byzantium', *Dumbarton Oaks Papers* 34–5 (1980–1), 1–16.

BYNUM, C. W., *Jesus as Mother. Studies in the Spirituality of the High Middle Ages* (California, 1982).

CUTLER, A., 'Art in Byzantine Society: Motive Forces of Byzantine Patronage', *Jahrbuch der Österreichischen Byzantinistik* 31/2 (1981), 759–87.

EPSTEIN, A. W., 'Formulas for Salvation: a Comparison of Two Byzantine Monasteries and their Founders', *Church History* 50 (1981), 385–400.

HODDER, I., *The Present Past* (London, 1982).

JUGIE, M., 'Un opuscule inédit de Néophyte le reclus sur l'incorruptibilité du corps du Christ dans l'eucharistie', *Revue des Études Byzantines* 7 (1949), 1–11; this text (in Paris, grec. 1189, folios 199v. to 200v.) was republished by Tsiknopoulos (1969), pp. 397–403.

KAZHDAN, A. and CONSTABLE, G., *People and Power in Byzantium* (Washington, DC, 1982).

MANGO, C. and HAWKINS, E. J. W., 'The Hermitage of St Neophytos and its Wall Paintings', *Dumbarton Oaks Papers* 20 (1966), 119–206.

MORRIS, C., *The Discovery of the Individual: 1050–1200* (London, 1972).

STOCK, B., *The Implications of Literacy. Written Language and Models of Interpretation in the Eleventh and Twelfth Centuries* (Princeton, 1983).

TSIKNOPOULOS, J. P., 'The Extraordinary Character of Neophytos, Priest, Monk and Hermit' (in Greek) *Byzantion* 37 (1967), 311–413.

TSIKNOPOULOS, J. P., *Kupriaka Tupika* (Nicosia, 1969).

TSIKNOPOULOS, J. P., *Life and Two Church Services of St. Neophytos (24 January and 28 September)* (in Greek) (Larnaca, 1953).

TSIKNOPOULOS, J. P., 'The Minor Works of Neophytos, Priest, Monk and Hermit' (in Greek), *Byzantion* 39 (1969), 318–419.

WALTER, C., *Art and Ritual of the Byzantine Church* (London, 1982).

WINFIELD, D. C., 'Reports on Work at Monagri, Lagoudera, and Hagios Neophytos, Cyprus, 1969/1970', *Dumbarton Oaks Papers* 25 (1971), 259–64.

WOLFF, J., *The Social Production of Art* (London, 1981).

ILLUSTRATION SOURCES

INDEX